On Prophecy

OTHER BOOKS BY THE AUTHOR

J. Vernon McGee

On Prophecy

Man's
Fascination With
The Future

THOMAS NELSON PUBLISHERS
Nashville

Copyright © 1993 by Thru The Bible Radio

Published in Nashville, Tennessee, by Thomas Nelson, Inc.

Unless otherwise noted, Scripture quotations are from the KING JAMES VERSION of the Bible.

Scripture quotations noted NKJV are from the NEW KING JAMES VERSION of the Bible. Copyright © 1979, 1980, 1982, Thomas Nelson, Inc., Publishers.

Scripture quotations noted Scofield are from the Scofield Study Bible. Copyright © 1967, Oxford University Press, Inc., New York.

Library of Congress Cataloging-in-Publication Data

McGee, J. Vernon (John Vernon), 1904–1988
   On prophecy : man's fascination with the future / J. Vernon McGee.
   ISBN 0-8407-6798-6
   1. Bible—Prophecies—Sermons. I. Title.
BS647.2.M385 1993
231.7'45—dc20   93–38942
                                        CIP

Printed in the United States of America
1 2 3 4 5 6 7 — 98 97 96 95 94 93

TABLE OF CONTENTS

Chapter 1

HOW GOD PREPARED THE WORLD FOR THE FIRST COMING OF CHRIST

But when the fullness of time was come, God sent forth his Son, made of a woman, made under the law, to redeem them that were under the law, that we might receive the adoption of sons. (Galatians 4:4, 5)

In amazing ways God prepared the world for the coming of the Lord Jesus Christ. The world consciously and unconsciously entered into God's plan. The four corners of the civilized world were made ready for His coming. Oh, I know they forgot to put the welcome mat out, and they went so far in one quarter as to even put up a sign that read in effect: "Keep off this world." The world then and now is saying, "Go home, God, we don't need You."

However, four great ethnic divisions of the human family were made ready for the first coming of Christ. First, the nation of Israel; second, the Oriental races; third, Greece; fourth, Rome. Each one of these performed its particular part in the coming of Christ into the world. Each one had a separate mission. When they all are fitted together, you can see that there was a pattern and a design on the part of God when He sent His Son into the world. It was when the fullness of the time was come that God sent forth His Son. He *prepared* the world for the coming of His Son. And when we look back over

1

the centuries and see that there is one design and one pattern, it should make the most skeptical, cynical person become a believer in Him. Let's consider these four different divisions of the human family and see how each was prepared.

ISRAEL

Look at Israel first because it is easiest to see. There is so much of Scripture that deals with the nation Israel in God's plan. Israel has special significance in the coming of the Savior into the world. Kurtz, the great German historian, said, "Judaism prepared salvation for man, and heathenism prepared man for salvation."

The Lord Jesus Christ said to the Samaritan woman at the well, "Salvation is of the *Jews*." He was accurate, of course. Paul, writing to the Romans, speaking of his people the Israelites, gave eight identifying fingerprints, and one of them was: ". . . of whom as concerning the flesh Christ came . . ." (Romans 9:5). Jesus Christ came out of Israel. He came into our world from this nation, and Israel had been prepared for His coming.

If you go back over the history of Israel, you will find that there are two major divisions in God's preparation of this nation. One is the period of *isolation;* the other is the period of *dispersion.* Or, to put it another way, one is the period of *segregation,* and the other is the period of *integration.* You ask, "Is God today for integration or is He for segregation?" God votes both ways.

For Israel there was the period of segregation (see Genesis 12–45). God reached down, first of all, into Ur of the Chaldees. You must remember that Jewish people came out of the East; they belong to the Orient. God drew Abraham out of the Tigris-Euphrates Valley and told him to leave not only the high civilization of Ur of the Chaldees, his business, and his friends, but also God wanted to get him away from all his relatives. He said, "Leave them all, and I'll bring you into a land that I will show you." He brought Abraham into the land of Canaan for a period of isolation during which God was preparing this man and his progeny, his race, if you please, for from Abraham came Isaac, Jacob, and the twelve sons of Jacob.

Then down into the land of Egypt they went, where there was that brief period of dispersion (Genesis 46—Exodus 12). They spent four hundred years in the land of Egypt, mixing with those heathen down there and adopting many of their customs. They became just as bad as the Egyptians as far as idolatry was concerned. Then God called Moses and said in effect, "I want you to take My people out of this land. I want you to bring them into the land of Canaan; I want to put them in a very special place." God took them out and brought them yonder to Mount Sinai and said, "There's one thing I have in mind, Moses, for these people, that they be a peculiar people." And everything that God gave them was different from the nations round about. If the surrounding nations went this way, God said to His people, "You go that way. I want to keep you separate." Finally, He put them in Canaan at the crossroads of the world where three continents mingled. The most amazing thing is that when the tramp, tramp, tramp of the nations of the world went by during the period in which the Israelites were faithful to God, He kept them a separate people. All that time He was preparing them for the coming of the Savior and preparing a lineage or line for His coming into the world.

Then the period of dispersion came, when God sent them back into the East from whence they had come, back to the Tigris-Euphrates Valley to mix with what were then the great nations of the world. They rubbed shoulders with the East, and they rubbed shoulders with the West. In their period of dispersion they carried to the world the greatest theological statement in the Old Testament: "Hear, O Israel: The LORD our God is one LORD" (Deuteronomy 6:4). Millions of nomads, Arabs wandering over the desert today, will listen to the summons to prayer from a minaret and say the same thing, "Allah is one God." Out to a polytheistic world Israel gave the message. One of the greatest historians said that once Greece rubbed shoulders with Judaism, polytheism was dead in Greece because Greeks were an intellectual people and would not follow idolatry, having come in contact with Judaism. Down yonder as Israel went into captivity, they disseminated the knowledge of the living and the true God. From then on, they walked the highways of the world, carrying a pack, doing business, building synagogues in every place, telling out: "Hear, O Israel, the LORD our God is one LORD— Jehovah our *Elohim* is one *Elohim*." That was their mission. All was preparation for the coming of the Messiah.

Then you come to the period of the prophets. Each prophet, as he spoke to the local situation, did not stop there but looked down through the ages and prophesied of events far in the future. When the prospect for national survival was darkest, the prophets saw it the brightest because God revealed to them the coming of the Messiah. They all pointed to His coming, so that when *the* fullness of *the* time was come, God sent forth His Son, born of a woman, born under the Law. The nation of Israel was prepared for the coming of the Messiah. From their Scriptures they knew *where* He was to be born (Matthew 2:6) and they should have known *when*. They believed the Old Testament Scriptures that He was coming, but they did not believe that He had arrived. God had prepared them for the coming of the Messiah.

ORIENTAL RACES

The second group, the Oriental races, were prepared for Christ's coming. That's where the majority of the population was in His day; it is where the majority of the population is today. Sometimes when I get on the freeway, I think that the majority of the population is here, but it is not. My friend, you find it in the Orient. That's where most people are.

The prophet Daniel saw the interpretation of the vision which God gave to Nebuchadnezzar. He saw an image composed of four different metals: the head of gold, the breast and arms of silver, the belly and thighs of brass, the legs of iron, the feet part of iron and part of clay (see Daniel 2). Those four different metals represented the four great world powers. Two of these nations were Oriental powers: Babylon, the head of gold, and Media-Persia, the arms and breast of silver. Both were descendants of Ham. They represent the Orient. You and I are living in a day when world control has been in the hands of the ethnological division of the human family descended from Japheth. I think that Japheth is coming to an end in his rulership of the world shortly. But the first great world powers were Hamitic.

The head of gold under Nebuchadnezzar and Babylon represented absolute autocracy. It represented a despotic power reposed in one man so that his whims became law. If he wanted men in a fiery furnace, they were thrown into a fiery furnace. Nobody questioned him. The kingdom that followed was Media-Persia. Media-Persia represents material riches. Probably no nation ever brought together so much of the wealth of the world as Media-Persia did. The world still stands in amazement at the wealth and the display of the Oriental courts of that day. These two nations, Babylon and Media-Persia, represent the Orient, the mysterious East, the land of the occult where there are contrasts and contradictions. Side-by-side, for centuries, wealth and wretchedness have been co-existing, squalor and splendor walk hand in hand, plenty and poverty go together, the purple and the perishing live in the same town and on the same side of the railroad tracks. Vast multitudes yonder in the Orient have been dying in rags right beside great riches. Solomon exemplified this also, for Solomon was the one who gathered together the wealth and the wisdom of the world. And Solomon made this statement, speaking for them: "He that trusteth in his riches shall fall . . ." (Proverbs 11:28). May I say to you, the East went down rich. Will Rogers said, when we in America entered the Depression, "America is the only nation on record that's going to the poorhouse in a Cadillac!" He was wrong, because he did not know history. That had been true of the Orient—they went to the poorhouse in purple and gold and silver in their day. But the gold and silver could not save them.

Abraham had come out of Ur of the Chaldees, out of that mysterious land. In captivity Israel went back into that land, and some never came out.

When the nations of the East lost their power, the East was like a dead battery that was run down. The ragged religions of that land didn't help any; they offered no hope. Zoroastrianism, Buddhism, Hinduism, Confucianism, Taoism, Shintoism, offered no help or hope for them. At the birth of the Lord Jesus Christ, the Orient was perishing, and there was a great longing in the hearts of the miserable mobs of the East. Also, an air of expectancy had spread throughout the world. Suetonius, the Latin historian, relates that "an ancient and definite expectation had spread throughout the East, that a ruler of the world would, at about that time, arise in Judea." Tacitus, the Roman historian, made a similar statement. And Schlegel, the German historian, states that Buddhist missionaries traveling to China met Chinese sages going to seek the Messiah about A.D. 33. Paul was saying no idle words when he witnessed of Christ's resurrection to a Roman king, "This thing was not done in a *corner!*" We find yonder on the day of Pentecost that there were Parthians and Medes in Jerusalem (see Acts 2:9). The East was represented.

It was an Ethiopian eunuch out of the dark continent of Africa who heard the Scriptures explained as he was returning from Jerusalem (see Acts 8). He was the first Gentile converted to Christ, and "he went on his way rejoicing." He took the gospel into Africa.

Thomas, the doubting apostle, did not go to the Roman Empire. Rather, there is an abundance of historical evidence that he went into India and even into China with the good news of Christ.

Out of that wretched and miserable East there came to Jerusalem wise men. Where men were suffering and dying they came with the urgent question, "Where is He that is born King of the Jews? We have seen His star in the East, and are come to worship Him." In the fullness of the time, God sent forth His Son, born of a woman, born under the law. The Orient had been made ready.

GREECE

Now we turn to the third ethnological division, the Greeks. The Greeks were the third world power that Daniel mentions. The Greco-Macedonian civilization was one of the greatest civilizations this world has seen. The basic philosophy of Greece was a striving to produce the perfect man. They tried to bring man to the place of physical and mental perfection. They didn't do much for him spiritually, but they certainly worked on him physically and mentally. The Greeks gave genius to the world as no other nation has. At the time that David was singing the sweet psalms in Israel, just a few miles away yonder in Asia Minor, the poet Homer was walking in rags and singing his story. As someone has commented, Homer went into twenty-five towns that would not give him bread but that afterward claimed to be the place of his birth.

Then several hundred years went by, and about the third century before Christ, in the Paraclean age, Greece erected upon the horizon of history a glory of Greece that covered the Acropolis and ran down to the ends of the earth—so much so that today it has affected every walk of life, even architecture. You can't build today a humble church or a courthouse that does not in some way reflect upon the genius of the Greeks. It was during that period that Socrates, Demosthenes,

Plato, Xenophon, Sophocles, and Euripedes appeared—each of them a genius in his line. Philosophy and poetry and drama and athletics and government were carried to the highest degree in this particular period. Then came Alexander the Great out of Macedon, uniting the Greek states for the first time and marching an army over the world to do something that, unbeknown to him, God wanted done. I want to give you Houson's statement regarding Alexander:

> He took up the meshes of the net of civilization, which were lying in disorder on the edges of the Asiatic shore, and spread them over all the countries which he traversed in his wonderful campaigns. The East and the West were suddenly brought together. Separated tribes were united under a common government. New cities were built, as the centers of political life. New lines of communication were opened, as the channels of commercial activity. The new culture penetrated the mountain ranges of Pisidia and Lycaonia. The Tigris and Euphrates became Greek rivers. The language of Athens was heard among the Jewish colonies of Babylonia; and a Grecian Babylon was built by the conqueror in Egypt and called by his name.

Alexander took Greek civilization to the ends of the earth, and may I say that he accomplished a purpose: God was disseminating a language that was to become the vehicle of the gospel, the Greek language. Every book of the New Testament was originally written in Greek. And that most amazing of all apostles, Paul, could stand and speak one language yonder in the "agora" (marketplace) in Corinth or on Mars Hill in Athens or in the amphitheater in Ephesus or in the Mamertine prison in Rome, and be understood by all. He was a master of the Greek language—his marvelous epistle to the Romans is proof of that. He *knew* the Greek language, and he could use it to preach Christ all over the Roman Empire. *God had prepared the Greeks for the coming of Christ into the world* at just the right moment. The Old Testament had previously been translated from Hebrew into Greek and was called the Septuagint. The Old Testament in Greek is one of the best of the translations that we have today. Luke wrote his gospel record to the Greek world and, in effect, said to them, "You have been seeking all these years for the perfect man. I present Him to you: the Lord Jesus Christ. I am a doctor, and I looked at Him physically. He grew physically in favor with God and man. He grew as a normal person down here upon this earth. But I examined Him," said Dr. Luke. "He was a *perfect* Man. He died upon a cross for the sins of the world, and He was raised from the dead." When Paul took that gospel throughout the Roman world, Luke traveled with him. One of the last things Paul wrote was "only Luke is with me." Luke, the man who in a sense put his stethoscope down on Jesus Christ, said to the Greek world, "You never found the perfect man, but here He is." In the fullness of the time, God sent forth His Son, born of a woman, born under the law.

ROME

God prepared the Romans for the coming of Christ. If you had told Caesar Augustus in the first century A.D. that he was nothing but a pawn on a chessboard carrying out God's wishes when he put his name to a tax bill, he would have laughed at you. But from our vantage point of about two thousand years we can look back to see that it is true. Of course, Augustus couldn't see it, but he was a puppet being moved by God's hand.

Rome was the empire of iron. Their philosophy in one word was power. Power. I'm afraid that Rome is misunderstood today, and we ought to know something about it in this hour—because, you see, Rome did not die. It lives on. The Roman Empire tried to solve the world's problems in another way. Again I would like to give you a quotation from Gregory concerning Rome. Notice that their philosophy sounds familiar:

> He [Rome] was to try whether human power, taking the form of law, regulated by political principles of which the regard for law and justice was most conspicuous, could perfect humanity by subordinating the individual to the state and making the state universal.

Neither Hitler, Mussolini, nor the Communists were the first to try making the state a sovereign and even a god. Rome did that. What a tremendous reminder! Look further at Rome. With physical force, the Roman conquered the world. With his executive power, he organized it, for he was an organizer. He gave good government—that is, if you can call his government *good*—to every people, tribe, and nation of the world. He built roads; he gave them *good* roads. God made sure of that because over those roads the gospel was to go to the hinterlands. Under Rome's domination law and order prevailed. Read the four Gospels again, and see how law and order prevailed in Jerusalem. Roman soldiers were there to enforce the law. That was the thing that Rome gave to the world, and their emphasis was on justice. Listen to Gregory again:

> It was justice practically omnipotent and omnipresent, and so neither to be resisted nor escaped, justice which never dreamed of mercy until the work of conquest and consolidation was done. It made men long for mercy because it demonstrated to them that there was no hope for them in righteous law.

What a picture! They upheld justice, and all over the Roman Empire which covered three continents in that day—all the way from the pillars of Hercules to the Euphrates River, all the way from the cold mountains of Scotland down to the burning sands of the Sahara Desert—there was law. There was that Roman judge like Pilate, and on his desk there was the image of Janus. We get our word January from him. He was represented with two opposite faces, that is, he looked in both directions, seeing both sides of a case. Rome said to every people they conquered, "We will not destroy your customs. You go right on living your lives. Only one thing: we will govern you. We will run things, and we will give you justice. Every one of you can come to us and get justice." Every Roman court stood for justice. Isn't it an anomaly, isn't it ironical, that Jesus Christ was crucified on a *Roman* cross? Crucified by the nation that boasted of *justice!*

By the time Paul the apostle, that little Jew, crippled and almost blind, started down those Roman roads, speaking the gospel of Christ, the world was ready to listen to him. One of the things that arrested their attention—oh, it is so important—he said, "I have obtained *mercy!*" The world was tired of justice.

You know that most people say today that they want justice from God. A man said to me in Altadena many years ago on his death bed, "You let me alone, preacher. All I ask of God is justice." I said, "Wait a minute, is it really justice you want or mercy?" He finally had to admit that what he actually wanted was mercy. You see, we have mercy and justice confused. Justice condemns you. The law condemns you, and the law was given that "every mouth may be stopped, and all the world may become guilty before God" (Romans 3:19).

And "by the deeds of the law there shall no flesh be justified in his sight" (Romans 3:20). Does God mean the Mosaic Law? *No*, He means *any* law. By deeds of Roman law, or any law, no one can be justified. Paul went out into the Roman world. He wrote the epistle to the Romans, in which he said, "By the deeds of law there shall no flesh be justified." That Roman world, down under the heel of Rome, hearing of nothing but justice, was crying out, not for justice, but for *mercy*! Paul came and said to them, "What the law could not do, in that it was weak through the flesh, God sending his own Son in the likeness of sinful flesh and for sin, condemned sin in the flesh" (Romans 8:3). But now "by *grace* are ye saved through faith . . . not by works"—not by works!

> **For by grace are ye saved through faith; and that not of yourselves, it is the gift of God, not of works, lest any man should boast.** (Ephesians 2:8, 9)

Oh, not by works but by grace! Out over that Roman Empire were sixty million slaves and sixty million free men, but none of them were free; they were all under Roman law. They all sighed for a salvation that could deliver them. In the fullness of time God sent forth His Son, born of a woman, born under the law.

Our contemporary world is equally as needy as it was under Roman rule. Honestly, we haven't come very far in that long span of time, except technologically. In our day there is both *plenty* and *poverty*. America has a headache with an abundance of surplus, and in India and in China, where most of the population of the world live, they go to bed with empty stomachs. And, my friend, they won't be filled on Thanksgiving or Christmas while the Western world sits down to gorge itself on food it doesn't need. The world is equally as needy, equally as wretched, as it was all those centuries ago.

WHY FOUR GOSPELS?

The Jew was the man of prophecy. When Matthew wrote his Gospel record he directed it to him, gathering up the Old Testament prophecies and presenting the Man who fulfilled them: "Here He is—the Messiah!"

The Oriental was the man of plutocracy and the man of poverty. The man who had pearls and gold and diamonds in such abundance that on the scales they would balance his body weight, had the same spiritual need as the man begging for bread. He was still hungry and still thirsty. The Gospel of John was written to him, and John quotes our Lord when He says, "I am the bread of life; he that cometh to me shall never hunger, and he that believeth on me shall never thirst" (John 6:35).

The Gospel of Luke was directed to the Greek, the man of perfection, the man of philosophy. Dr. Luke wrote, "Look, here He is, the perfect Man."

The Roman was the man of power, the man of politics. With him in mind Mark wrote a brief Gospel in staccato fashion, one miracle after another. He presented Jesus Christ as the Man of action.

But the world is needy still. Idealism is all but dead. Mankind is bankrupt intellectually. There is not a leader in the world who is outstanding, not one. We are not producing giants in any field of endeavor. Modern literature reflects this. One of our modern writers gives her estimation: "Modern literature is a mirror on the ceiling of a brothel." What a picture!

In these four Gospels is the Man Christ Jesus, God, who took upon Himself human flesh. My friend, He can meet your need. Are you hungry? Are you thirsty? Are you tired of life? A young lady on the telephone said to me not long ago, "If you don't give me a reason for living, I intend to take my own life." Are *you* tired of life today? Maybe you have been looking in the wrong areas, maybe you have been going to the wrong places, maybe you are listening to the wrong voices. I point you to Jesus Christ, who still is the Savior of the world.

It's black outside right now. You know it. I don't have to tell you that. Men in high places are pessimistic and frightened about the future.

My friend, I have some good news for you. There is a little glimmer of light breaking on the horizon right now, and it shows up brighter because it is so dark down here. This One who came about two thousand years ago is coming again! I'm willing to risk being called a fanatic in saying that I think God is preparing the world right now for the return of Jesus Christ. He is coming again! This is the hope of the world. I point you to Him, the mighty Son of God, the Savior of the world and the only One who can meet your need.

Chapter 2

THE TIMES OF THE GENTILES
Daniel 2

There are two worldwide kingdoms ahead of us, and we may be closer to them than we think. The first will be the kingdom of Antichrist, set up by man's philosophy and man's psychology. It will deify human beings and attempt to prove that they can unite and bring about a world of order, peace, and equality without God.

Because God instituted moral absolutes to govern the human family, man claims that Utopia can come only through the rejection of these absolutes. It is this kingdom that the Lord Jesus will destroy at His coming. All of man's supposed superiority will lie in the ashes and dust of the fallen empires, leveled by the Stone that smashes the image and grinds it to powder.

Gentiles have not done a very good job of running the world. We can see the beginning of this in the Book of Daniel, dating back to around 600 B.C. You and I have moved down pretty close to the end of Gentile rule, to a day when the Lord Jesus Christ will come forward and take the scepter of world dominion back into His own hands. The story of the "times of the Gentiles" is remarkably told in Daniel 2.

And in the second year of the reign of Nebuchadnezzar, Nebuchadnezzar dreamed dreams, wherewith his spirit was troubled, and his sleep brake from him.

Then the king commanded to call the magicians, and the astrologers, and the sorcerers, and the Chaldeans, for to show the king his dreams. So they came and stood before the king.

> **And the king said unto them, I have dreamed a dream, and my spirit was troubled to know the dream.**
>
> **Then spake the Chaldeans to the king in Syriac, O king, live for ever: tell thy servants the dream, and we will show the interpretation.**
>
> **The king answered and said to the Chaldeans, The thing is gone from me. . . .** (Daniel 2:1-5)

Because of this translation, the impression has been given that the king had forgotten his dream and could not recall it. That, of course, is not true. He did know what his dream was. What he said is better translated "The word is gone forth from me," or putting it another way, "The word from me is sure." The king recognized that his wise men were hedging; they were stalling for time. He said in effect, "I want you to know that the thing that I've said is sure, my decision is firm. I do not intend to tell you the dream; I intend for you to tell *me* the dream and its meaning." Of course he knew what his dream was.

> **. . . If ye will not make known unto me the dream, with the interpretation thereof, ye shall be cut in pieces, and your houses shall be made a dunghill. But if ye show the dream, the interpretation thereof, ye shall receive of me gifts and rewards and great honour: therefore show me the dream, and the interpretation thereof.**
>
> **They answered again and said, Let the king tell his servants the dream, and we will show the interpretation of it.**
>
> **The king answered and said, I know of certainty that ye would gain the time, because ye see the thing is gone from me.**
>
> **But if ye will not make known unto me the dream, there is but one decree for you: for ye have prepared lying corrupt words to speak before me, till the time be changed: therefore tell me the dream, and I shall know that ye can show me the interpretation thereof.** (Daniel 2:5-9)

You will recall the story of how Daniel intervenes and God gives to him the dream and the interpretation of it. I think Daniel asked God to let him dream the dream so he would know exactly what it was and that God actually caused him to do so. Then he gets an audience with King Nebuchadnezzar, and here is his interpretation:

> Thou, O king, sawest, and behold a great image. This great image, whose brightness was excellent, stood before thee; and the form thereof was terrible.

> This image's head was of fine gold, his breast and his arms of silver, his belly and his thighs of brass, his legs of iron, his feet part of iron and part of clay.

> Thou sawest till that a stone was cut out without hands, which smote the image upon his feet that were of iron and clay, and brake them to pieces.

> Then was the iron, the clay, the brass, the silver, and the gold, broken to pieces together, and became like the chaff of the summer threshingfloors; and the wind carried them away, that no place was found for them: and the stone that smote the image became a great mountain, and filled the whole earth.

> This is the dream; and we will tell the interpretation thereof before the king.

> Thou, O king, art a king of kings: for the God of heaven hath given thee a kingdom, power, and strength, and glory.

> And wheresoever the children of men dwell, the beasts of the field and the fowls of the heaven hath he given into thine hand, and hath made thee ruler over them all. Thou art this head of gold.

> And after thee shall arise another kingdom inferior to thee, and another third kingdom of brass, which shall bear rule over all the earth.

> And the fourth kingdom shall be strong as iron: forasmuch as iron breaketh in pieces and subdueth all things: and as iron that breaketh all these, shall it break in pieces and bruise.

> And whereas thou sawest the feet and toes, part of potters' clay, and part of iron, the kingdom shall be divided; but there shall be in it of the strength of the iron, forasmuch as thou sawest the iron mixed with miry clay.

> And as the toes of the feet were part of iron, and part of clay, so the kingdom shall be partly strong, and partly broken.

And whereas thou sawest iron mixed with miry clay, they shall mingle themselves with the seed of men: but they shall not cleave one to another, even as iron is not mixed with clay.

And in the days of these kings shall the God of heaven set up a kingdom, which shall never be destroyed: and the kingdom shall not be left to other people, but it shall break in pieces and consume all these kingdoms, and it shall stand for ever.

Forasmuch as thou sawest that the stone was cut out of the mountain without hands, and that it brake in pieces the iron, the brass, the clay, the silver, and the gold; the great God hath made known to the king what shall come to pass hereafter: and the dream is certain, and the interpretation thereof sure. (Daniel 2:31-45)

May I say at the outset that the subject before us about "the times of the Gentiles" is not an invention of a propagandist or a monger of sensationalism. The subject may sound sensational, but it is actually one our Lord Himself discussed. In the Gospel of Luke our Lord used that expression in language like this:

And they shall fall by the edge of the sword, and shall be led away captive into all nations: and Jerusalem shall be trodden down of the Gentiles, until the times of the Gentiles be fulfilled. (Luke 21:24)

The "times of the Gentiles" happens to be a period of time that you can pinpoint. You can identify the beginning of it, and you can project the ending of it—which is still yonder in the future. There are other expressions used in Scripture that are not synonymous to this at all, and we need to be very careful.

For instance, Paul spoke to the Roman Christians about the fullness of the Gentiles.

For I would not, brethren, that ye should be ignorant of this mystery, lest ye should be wise in your own conceits; that blindness in part is happened to Israel, until the fulness of the Gentiles be come in. (Romans 11:25)

Now the fullness of the Gentiles is that period when God is calling out from among the Gentiles a people to His name. In Acts 15 we read that James got up before the early church which was one hundred percent Jewish, and in substance he said to them, "Men and brethren, the prophets speak of the fact that God is going to take out of the Gentiles a people to His name. And after that He will return and will build again the tabernacle of David which is fallen down. Then all the Gentiles will call upon Him."

That time which is labeled here "the fulness of the Gentiles" is the period in which you and I are now living. It will end with the Rapture of the church.

As you can see, the *fullness* of the Gentiles differs from the *times* of the Gentiles, although they run concurrently part of the way. The *fullness* of the Gentiles ends at the Rapture; the *times* of the Gentiles continues on until Christ returns to the earth to establish His Kingdom.

Our Lord linked the times of the Gentiles with the city of Jerusalem. He said,

. . . And Jerusalem shall be trodden down of the Gentiles, until the times of the Gentiles be fulfilled. (Luke 21:24)

In other words, the period that is labeled the times of the Gentiles is the period in which Jerusalem is trampled underfoot by the Gentiles.

The beginning of the times of the Gentiles is something you can pinpoint in history. Actually, I do not think this is even a debatable point anymore in the study of prophecy. It began with Nebuchadnezzar. He is the first one to lay siege to Jerusalem and to destroy it after David had become king.

Nebuchadnezzar's invasion was several hundred years after David's reign, but you'll notice that Egypt is not included in the dream of Nebuchadnezzar as one of the world empires, and yet Egypt had been a great world empire.

Neither was the Assyrian empire included, though Assyria did lay siege to Jerusalem around 700 B.C. Isaiah 37 records God's deliverance of Judah, not permitting even one arrow of the Assyrian army to be shot into the city. God would not allow Assyria to take Jerusalem— He was holding them away to give His people a full opportunity to return to Him.

You see, when David had been king over Israel, God had said to him, "I'm going to give you an *everlasting* kingdom." He also said to David, "It will be a *worldwide* kingdom, not just over Palestine but over this entire earth." The psalmists picked up this promise and the prophets repeatedly spoke of it. For instance, let me direct your attention to only one Scripture, Isaiah 2:1–3, so you may see that this kingdom which the prophets talked about was not just confined to Palestine but was to be worldwide.

> **The word that Isaiah the son of Amoz saw concerning Judah and Jerusalem. And it shall come to pass in the last days, that the mountain of the LORD's house shall be established in the top of the mountains, and shall be exalted above the hills; . . .**

The Kingdom shall be established in the top of the "mountains," meaning earthly kingdoms, and shall be exalted above the "hills," referring to the little nations.

> **. . . And all nations shall flow unto it. And many people shall go and say, Come ye, and let us go up to the mountain of the LORD, to the house of the God of Jacob; and he will teach us of his ways. . . .**

That prophecy can be multiplied, not only once, twice, or three times, but I believe that I could give you five hundred prophecies from the Old Testament concerning that Kingdom which is yet to be established upon this earth—universal and everlasting. That Kingdom was represented by the scepter of David, and God kept telling those who followed in David's line that if they continued in sin He would take that scepter away from them, away from them temporarily until the times of the Gentiles would be fulfilled. However, they did not listen to the prophets whom God sent to them, and our Lord Jesus reminded the Jews of His day of that fact. So the day came when God took the scepter out of the hands of Jehoiakim, king of Judah, and He placed it into the hands of Nebuchadnezzar, king of Babylon. He took the scepter of worldwide rulership and put it into Gentile hands. My friend, that was well over twenty-five hundred years ago, and that scepter today is still in the hands of the Gentiles.

The scepter represents world rulership, if you please. Nebuchadnezzar found himself, overnight, a world ruler. He had defeated Necho, king of Egypt, and then was warring in the Delta of the Nile and was overcoming it—everything fell before him—when news came to him of the death of his father, Nabopolassar, which made this man

Nebuchadnezzar the undisputed ruler of the world. Since he had overcome everything else, a little tribal deity up in Judah by the name of Jehovah didn't amount to very much, he thought. He could overcome there also. Who was to stand in his way?

When Nebuchadnezzar returned to Babylon, he could look over that great city that boasted a civilization second to none. To this day we have not presented to the world a civilization any greater than the Babylonian. There came a question into his mind and to his heart about the future: *Here all of a sudden I find myself a world ruler. In my hand has been placed a scepter. It has come from somewhere. Who will it go to, and what will happen to it? What will be the final outcome?* Do you know that after about twenty-five hundred or three thousand years of human history since Nebuchadnezzar, the world is still wondering about that? We have the answer in this image.

So God spoke to this king through a dream one night. He answered his questions to let him know the future and also to let him know that these despised people whom he had brought into captivity were still His *chosen* people. It would be one of them who would be the instrument to reveal to the king the vision and the interpretation of it.

Now the man had a dream. It was a dream that he could certainly recall. Don't ever think for one moment that Nebuchadnezzar would have forgotten this dream! He saw an image, tremendous and awesome. God spoke to him in the kind of language he understood—Babylon was the very fountainhead of all idolatry. I suppose that Babylon had as many idolatrous images as Memphis in Egypt had. In fact, all idolatry can be traced back to the Tower of Babel and this city of Babylon. You can see that God communicated to this king by way of an image, a language he understood.

Nebuchadnezzar wondered about this great image that did nothing but just stand before him. There was no movement at all. It just stood there in its brightness—multicolored, polychrome, a multi-metallic image. He'd seen nothing like it. It was stupendous and awe-inspiring. It was fierce in its countenance. It was that which would incite terror!

The king wondered about it and was so troubled he summoned his cabinet. He wanted to make sure he would get accurate information. I think he said to himself, *I've been suspecting these wise men of getting free board here, they're just hangers on, they've just been giving me a lot of malarkey. I'm going to find out whether they're genuine or not.* When they came and stood before him, he said, "I had a dream, and I want you to know it's an important dream—you can be sure of that! I want you to tell me what the dream is, and then I want you to give me the interpretation of it." These wise men were the brain trust of Babylon. Because they couldn't come up with the answer, do not think that these men did not represent the best brains of the day; they did. They said, "We can tell you the interpretation if you'll tell us the dream, but we don't know what the dream is."

And Nebuchadnezzar said, "You'll have to tell me the dream. Because I'm tremendously concerned about it, I'll not know that your interpretation is valid unless you can tell me the dream."

For this cause the king was angry and very furious, and commanded to destroy all the wise men of Babylon. (Daniel 2:12)

This was Satan's effort, of course, to destroy Daniel because he had already become a conspicuous man, a man of purpose in that court. Daniel had been faithful to God, and the devil wanted to destroy him.

When word is brought to Daniel that all of the wise men are to be destroyed unless the dream can be given, this man Daniel, with real confidence and faith in God, asks for an audience with the king. When he is ushered into Nebuchadnezzar's presence, he says, "Just give me time and we'll give you the interpretation." The king says, "All right, if you think you can do it, young man, I'll give you the opportunity. I admire your spunk. If you feel that you can bring forth the dream, I'll be willing to wait." So Daniel goes and calls his three friends together, and they have a prayer meeting. I'll bet you this is the greatest prayer meeting ever to be held in the city of Babylon. They pray fervently that night. They lay hold of God that night, and God gives to Daniel in a night vision the dream and the interpretation of it. Then Daniel asks for another audience with Nebuchadnezzar, and the captain of the guard quickly ushers him in to the king. Daniel says in substance to the king, "I'm going to give you the dream and I'm going to give you the interpretation. But I want you to understand one thing: it's not because of anything in me. Don't you give me credit for it. I want you to know that there is a God in heaven who reveals secrets."

By the way, I personally think that Nebuchadnezzar came to know that there is a God in heaven and became a converted man through this experience. I expect some day to meet him on Hallelujah Boulevard in heaven.

Now Daniel describes the dream, "You saw in your dream a great image." The minute he said that, I think Nebuchadnezzar's eyes lit up. He might have been skeptical at first as he looked down on this young man, *He's rather presumptuous to think he can do a thing like this!* But the minute Daniel said to him, "You saw in your dream a great image," I think Nebuchadnezzar moved to the edge of his throne and said, "Go on, young man. You're on the right track."

Then Daniel continues, "You saw a great image of splendor. It was frightful to look upon. That image just stood there. It had a head of gold. It had chest and arms of silver. It had an abdomen and thighs of brass. It had legs of iron and feet of iron and miry clay."

Nebuchadnezzar says, "You're right. That's what I saw. That was my dream."

"And then you saw a *stone* cut out without hands. You saw it smite the image on the feet, and it pulverized it."

"That's right. That's what happened."

"Now I'll give you the interpretation of it." Daniel said first to him, "Thou, O king . . . thou art this head of gold." Then in substance he said, "What you have just seen, Nebuchadnezzar, is what God is going to do in the latter days, and God has given you the entire briefing of future rule. He has set before you the course of Gentile domination down to the very end of Gentile world history."

Our Lord said, ". . . Jerusalem shall be trodden down of the Gentiles, until the times of the Gentiles be fulfilled" (Luke 21:24). For twenty-five hundred years the armies of these nations mentioned here, and others, have marched through Jerusalem. To me, one of the most thrilling things is this: When the United Nations made the Jewish population of Israel a nation, the Jews wanted above everything else the ancient city of Jerusalem. I held my breath when the United Nations was making that decision, and up to that time Russia and the United States hadn't agreed on anything in the United Nations, but they agreed they'd keep Jerusalem an international city. Jerusalem shall be trodden down of the Gentiles until the times of the Gentiles be fulfilled. Over there today Jerusalem is not in the hands of the little nation of Israel. They have only the new city; the old city is in the hands of the Arabs. Interesting, isn't it, my beloved, when you have the Word of God before you which has made this so crystal clear.

The kingdoms represented by the metals of the image are clearly identified. We do not have to speculate. Before we finish reading the Book of Daniel we find that God actually names the first three king- doms: Babylon; Media-Persia; Greece; and He so well describes the fourth kingdom as to leave no doubt that it is the Roman Empire.

I'm not going into details concerning these empires other than to say that historically each empire has followed the other exactly as God said it would, each one becoming a little stronger and a little larger than the other, but also each becoming a little inferior to the one that preceded it.

This man Nebuchadnezzar was an absolute monarch in the Babylo- nian Empire. He never asked anybody, not even his wife, about anything. He never shared rulership with anyone. When this man said, "Peace," there was peace in the world because he said it. A little bird didn't even chirp without his permission. (But do you want that kind of peace?)

After him came that oriental empire that dazzled the world, the Media-Persian Empire with all of its riches and oriental splendor. When Xerxes, lusting for power, moved toward the West, God stopped him at Thermopylae. The Greeks said the "gods" helped them there. But it wasn't gods (plural), it was singular—God did help the Greeks in that He stopped the invading Media-Persian Empire. Three hundred ships were destroyed, and Xerxes lost a million men in that expedition.

Then God took the scepter of world dominion out of the hand of oriental rulers and passed it to Greece, placing it in the hands of the young man, Alexander the Great, who in just a brief span of eleven years conquered the world. But Greece couldn't hold it. After the death of Alexander at the age of thirty-two, the empire was divided among his four generals. Then the scepter was passed to Rome, and Rome ruled.

The Media-Persian Empire had ruled from the Hellespont to the coral strands of India, from the top of the Euphrates down to the Persian Gulf, but now Rome comes on the scene and conquers the then-known world. All the way from the rockbound coast of Scotland to the burning sands of the Sahara Desert, all the way from the Rock of Gibraltar to the Euphrates River, the great Roman Empire ruled. It is the fourth and the last.

Now, my friend, although the boundaries widened, as you move down in history you see there is deterioration from one empire to the next empire. How different it is from man's outline of history! H. G. Wells wrote a book years ago entitled *The Outline of History*. He traced the history of man all the way up from the very beginning, from the Paleozoic to the Paleolithic to the Neolithic ages and up. It is onward and upward forever, bigger and better. That's the story of man according to H. G. Wells. But the interesting thing is, this man lived to see World War II, and before he died he said this: "The world has come to the end of its tether, and civilization has come to an end. We are standing on the brink, and we will fall over one of these days." It doesn't sound like we're getting bigger and better. God said there would be no improvement.

God said there would be deterioration, and there is deterioration in four different aspects, as graphically depicted by the image. First of all, there's deterioration in the worth of the metals. Gold is certainly more valuable than iron, and it's gold to silver to brass to iron and then to clay.

Then there's deterioration in position. Nebuchadnezzar was the head of gold, and certainly the head occupies a more honored position than the foot occupies. There is deterioration here according to the clear-cut statement of Scripture: "After thee shall arise another kingdom inferior to thee." God makes it clear that each one in succession was to be inferior to the other.

Then there's something that Tregelles, the great Hebrew scholar, called attention to, and if you have studied even basic chemistry you will recognize this: even the specific gravity of these metals becomes less as you move down. All the way from the head of gold down to the feet of iron and clay there is deterioration.

Something else that we must call to your attention here in conclusion is very important. We are told that when Daniel appeared before King Nebuchadnezzar he said,

> **But there is a God in heaven that revealeth secrets, and maketh known to the king Nebuchadnezzar what shall be in the latter days. . . .** (Daniel 2:28)

Note the expression "in the latter days," which has a very specific meaning. Those of you who are students of Scripture, and especially of prophecy, will recognize that this expression occurs again and again in the Old Testament. You ought never to confuse the last days of Israel with the last days of the church. They're not the same at all. And the mentioning of the last days of Israel began way back, long before the people became a nation. When old Jacob was on his death-bed, he called his twelve boys to come around him, and he made a prophecy concerning them. Here's what we're told in Genesis 49:1: "And Jacob called unto his sons, and said, Gather yourselves together, that I may tell you that which shall befall you in the last days"—the last days, in the latter times. You will find that the prophets all looked down the centuries to the last days. These last days concern the nation Israel.

Now what are these last days, these latter times, that God is talking about? Well, the fourth kingdom takes place, of course, in the latter days. That fourth kingdom is Rome. Now, my friend, I want you to look at something that is without doubt one of the most amazing things in the prophetic Word. No man could have guessed like this. There are only *four* worldwide kingdoms represented by these four different metals. There is first of all the head of gold, specifically stated to be Nebuchadnezzar in Daniel 2:38. There are the chest and the arms of silver, clearly identified as Media-Persia, and the brass abdomen and thighs of Greece, the Graeco-Macedonian Empire. Then there are the legs of iron with feet of iron and clay, the Roman Empire, and there are no more kingdoms after that. Rome is the last worldwide kingdom.

Now you will notice, Rome came to a dissolution about the fourth century A.D. It was in the fifth century that the barbarian hordes poured into the Roman Empire, and my ancestors and maybe yours were in those barbarian hordes. It's awful to think that you and I had barbarian ancestors, but we did. The barbarians poured into that empire. It fell apart because it was rotten to the core. It was a dictatorship, the like of which the world had never seen. Edward Gibbon, in his *Rise and Fall of the Roman Empire*, has written:

> The empire of the Romans filled the world, and when the empire fell into the hands of the single person, the world became a safe and dreary prison for his enemies. To resist was fatal and it was impossible to fly.

Robert Culver who more recently has written a brilliant book on Daniel says,

> Two millennia ago, Rome gave the world the ecumenical unity which the League of Nations and the United Nations organizations have sought to revive in our time. The modern attempts are not original at all (as many of our contemporaries suppose), but are revivals of the ancient Roman ideal which never since the time of Augustus Caesar has been wholly lost.

Rome did not end. Rome fell apart, just came loose at the seams. It never died. Rome lived on and Rome lives today in the broken fragments of many countries of Western Europe. Isn't it interesting that when Rome fell apart the barbarian hordes poured in? Attila the Hun sacked Rome, and was awestruck by what he saw. When he looked about and realized he could not handle such an empire, he took his army and left the city. There arose no *fifth* empire, and there hasn't for fifteen hundred years been a world empire. That's something to think about.

In the seventh century, out of the East came the Arab hordes. They came from both East and West under the crescent—Moslems, fanatics to the core and armed with a sword to convert the world. They almost destroyed the civilization of Western Europe at that time, what little there was. But they built no *empire*. The crescent of the Moslems was lifted over Constantinople, the capital of the eastern branch of the Roman Empire. You might have expected one of the caliphs to ascend the throne of the Caesars, but none ascended it.

Tartars and Turks moved through Asia. Genghis Khan, Suleiman the Great—neither of them became a world ruler. Napoleon tried it, but on his way to Warsaw God stopped him with the weakest thing in the world, a snowflake. Bismarck, the iron chancellor of Germany, tried to put Western Europe together and revive the Roman Empire.

He failed. Kaiser Wilhelm tried, Hitler tried, and Mussolini tried. All failed.

I say to you, my beloved, there have been only four empires, and for fifteen hundred years the nations of Europe have been at each other's throats. There has been warring back and forth among those nations that composed the Roman Empire, and as of this writing the revived Roman Empire is somewhere down in the feet of the image where there are ten toes.

Now don't attempt to identify the nations represented by the toes. I can't; no one can yet. But they will fall into place after the church is removed at the Rapture. I have a friend who is always trying to locate which is which, and I like to kid him about it and say, "You remind me of going into the nursery and playing with the little baby's toes—this little piggy went to market, this little piggy stayed home. . . ." Although we cannot identify the nations that will compose the revived Roman Empire, at this point we are somewhere down in the time of the feet of the image. Notice again that there will be division. At the beginning there are two legs of iron and now there are ten toes representing the division of the empire. And they are made of clay and iron, the clay denoting weakness and iron denoting strength. You and I know that in Europe there are both today.

Do you know what Western Europe is waiting for at this hour? It waits for a man big enough and strong enough to come along and put Western Europe back together again, and they are making progress. Europe for years was caught between two colossi, two great juggernauts—Russia on one side, the United States on the other. The little nations of Europe are now moving together and are quickly gaining economic power. No longer do you have difficulty crossing over from Germany to France and from one country to another. They are breaking down the barriers. A brilliant young German said not long ago, "We are European." Will that be the name of the new nation that will come out of this? Western Europe will come back together, and we're told in the Word of God that this last empire will be headed up by the Antichrist, for he alone will bring it back together again. And he will accomplish it in the last days.

This will end the times of the Gentiles, for when it comes back together it will defy God again. Remember, this is the empire that crucified our Lord Jesus. This empire in the days of Caesar Augustus sent out a decree that the whole world should be taxed. Boy, does that sound familiar! Mary had to go down from Nazareth to Bethlehem, because she was of the house and lineage of David, in order to enroll for the taxation made by Rome. And Rome will defy our Lord again and will seek to destroy Him. Then, my beloved, Christ Jesus will come forth. And this time—it is His second coming to earth that is before us—He is represented by the stone, the smiting stone.

Daniel continues,

> **Thou sawest till that a stone was cut out without hands, which smote the image upon his feet that were of iron and clay, and brake them to pieces. Then was the iron, the clay, the brass, the silver, and the gold, broken to pieces together, and became like the chaff of the summer threshingfloors; and the wind carried them away, that no place was found for them: and the stone that smote the image became a great mountain, and filled the whole earth.** (Daniel 2:34, 35)

Nebuchadnezzar beheld the image in awe and wonder. The stone, coming from beyond the environs of the image and without human origin or motivation, smote the image on the feet of iron and clay with such force that all the metals were pulverized. And a wind blew the dust of the image away so that it entirely disappeared. Then the stone began to grow as a living stone, and it filled the whole world, taking the place of this image.

My friend, you and I are living in a world where men in the religious community have been saying for years that the church is going to convert the world, that the Kingdom of God will be established by human effort. The Bible has been saying the contrary. When God is ready to set up His Kingdom, He won't need help from any church! This age in which we live will not end with a converted world. This age is to end by the catastrophic and cataclysmic coming of Jesus Christ to this earth to put down Gentile misrule and to take for Himself the scepter of world dominion. He is the smiting Stone of destruction.

The reason that Stone has not yet struck is because the last part of the prophecy has not quite been fulfilled. Antichrist is yet to appear, but God is holding him back. Europe is crying out for him. If any man will appear in Europe who can put the countries of the Roman

Empire back together again, they'll not ask and they won't care whether he comes from heaven or hell. They'll take him if he will just promise to bring them together and give them a measure of peace, for that is exactly what the Antichrist will promise and accomplish for a brief time when he comes. But there's no real peace for this earth until Jesus comes.

In the meantime, in patience our Lord is dealing with this world, and in mercy He's holding back the judgment. On an occasion when the Lord Jesus confronted the Pharisees, He said,

> **Therefore say I unto you, The kingdom of God shall be taken from you, and given to a nation bringing forth the fruits thereof. And whosoever shall fall on this stone shall be broken: but on whomsoever it shall fall, it will grind him to powder.** (Matthew 21:43, 44)

My friend, if you fall upon this Stone, you can obtain mercy and you can be saved.

> **The Father loveth the Son, and hath given all things into his hand. He that believeth on the Son hath everlasting life: and he that believeth not the Son shall not see life; but the wrath of God abideth on him.** (John 3:35, 36)

You and I have moved down pretty close to the end of the age, to a day coming when the Lord Jesus will come forward and take the scepter back into His own hands. And, friend, there will never be peace on this earth until that scepter is held by nail-pierced hands, until Jesus Christ rules on this earth. It's not until then that peace and righteousness will cover this earth as the waters cover the sea. That is the hope of the earth.

Chapter 3

WHY GOD GAVE PALESTINE TO ISRAEL

Whether Israel has been in the news recently or not, that land happens to be the very center of God's earthly program, and God's people have learned to keep their eye on it. Now there are certain questions which arise in connection with Israel and that land. Why did God give that land to Israel? You can turn the question around— why did God give Israel to that land? They both go together.

Now here are some of the questions that have been raised. Why would God put one people out of the land and put another people into the land? Why did God put the Canaanites and all of the others out of that land and put the Israelites into the land? How can you justify such actions? Wasn't it rather arbitrary on the part of God to do such a thing as that?

And then another question: What superiority did Israel possess that would justify God's putting them in the land? Now over the centuries these have been the questions that the cynic and the skeptic have asked, and they have disputed the rightness of God in putting these people in the land. We find the same questions have been raised in our day about the present situation over there. However I'm not discussing the present situation at this time but am confining what I have to say to the basis upon which God put the people of Israel into that land at the time of Joshua.

Years ago someone, apparently an anti-Semite, wrote these words on a fence:

It's odd that God should choose the Jews.

A Jew had come along and written under it,

God chose, which shows God knew His Jew.

A Christian came along and wrote under that,

> This Jew spoke true. God knew His Jew as King would bring to
> earth new birth.

May I say, that is one of the reasons, and it's a valid reason, why God drew these people aside and used them as the instrument through whom He would bring the Messiah into the world. But that's a phase we're not discussing now.

I want to consider some of the facets of this problem about God's putting these people in that land. We need to get a full-orbed picture with a correct perspective, and I personally believe that the Book of Deuteronomy is the one that will give us that picture.

A precise point which I have attempted to establish in teaching the entire Word of God has been this: there is a two-fold purpose of God in giving the Law. First of all, He gave the Law to a people, and second, He gave the Law for a land, a particular land and not just any land. The people to whom God gave the Law was the nation Israel. The land for which God accommodated the Law was the land of Canaan (later called Palestine). Although the nation Israel never did fully occupy it (probably only one tenth of it), today they occupy even less. Yet that land is the place that is concerned with the Mosaic Law. The Law was accommodated to the land.

Now if you will note the Scriptures that we cite, you will see this suggestion. We will turn first to Deuteronomy 6:10:

> **And it shall be, when the LORD thy God shall have brought thee
> into the land which he sware unto thy fathers, to Abraham, to
> Isaac, and to Jacob, to give thee great and goodly cities, which
> thou buildest not.**

God is constantly, in the Book of Deuteronomy, reminding the people of Israel, "When you get into the land, this is the way it's going to be, and this is the thing you are to do." You find this also in the Book of Exodus, and you find it in the Book of Leviticus: God's saying that the Law is to be applicable to the land of Canaan. Again and again God said, "This is what it shall be, and this is what you shall do when you enter the land."

Therefore much of the Mosaic Law and system is applicable to the Promised Land. It was not applicable to the wilderness; it was not until they entered the Promised Land that a great deal of it could even go into effect. It wasn't feasible for them until then.

And it wasn't meant for California either. It's not geared to our freeway system at all. Let me remind you of one or two things. God gave to these people cities of refuge, places they could flee to when they accidentally killed someone. Well, may I say, it just wouldn't work here, it wouldn't fit into our system today at all. Also they were given a certain right regulating the mortgaging of land. They could put up only a forty-nine-year mortgage, because every fifty years every mortgage was canceled and the land went back to the original owner. I'm confident that loan associations in the United States would not want to work on that kind of a program, when today a ninety-nine-year lease is the one they use. And then the year of jubilee was certainly suitable and made to fit into the society and the social structure of the Holy Land. The tribes of Israel and the land of Canaan belonged together like ham and eggs. (I probably ought not use that metaphor, because they were not to eat ham!)

LOVE IS PRIMARY

It's imperative that we state here and now that the primary motivating power and the explanation of why God put these people in the land was love. He loved them. He made that as the basis. Will you listen to Him again:

And because he loved thy fathers, therefore he chose their seed after them, and brought thee out in his sight with his mighty power out of Egypt; to drive out nations from before thee greater and mightier than thou art, to bring thee in, to give their land for an inheritance, as it is this day. (Deuteronomy 4:37, 38)

Now the question arises, didn't God love the other nations? Why would He put them out? Didn't He love them? Moses answers that question:

He [God] doth execute the judgment of the fatherless and widow, and loveth the stranger, in giving him food and raiment. Love

ye therefore the stranger: for ye were strangers in the land of Egypt. (Deuteronomy 10:18, 19)

God tells His people, "I love the stranger. And you are to love the stranger. If you want the evidence for that, I feed them and I take care of them." My friend, today as you look throughout this world, in spite of the fact that the curse of sin is on this earth, it does produce enough to feed everybody. The trouble is that men, because of their sin and their selfishness, have blocked the avenues that would adequately distribute this bounty, and that's the reason today multitudes have to go hungry. It is man's inhumanity to man!

God loves the stranger. God loves the people. God says here in Deuteronomy, "I'm putting you in the land. I'll put these others out, but I want you to know that I love them also."

Again this is called to our attention when we get to the New Testament: "God so loved the world. . . ." He loved the cosmos.

He loved the world of humanity.

For God so loved the world, that he gave his only begotten Son, that whosoever believeth in him should not perish, but have everlasting life. (John 3:16)

So that's the motivating power that caused God to move as He did. He said, "It was because I loved you. I moved in your behalf because of my love for you."

WAS GOD UNJUST?

Now that has not answered the question of why God put these other nations out of the land. That question is raised today by many, and the implication always is that God was unjust; He was narrow and He was mean in so doing. The liberal theologian has called the God of the Old Testament a big bully! "He had no right to go in there and put these people out of the land! He was wrong when He did that. These were poor, innocent, lovely, cultured, refined people, and God pitched them out! Why would God do such a thing as that?" Now today will you look at what God says. I do think He needs to be heard in this matter, and He hasn't been heard. I get a little provoked when I hear a liberal who makes a boast of intellectuality, and then he does not examine the evidence; God makes it clear if you let Him explain His case. He should be heard in court. I want you to notice this very carefully:

> **When the LORD thy God shall bring thee into the land whither thou goest to possess it, and hath cast out many nations before thee, the Hittites, and the Girgashites, and the Amorites, and the Canaanites, and the Perizzites, and the Hivites, and the Jebusites, seven nations greater and mightier than thou; and when the LORD thy God shall deliver them before thee; thou shalt smite them, and utterly destroy them; thou shalt make no covenant with them, nor show mercy unto them: neither shalt thou make marriages with them; thy daughter thou shalt not give unto his son, nor his daughter shalt thou take unto thy son. For they will turn away thy son from following me, that they may serve other gods: so will the anger of the LORD be kindled against you, and destroy thee suddenly. But thus shall ye deal with them; ye shall destroy their altars, and break down their images, and cut down their groves, and burn their graven images with fire.** (Deuteronomy 7:1-5)

The people that were in that land were an idolatrous people. They had turned their backs upon God. They had rejected the living and true God, and the type of idolatry they were in was grossly immoral. For a picture of that we'll go to Leviticus 18, and again God will make it very clear. I'm going to lift out just one little segment, verses 21-28, to let you see the immorality that was in that land when God put His people in there. Notice this:

> **And thou shalt not let any of thy seed pass through the fire to Molech, neither shalt thou profane the name of thy God: I am the LORD.**

What He meant by "your seed" was, of course, their children. You see, in that land there was the worship of Molech, and the image of Molech was either sitting with his lap open or his arms held out. From the inside, that image was heated red-hot, and then little children were put into the arms or lap of that image as human sacrifices. God rejected that. God was saying, "Don't you ever commit your children, your seed, to go through the fire of Molech." That's what the people of the land were doing.

That's one of the reasons God put them out, but that's not all. Listen to this:

> **Thou shalt not lie with mankind, as with womankind: it is abomination.**

That's what they were doing in that land.

> **Neither shalt thou lie with any beast to defile thyself therewith: neither shall any woman stand before a beast to lie down thereto: it is confusion.**

That's what they were doing in that land.

> **Defile not ye yourselves in any of these things: for in all these the nations are defiled which I cast out before you.**

God says, "This is what these nations were doing and that's the reason I'm putting them out."

Doesn't an owner of property have a right to put out a tenant who is destroying his property, who won't pay rent, who doesn't recognize him at all and who has turned his house into a place of ill repute? God says, "They must leave that land. It's on the bridge of three continents. It is defiling the entire human race! I must put these people out of that land."

> **And the land is defiled: therefore I do visit the iniquity thereof upon it, and the land itself vomiteth out her inhabitants.**

They were so rotten and corrupt in their immorality that God likened it to the land itself vomiting them out—it made the land sick, if you please.

> **Ye shall therefore keep my statutes and my judgments, and shall not commit any of these abominations; neither any of your own nation, nor any stranger that sojourneth among you: (for all these abominations have the men of the land done, which were before you, and the land is defiled;) that the land spue not you out also, when ye defile it, as it spued out the nations that were before you.**

Now the Lord makes it very clear that these people were living in gross immorality and that their idolatry was dragging not only them down, but actually it was also dragging other nations down.

Now again, will you listen to the Lord in Deuteronomy 8:20:

As the nations which the LORD destroyeth before your face, so shall ye perish; because ye would not be obedient unto the voice of the LORD your God.

Now God warned His people. He said, "If you go into that land and you repeat the things they are doing, as sure as I put them out I'll put you out." Did God put His own people out? Yes, there came such a day. Because of the fact that privilege always creates responsibility, God punished His people far greater than He ever punished these idolatrous nations that were in the land.

That's the reason I say again that I believe America is far more responsible to God than an atheistic country is. I believe the people in America are more responsible to God than the people who have not heard what God has said in His Word. But you have heard, and the people listening to Christian radio programming have heard. I don't know how much longer it's going to continue, but I do want to say this: we can hear the Word of God in America and responsibility becomes ours because we do have light. His people, the children of Israel, had light. And so there came a day of reckoning for them.

Notice in 2 Kings 24:2–4, there came the day when God put His own people out:

And the Lord sent against him bands of the Chaldees, and bands of the Syrians, and bands of the Moabites, and bands of the children of Ammon. . . .

The very people that Israel put out! God permitted them later to come and put the children of Israel out.

. . . and sent them against Judah to destroy it, according to the word of the LORD, which he spake by his servants the prophets. Surely at the commandment of the LORD came this upon Judah, to remove them out of his sight, for the sins of Manasseh [probably the worst king that Judah ever had], according to all that he did; and also for the innocent blood that he shed: for he filled

Jerusalem with innocent blood; which the LORD would not pardon.

Why? Manasseh had light. And since he had light, now God says, "You go into captivity because you've done exactly what the heathen did."

So when you say that God is playing favorites with the nation Israel, you are wrong. History does not bear that out. God treated them even more severely than He treated these other nations. He told them at the beginning, "If you do the things these nations are doing, out you go." My friend, of the seventeen great civilizations that have gone down, they all started their decline the moment they repudiated God.

The signs in America today are not good. We see even our Supreme Court deciding that a man does not have to put his hand on the Bible as he takes an oath that he will support our constitution and that he will carry out his office. They suppose that the Bible is not necessary because we no longer believe it is the Word of God. Other nations have gone down that repudiated God like that.

At Jericho you will recall that God forbad His people to take any of their booty. When a wedge of gold and a Babylonish garment were taken, God judged Israel, led them to defeat because of that. We today may look back at that and question it, but now the archaeologists can tell you why God was so severe. These people in Jericho were eaten up with venereal disease. God says, "Don't put your hand upon a thing. Don't you dare take anything for yourselves because these are a rotten and corrupt people—they must be destroyed." May I say that it was the judgment of God upon them. God was justified in putting these nations off His land.

Furthermore let me add this, God actually was merciful to these nations. We are trying to get a full-orbed picture of this, so let's go back to the Book of Genesis. At that time there was no nation of Israel, only Abraham. And God is speaking to Abraham:

And he said unto Abram, Know of a surety that thy seed shall be a stranger in a land that is not theirs, and shall serve them; they shall afflict them four hundred years. (Genesis 15:13)

Why would God send His people out of that land for four hundred years? Here's the reason:

And also that nation, whom they shall serve, will I judge: and afterward shall they come out with great substance. And thou shalt go to thy fathers in peace; thou shalt be buried in a good old age. But in the fourth generation they shall come hither again: for the iniquity of the Amorites is not yet full. (Genesis 15:14–16)

In Abraham's day God said, "I can't put you here now, because the Amorites have not yet sinned away their day of grace. I'm going to give them four hundred more years to make up their minds whether they will turn to Me or not." Now isn't that being merciful? I wonder today if even the worst critic of the Word of God wouldn't agree that four hundred years is long enough to give anybody? I wouldn't want to ask God to extend it longer than that. God says, "For four hundred years I'll keep you out of this land, and I won't let you in because the iniquity of the Amorites is not yet full." God is being gracious in dealing with these people.

Then when the children of Israel finally came into the land they sent in spies to Jericho, and these spies took refuge in the home of Rahab. I want you to see something quite interesting that Rahab said to the spies:

And she said unto the men, I know that the LORD hath given you the land, and that your terror is fallen upon us, and that all the inhabitants of the land faint because of you.

Now listen to this:

For we have heard how the LORD dried up the water of the Red Sea for you, when ye came out of Egypt. . . . (Joshua 2:9, 10)

How long ago was that? Forty years before, God had brought them across the Red Sea. And one of the reasons He kept them out in that wilderness after Kadesh-barnea was to see if somebody in that land would turn to Him, would believe. And Rahab heard! We're told by the writer to the Hebrews,

By faith the harlot Rahab perished not with them that believed not, when she had received the spies with peace. (Hebrews 11:31)

Here is one woman who believed God during those forty years. God saved her. I've a question to ask you. If Rahab the harlot would be saved by turning to God, what about the mayor of Jericho? Do you think God would have saved him? I think so. Do you think God would have saved the captain of the hosts of Jericho? I think He would have. Do you think God would have saved the so-called "better" people of town—those who lived on the best side of the railroad tracks? I think He would. He saved Rahab. And for forty years after those people had heard, they still had an opportunity to turn to God. Oh, how merciful God was to those corrupt people in that land! They could have turned to Him. May I say to you, when God put these people out He was justified in doing so.

WAS ISRAEL SUPERIOR?

Did God think the people of Israel were a superior people? The anti-Semite raises this question, then he proceeds to censure these people and call them rascals, and scoffing he says, "God chose them, and He thinks they were superior!" Well, did God think they were superior? Will you listen to the Lord now—He needs to be heard in this day:

> **The Lord did not set his love upon you, nor choose you, because ye were more in number than any people; for ye were the fewest of all people.** (Deuteronomy 7:7)

You see, if God were depending on their vote to get into office, He was playing with the wrong people. They were a minority group. They couldn't help Him win an election. Napoleon said, "God is on the side of the biggest battalion"—and of course Napoleon proved himself wrong. He had the biggest battalions and he lost. Here God says, "I didn't choose you because you were superior in number. I didn't choose you for that reason at all."

And it was not because of their superior ability and aptitudes. Notice how the Lord warns them through Moses:

> **. . . The LORD thy God . . . who fed thee in the wilderness with manna, which thy fathers knew not, that he might humble thee, and that he might prove thee, to do thee good at thy latter end;**

and thou say in thine heart, My power and the might of mine hand hath gotten me this wealth. But thou shalt remember the LORD thy God: for it is he that giveth thee power to get wealth, that he may establish his covenant which he sware unto thy fathers, as it is this day. (Deuteronomy 8:14, 16–18)

Now Moses is saying to these people, "When you get in that land and you are prospered—and God will prosper you if you serve Him—don't you get the notion that it's because you have superior ability or you have aptitudes that other people do not have. You do not. God is the One who will give you that ability, and God is the One who will help you when you are in that land." Don't for one moment think God ever put Israel in the land of promise because they had superior ability and aptitude.

And it was not because they would keep His commandments. Oh, we need to see that! Over in Deuteronomy 5:29 is the heart-cry of God:

O that there were such an heart in them, that they would fear me, and keep all my commandments always, that it might be well with them, and with their children for ever!

These people were very presumptuous at Mount Sinai. They asked for the Law and didn't even know what it was. When God sent Moses into their midst, He said, "Ask them, would they like to go on eagle's wings, or would they prefer the Law?" And they sent back word, "Bring it on. We'll keep it." They didn't even know what it was.

That is the attitude of a great many people today. There are so many folk who think they please God. But oh, if you and I could see ourselves as God sees us! If you and I were taken to heaven tonight we would wreck the place before morning. We think we're going to adorn the place and that we will be an asset up there. But we would be the biggest liability God ever had if He took us as we are right now. We're not attractive. We're not godly. We are very unlovely. We are sinners. God knows our weaknesses, and God knows our littleness, and God knows our sin. And as He put these people of Israel in the land on the basis of the Law, God's heart cried out, "O that they had a heart to keep My law." He knew what would happen.

I do not know about you, but when I hear people say they can keep the Law and please God, it makes me shudder. My friend, you can't please Him. That's the reason He sent His Son to die for you. He loved you and knew you couldn't do a thing to please Him. God did not put these people in this land because they were going to keep His commandments. He knew they would not.

And it was not because of Israel's superior goodness and righteousness. Now if this wasn't so serious you would just have to laugh—I think God must have smiled. Notice Deuteronomy 9:4–6:

> **Speak not thou in thine heart, after that the LORD thy God hath cast them out from before thee, saying, For my righteousness the Lord hath brought me in to possess this land: but for the wickedness of these nations the LORD doth drive them out from before thee.**

God says, "I'm not putting you in this land because you are righteous. You are not."

> **Not for thy righteousness, or for the uprightness of thine heart, dost thou go to possess their land: but for the wickedness of these nations the LORD thy God doth drive them out from before thee, and that He may perform the word which the LORD swore unto thy fathers, Abraham, Isaac, and Jacob.**

Now notice this:

> **Understand therefore, that the LORD thy God giveth thee not this good land to possess it for thy righteousness; for thou art a stiff-necked people.**

A stiff-necked people! It sounds like God was anti-Semitic, doesn't it? And He was. And I want to say this, He's anti-Gentile also! If you think that you have any righteousness that He can accept, you are wrong. These people had none, and they had the Mosaic Law that was accommodated to the land, where it would be easier to keep. But they failed, and they stand as a monument in history as evidence that no people can measure up to God's standard. You have to come some other way.

God said, "You are not going into that land because of your righteousness." God said, "Why, you are a stiff-necked people." And my friend, God has not saved you or me because of any goodness in us.

He found none. Oh, if we could only learn that. There are some folks who seem to think, *He saved me as a sinner, but He got a pretty good fellow.* He didn't get a good fellow! I marvel that God ever saved me. He shouldn't have done it, but I thank Him that He did. And it was all because of His mercy.

I've seen those pictures, as you have, of people pouring out of one country then another, hungry people. My friend, you'd better stop and think it over. Do you think that you are any better than they are? Not in God's sight. Why has God saved you? Because of His *mercy.*

God said of Israel, "I'm putting them in the land, but not because they are righteous. They are not a superior people."

GOD KEEPS HIS PROMISES

God did give the children of Israel the land because of His covenant with Abraham, Isaac, and Jacob. In the Book of Genesis God called Abraham out of Ur of the Chaldeans and promised him three things. One of those things was the land which became known as the Promised Land. He reaffirmed that promise when Abraham got into that land. The Lord said to Abraham:

> . . . **Lift up now thine eyes, and look from the place where thou art northward, and southward, and eastward, and westward: for all the land which thou seest, to thee will I give it, and to thy seed for ever.** (Genesis 13:14, 15)

"This is it, Abraham, I give it all to you." He reaffirmed this covenant with Abraham's son Isaac and with his grandson Jacob—He said, "This is your land." When the land was stricken with a seven-year famine, God provided a place of survival for Jacob and his family in Egypt:

> **And he said, I am God, the God of thy father: fear not to go down into Egypt; for I will there make of thee a great nation: I will go down with thee into Egypt; and I will also surely bring thee up again. . . .** (Genesis 46:3, 4)

He said, "Jacob, you can go on down into Egypt. I'll hold this land in fee simple for you. It's yours." In time God brought them out of

Egypt under Moses and back to their own land because of His promise
to Abraham, Isaac, and Jacob. Again and again in Deuteronomy He
reminded the children of Israel of that:

> **The Lord did not set his love upon you, nor choose you, because
> ye were more in number than any people; for ye were the fewest
> of all people: but because the Lord loved you, and because he
> would keep the oath which he had sworn unto your fathers. . . .**
> (Deuteronomy 7:7, 8)

God had said to Abraham, "I'll give it to you." And God keeps His
promises.

My friend, when God saves you and me, it's no transaction that
you and I have made with God. It's a transaction that back in eternity
the Son made with the Father that He would come to this earth and
die for Vernon McGee and for you. God saves us because He made
that covenant:

> **For God so loved the world, that he gave his only begotten Son,
> that whosoever believeth in him should not perish, but have
> everlasting life.** (John 3:16)

It is God's covenant! He's a covenant-making and covenant-keeping
God.

God has a plan, and we find it briefly stated in the great Palestinian
covenant of Deuteronomy 30. There are seven great promises God
makes here, and there are no "if's" in this covenant. These statements
are unconditional. Verse one says that the people of Israel will be
dispersed among all the nations, that the nation will be plucked off
the land for its unfaithfulness. That has taken place. Verse 2 tells that
there will be a future repentance of Israel in the dispersion. They are
going to come back to God.

> **. . . The LORD thy God will turn thy captivity, and have compas-
> sion upon thee, and [Messiah] will return and gather thee from
> all the nations, whither the LORD thy God hath scattered thee.**
> (Deuteronomy 30:3)

This verse gives the first mention in Scripture of the return of Christ
to the earth. It is a remarkable prophecy, and it has not yet been

fulfilled. Not until its fulfillment will the land be blessed and be at peace.

And the LORD thy God will bring thee into the land which thy fathers possessed, and thou shalt possess it; and he will do thee good, and multiply thee above thy fathers. (Deuteronomy 30:5)

The fourth great promise of God is that Israel is to be restored to the land. This is an unconditional promise. No amount of scattering can change the fact that in the future God will bring them into the land.

The fifth promise is that there will be a national conversion:

And the LORD thy God will circumcise thine heart, and the heart of thy seed, to love the LORD thy God with all thine heart, and with all thy soul, that thou mayest live. (Deuteronomy 30:6)

In verses 7–10, we read that Israel's enemies will be judged. And finally, the seventh promise, Israel will then receive her full blessing. Jeremiah wrote of this in Jeremiah 31:31–33:

Behold, the days come, saith the LORD, that I will make a new covenant with the house of Israel, and with the house of Judah: not according to the covenant that I made with their fathers in the day I took them by the hand to bring them out of the land of Egypt; which my covenant they brake, although I was an husband unto them, saith the LORD: but this shall be the covenant that I will make with the house of Israel; After those days, saith the LORD, I will put my law in their inward parts, and write it in their hearts; and will be their God, and they shall be my people.

And the writer to the Hebrews referred to this new covenant:

For finding fault with them, he saith, Behold, the days come, saith the Lord, when I will make a new covenant with the house of Israel and with the house of Judah. (Hebrews 8:8)

Christ is the One to institute this new covenant which is yet future.

Moses told the children of Israel that their stay in the land would be determined by their obedience. He outlined their history and said they would be expelled from that land when they disobeyed. But God promised to bring them back. Finally, He will return them to the land, and they shall never, never go out again. Why? Because they will have obeyed Him? No. Because God makes good His covenant. He will bring them back, and then they will obey Him.

It is exactly the same with us. God asks us to trust the Lord Jesus Christ as our Savior. After that He talks to us about obedience—"If ye love me, keep my commandments" (John 14:15).

GOD IS GOD!

Now I move to the last point. God put them in that land, and He will bring them back into the land, because of the sovereignty of God! And I just love the following verse:

> **Know therefore this day, and consider it in thine heart, that the LORD he is God in heaven above, and upon the earth beneath: there is none else.** (Deuteronomy 4:39)

God says, "I am unique. There's only one of Me." Only one God. God does not have to report to a superior. He doesn't turn in a report every week. God has no boss to whom He's responsible. He never punches a timeclock. He has no one that He has to answer to—He has no equal, no one over Him. By the same token, there is no one beneath Him that He has to answer to.

Even the Democrats and the Republicans try to please the people beneath them. But God doesn't have to. God does not depend upon the vote of the majority to stay in office. He is sovereign.

And in this same connection God spoke to Moses:

> **What shall we say then? Is there unrighteousness with God? God forbid.** [Anything God does, He is right in doing.] **For he saith to Moses, I will have mercy on whom I will have mercy, and I will have compassion on whom I will have compassion.** (Romans 9:14, 15)

Moses, you remember, came to God, and God heard his prayer. But God said to Moses, "I want you to understand one thing. My answering your prayer is not because you are Mr. Moses. It's not because of who you are. It's not because you've been my leader all these years; it's not because you've followed me faithfully. 'I will have mercy on whom I will have mercy, and I will have compassion on whom I will have compassion. So then it is not of him that willeth, nor of him that runneth, but of God that sheweth mercy'" (Romans 9:15, 16).

Oh, how in America, even in our so-called Bible churches, we need to learn this: God put Israel in that land we call the "Holy Land." He gave it to them because He wanted to, and He doesn't have to answer to you! And in the future He will return them to that land for the same reason. Let's learn that God doesn't have to turn in a report to you or to me tomorrow morning and explain why He does certain things. God is riding triumphantly in His own chariot, and there's no unrighteousness with Him. Whatever He does is right.

What I need to learn, and what you need to learn, is to bow before Him. He is God. You and I are not God. We do not have to be responsible, but God—beloved, oh, how we need to learn it—God is sovereign. And He said to Israel, "There is none like Me. I am God. I'm right in what I'm doing." You don't like it? It is too bad for you, my beloved. Why do you keep fighting God? Why do you keep resisting Him? Why do you keep questioning Him? Don't you know that He is right, and you are wrong?

There was a Greek proverb that said, "The dice of the gods are loaded." God says in effect, "Don't roll dice with me. I roll only loaded dice. I know exactly how they're coming up, and you don't. So don't gamble with Me. You'll lose."

A sovereign God took these people, small in number, unworthy, and He gave them that land. He put out the former inhabitants after He had been merciful to them by giving them forty more years of opportunity. And today my friend, that same God moves in a sovereign way, but He comes to the door of your heart and stops, and He knocks, saying in effect, "You will have to be the one to let Me in. I won't force my way in. But I want to come into your life, not because you are wonderful, but because you are a sinner. I'm not coming to you because you are great, but because you are little. I'm not coming in because you are good. You are not good in my sight. But I love you. My death on the cross paid the penalty for your sin. I want to save you. I am God."

Come now, and let us reason together, saith the LORD: Though your sins be as scarlet, they shall be white as snow; though they be red like crimson, they shall be as wool. (Isaiah 1:18)

Chapter 4

DEAD BONES
IN DEATH VALLEY
Ezekiel 37

It was William Lewis Manly, a tenderfoot from Vermont, and his partner John Rogers who were the first to cross Death Valley in California. They did it to bring supplies to the Bennett-Arcane party that had been stranded during their trip from the East among the '49ers. Manley and Rogers were the first two white men, as far as we know, who ever looked upon the grandest scene of desolation and death that any man had seen—Death Valley in California.

Now there is one exception to this. Twenty-five hundred years before Death Valley was discovered in California, Ezekiel was given a vision of another death valley that was more desolate, more fearsome and awesome than any man had seen before or has seen since then. The valley that Ezekiel saw was a valley filled with dry bones. And believe me, he emphasizes it: they were very dry indeed.

Ezekiel was with the captives by the river Chebar. This was the place where they had been taken as slaves. They had been captured and taken into captivity for seventy long years. There, as Psalm 137 says, they hung their harps upon the willows, and they sat down and wept when they remembered Zion. All hope was gone. They thought God had deserted them and that they were in a predicament out of which they could never be delivered. But this man Ezekiel was called to prophesy to these poor, downtrodden, helpless, hopeless captives. I believe he prophesied at the darkest moment in the history of the nation. But it's interesting that the darker it got, the brighter the prophecies were. Isaiah's prophecies are bright; Jeremiah's brighter;

but Ezekiel's are the brightest of all. The greatest prophecies in Scripture come from Ezekiel.

Now this prophecy in particular has to do with the nation Israel in the deplorable and degraded state that they were in during the sixth century B.C.:

The hand of the LORD was upon me, and carried me out in the Spirit of the LORD, and set me down in the midst of the valley which was full of bones, and caused me to pass by them round about; and, behold, there were very many in the open valley; and, lo, they were very dry. And he said unto me, Son of man, can these bones live? And I answered, O Lord GOD, thou knowest. Again he said unto me, Prophesy upon these bones: and say unto them, O ye dry bones, hear the word of the LORD. Thus saith the Lord GOD unto these bones; Behold, I will cause breath to enter into you, and ye shall live. And I will lay sinews upon you, and will bring up flesh upon you, and cover you with skin, and put breath in you, and ye shall live; and ye shall know that I am the LORD. So I prophesied as I was commanded. And as I prophesied, there was a noise, and, behold, a shaking, and the bones came together, bone to its bone. And when I beheld, lo, the sinews and the flesh came up upon them, and the skin covered them above, but there was no breath in them. Then said he unto me, Prophesy unto the wind, prophesy, son of man, and say to the wind, Thus saith the Lord GOD: Come from the four winds, O breath, and breathe upon these slain, that they may live. So I prophesied as he commanded me, and the breath came into them, and they lived, and stood up upon their feet, an exceedingly great army. Then he said unto me, Son of man, these bones are the whole house of Israel; behold, they say, Our bones are dried, and our hope is lost; we are cut off on our part. Therefore, prophesy and say unto them, Thus saith the Lord GOD: Behold, O my people, I will open your graves, and cause you to come up out of your graves, and bring you into the land of Israel. And ye shall know that I am the LORD, when I have opened your graves, O my people, and brought you up out of your graves. . . . And say unto them, Thus saith the Lord GOD: Behold, I will take the children of Israel from among the nations,

to which they are gone, and will gather them on every side, and bring them into their own land. (Ezekiel 37:1–13, 21)*

Ezekiel tells us that God picked him up in the spirit and took him out there to show him this valley covered with bones, and they were human bones. They were scattered so that apparently no skeleton was intact. All the bones were separate and scattered all over the valley, and they were very dry indeed.

And then God asked Ezekiel a question, "Son of man, can these bones live?" This man Ezekiel is, to my judgment, a skeptic. He said, "O Lord GOD, thou knowest," which is an idiomatic expression that means, "As far as I'm concerned they can't live. They're dead. There's no possibility of their ever living." That is exactly what his answer implies. "O Lord God, Thou knowest, I don't." To translate it into good old Americana, I suppose it would be something like this: "If they live You will have to do something because, as far as I'm concerned, they're just as dead as a dodo bird, and there's no possibility of any life being in this valley of death I'm looking at."

Now God tells Ezekiel to do something that I'm confident seems silly to him. "Again he said unto me, Prophesy upon these bones: and say unto them, 'O ye dry bones, hear the word of the LORD.'"

I think maybe Ezekiel protested, "You don't mean for me to talk to these bones!"

God says, "I certainly do."

"But I don't think I ought to say anything to them, because they can't hear."

"I say to you, prophesy to these bones! Speak to them, and say to them, 'O ye dry bones, hear the word of the LORD!'"

May I say to you, that is the predicament of every person who speaks to an unsaved individual or speaks to an unsaved congregation. Do you know that you are speaking to those who are dead? We're all dead in trespasses and sins before we are saved. To speak to a person who is unsaved is to speak to a person who can't hear you. He can't respond to you. He has no will to act upon what you have to say. Yet you and I are told that we are to witness. We are to talk to dead people! My friend, as all unsaved people are dead, so you and I were dead in trespasses and sins before we came to Christ. Ephesians 2:1

---

*All Scripture from the New Scofield Reference Edition, © 1967.

tells us: "And you hath he made alive, who were dead in trespasses and sins." Now that's the condition of the human family.

There's something that I always did during all my years as pastor of the Church of the Open Door. Every Sunday morning before coming out to the pulpit the last thing I'd tell the Lord was, "If anything happens today You will have to do it because I'm speaking to folks that are dead"—that is, the unsaved. I think sometimes the saved come under that category too, but certainly the unsaved do—dead in trespasses and sins. They can't hear, and they're not going to hear unless the Spirit of God speaks to them. Yet God says to me and to you, "Speak to these dry bones, and say something to them, and witness to them."

Oh, my friend, though we may be very helpless in ourselves, we always have the Spirit of God, and the Spirit of God can make dead ears hear. He can make a dead heart respond. He can make a dead will act, if you please. God can do that, and He alone can do it. You and I can't do it. Therefore we may be the most helpless people in the world, and yet we're the strongest because the Spirit of God is with us, for we are saying what the Spirit of God can use.

Now will you notice that Ezekiel is supposed to speak to these dry bones. And he has quite a message for them, a very encouraging message. He says, "Dry bones, you're going to live. You're going to come back."

You can see the pertinency of that message for Ezekiel's day. He is talking to a group of discouraged people who have sat down yonder by the river in Babylon. They're weeping; they can't sing the songs of Zion. He says to them, "You may be dry bones, but there's one thing for sure, there's a day coming when you're going to live again."

Now this passage of Scripture is used in several different ways. I just got a new book on Ezekiel, and the first place I turned was to Ezekiel chapter 37, as I always do to see how the expositor interprets it. Well, the author went down the old familiar line that what Ezekiel is talking about here is revival; this is the way you promote a revival, we need to stir the old dry bones, and that type of thing. Another interpretation, and this author gives it too, is that the passage speaks of resurrection, physical resurrection.

Now may I say to you that I do not object to drawing wonderful, marvelous applications from this prophecy. I'm sure you can get a lesson here on revival if you look for it, and you will probably get a lesson on resurrection if you look for it. But we're not left to our own devices in interpretation. In this passage of Scripture we are told what it means—we are not left to guess what God is talking about:

> **Then he said unto me, Son of man, these bones are the whole house of Israel. . . .**

So I understand that these dead bones represent the whole house of Israel, and they do not mean primarily anything other than that.

> **Behold, they say, Our bones are dried, and our hope is lost; we are cut off on our part.**

He's talking to the nation Israel. He's talking to them about their hope for the future, whether God is through with them or not.

Now, God doesn't end with that.

> **Therefore, prophesy and say unto them, Thus saith the Lord GOD: Behold, O my people, I will open your graves, and cause you to come up out of your graves, and bring you into the land of Israel.**

Some expositors say, "Yes, but He's talking now about resurrection, and He's talking about raising them from the dead, probably beginning with Abraham, Isaac, and Jacob." And I say to you that He has nothing like that in mind at all. He makes it very clear what He means. He says,

> **Thus saith the Lord GOD: Behold, I will take the children of Israel from among the nations [Gentiles], to which they are gone, and will gather them on every side, and bring them into their own land.**

God is going to reach out among the nations of the world, and He's going to bring the whole house of Israel back into that land. And that's what He means.

Somebody counters, "But He talks about resurrection and life from the dead." Sure. In our Lord's parable of the prodigal son, do you remember what the father said when his boy came home? "This my son was dead. He's alive again." Was the boy actually physically dead? No. He was not. He was dead to the father in the sense of fellowship, in relationship, in enjoyment. And the children of Israel for twenty-five hundred years as a nation have been out of fellowship, out of relationship with Almighty God. They are dead to Him as far as His purposes with this nation are concerned. That's been true since the days of Ezekiel, if you please.

We are not left to guess, you see. We are told that God is talking about the whole house of Israel. He is talking about the fact that He, in the future, is going to reach out among the nations (called "heathen" in some translations, meaning the Gentile nations of the world), and He's going to bring Israel back into the land He promised to give them.

THE VISION IN THREE STAGES

What we have given to us here is a process. In fact, three stages are mentioned in this passage concerning the condition of these bones.

First Stage

The first condition, we are told, was that the bones were dry, and they were scattered all over the valley. You couldn't find the ankle bone that belonged to the leg bone. They were scattered, and you couldn't tell which one was to be joined to the other. These bones were not only scattered, they were also dry. This was a scene of desolation. And if you look at the history of the nation Israel for twenty-five hundred years, that has been their condition. Because of that condition, a great many expositors say, "God is through with the nation Israel." Theologians argue, "You mean to tell me these bones can live? Of course they can't—they're dry. They're dead. They can't live." May I say, I'm on Ezekiel's side. They can't live as far as I'm concerned—I agree with Ezekiel on that—but God can make them live, you see. The whole question is, what is God's plan and purpose?

Now God speaks to Ezekiel saying, "Prophesy upon these bones: and say unto them, O ye dry bones, hear the word of the LORD." And I think that Ezekiel, in an aside, said, "Isn't this silly?" But he does it—"O ye dry bones, hear the word of the LORD." God says, "That's what you're to say, because those dry bones are going to live. They are going to hear you, Ezekiel."

Second Stage

And I will lay sinews upon you, and will bring up flesh upon you, and cover you with skin, and put breath in you, and ye shall live; and he shall know that I am the LORD. So I prophesied as I was commanded. And as I prophesied, there was a noise and, behold, a shaking, and the bones came together, bone to its bone.

Maybe the song is right—"the ankle bone connected to the leg bone, the leg bone connected to the knee bone," etc. I don't know, but the bones came together, and on those bones the muscles, the sinews came that held the bones together, and then flesh came upon them, and skin came upon them. Now what do you have? You have a morgue. All you have now are a lot of corpses lying around. That is the second stage.

Third Stage

Then said he unto me, Prophesy unto the wind, prophesy, son of man, and say to the wind ["wind" can be translated *Spirit*], Thus saith the Lord GOD: Come from the four winds [spirits], O breath [or spirit], and breathe upon these slain, that they may live. So I prophesied as he commanded me, and the breath came into them, and they lived, and stood up upon their feet, an exceedingly great army.

Now that's the third and final stage. All of these that were nothing in the world but dead bodies came alive! They lived.

Has this reminded you of the creation of man? The creation of man was a twofold work of God. God created the body of man first, the earthly tabernacle, the physical form, and then we find that He breathed into man the breath of life. You have in Genesis the same stages as here in Ezekiel. In the two situations, you have the forming of the physical body, then the breathing into it of life.

ISRAEL'S THREE STAGES

Now my beloved, these are the three stages of the coming together of the nation of Israel. First of all, they are scattered. They are dry bones, scattered, then comes a second stage where they come back together. I do not want to be too dogmatic about this, but I do believe that we have come to the second stage, that you and I in our day have witnessed that second stage. But don't become too enthusiastic, for the simple reason that at this writing we see no life. What you see in Israel today is a first-class corpse. As a nation there's no spiritual life there whatsoever, no turning to God. But we've at least seen something tremendous happen in our day, though for some reason it is not making an impression upon Christians as it should.

However, it has made an impression upon certain outstanding men. Dr. William F. Albright, a Gentile professor of archaeology at Johns Hopkins University, spoke some years ago at the Jewish theological seminary in New York. He said:

> It is without parallel in the annals of human history that a nation carried into captivity for seventy years should return to resume its national life, that after nearly six hundred years this same nation should again be scattered worldwide for nearly two thousand years and retain its identity, and that this people should then return to rebuild its ancient homeland and achieve statehood among the family of nations.

Now that is remarkable coming from this outstanding scholar. He goes on:

> Many nonprophetic souls, of whom I was one, declared that such a thing was impossible.

I had a professor in seminary back in 1931 or 1932 who said to me, "You come to me and talk to me about becoming a premillennialist when the nation Israel becomes a nation again." May I say to you that what seemed back then to be very far-fetched has come to pass today. Dr. Albright continues with this:

> And yet we have seen it. Since the words of the Old Testament prophets have been literally fulfilled we should expect the remainder of their predictions concerning the nation Israel likewise to be fulfilled.

Now that is good logic.

Many years ago Mark Twain visited Palestine, and he said,

Palestine sits in sackcloth and ashes, desolate and unlovely. It's a hopeless, dreary, heartbroken land. And why should it be otherwise? Can the curse of the Deity beautify a land? Palestine is no more of this workday world. It is sacred to poetry and tradition. It is dreamland.

In other words, when this man Mark Twain, who was not a Christian at all, looked at Palestine, he said that it was nonsense to talk about Israel coming into existence as a nation again—it was dream stuff to talk like that. Well, the twentieth century has seen two World Wars, which didn't accomplish very much. But they did do one thing. Even before the first World War began, Dr. Theodor Herzl, who was a Jewish playwright and who really beat the tom-toms for the Jew going back to Palestine, popularized this slogan:

There is a land without a people. There is a people without a land. Give the land without a people to the people without a land.

That was his watchword as he went about in his day.

Also in World War I there was the man who did a very outstanding piece of work as a chemist. He was able to get an acid that Great Britain did not have by extracting it from that which they did have, and it enabled them to win the war. Then the chemist exacted one promise, which became the Balfour Declaration: the Allies would permit the Jews to go back to Palestine.

Then Dr. Chaim Weizmann, the first president of Israel, made this statement before the Anglo-American Commission of Inquiry:

The Jewish nation is a ghost nation. Only the God of Israel has kept the Jewish people alive.

Mr. David Ben-Gurion, the premier of Israel until 1963, said:

Ezekiel 37 has been fulfilled, and the nation of Israel is hearing the footsteps of the Messiah.

The Arabs who surround that land today have had some interesting things to say about Mr. Ben-Gurion. Jordan's education minister made this statement concerning Ben-Gurion:

He's a man nobody can talk to, reason with or deal with. He is the most dangerous man in the Middle East.

And then the leader of the Arab refugees in Jericho said,

> Ben-Gurion is not a full man; he's a poet not a man of fact [notice this]—he wanted to build a new nation by raiding cemeteries and making a people from the bones of history.

That's an interesting statement! The only thing is, Ezekiel beat him to it twenty-five hundred years ago and said that's exactly what would happen: the bones of history would come together again. We saw in 1948 probably the only constructive thing the United Nations has done; and that is, they recognized the little nation of Israel. Now Israel has a premier. It has a government. It has law. It has a flag. Israel is a nation today, and there's nothing to parallel this in the history of the world.

Ezekiel prophesied to the dead bones, saying they were going to come together again. Theologians down through the centuries have said, "Don't you believe it. Those bones can't come together. They're as dead as they possibly can be." But God said they would come together again. The very interesting thing is that they *have* come together, and remarkable things have taken place.

The Jews, when they were taken into captivity in Babylon, stayed seventy years, then were permitted to return to their homeland. Actually very few of them—no more than sixty thousand—went back under Ezra, Zerubbabel, and Nehemiah. Yet those few constituted the nation. And the temple was rebuilt. It was to that small returned remnant that the Lord Jesus Christ came and offered Himself as the Messiah. Then, when they rejected Him, He wept over the city of Jerusalem, knowing what was going to happen.

In A.D. 70 the army of Rome under Titus camped about that city. That Tenth Roman Legion made a vow that Jerusalem should never rise again. To this day the Jews don't have the temple area—but they will get it. The nearest thing they have to it today is the convention center, and when they were clearing off the ground and making the excavation for the foundation of the convention center, they found evidence that that's where the Tenth Roman Legion had camped outside the walls of Jerusalem. That very place, my beloved, has become the center of worship.

It has been quite interesting to see these things take place in our day. Now several million Jews are back in that land, and the number continues to grow. Yet they have never occupied all that God gave them. He gave them 300,000 square miles and specified boundaries. But even in their heyday during the time of David and Solomon they occupied only thirty thousand square miles. Today they have only about eight thousand square miles. They occupy very little of the land, but they are a nation today.

However Israel is only a corpse. There's no spiritual life there. They are dead to the things of God, dead to the glorious future that is theirs. But the Word of God says there is a day coming when again Jerusalem will become the center of the earth. As one commentator said years ago,

> Palestine became the nerve center of the earth in the days of Abraham. Later on it became the truth center because of Moses and the prophets. It finally became the salvation center when Christ was nailed to the cross. And then after His rejection it became the storm center of the world. The Scriptures say that someday it will be the peace center under the reign of the skies, and it will finally become the glory center of this earth.

We do not know where or how far we are in God's program. I do know that God's timepiece is not B-U-L-O-V-A or T-I-M-E-X but God's timepiece is I-S-R-A-E-L. It is thrilling to see these things begin to take place in our day. Is there a corpse over there in the Middle East today? It looks like it. The bones were scattered, they have come back—but they've come back in unbelief; let's understand that. They have not come back in faith at all.

Oh, I know they recognize something has happened. One of those involved in the new State of Israel said this:

> We've done wonders in our time such as our fathers and their fathers before them had not seen since the Exodus from Egypt. We've witnessed the courage of our brothers and some who have not faltered for a moment in offering themselves as sacrifices on the altar of their love for land and people. With our own eyes we've been allowed to see miracles and salvation as in the days of the Hasmonaean, and before our very eyes there arose the great miracle of the ingathering of our exiled sons from the four corners of the earth in a greater measure than in the days of Zerubbabel and Nehemiah.

Although they sense something is taking place, that does not mean there is any turning to God. But this which is happening over there has attracted the interest of many folk.

Stanton Delaplane, a columnist who has traveled all over the world, made a trip to Israel in 1960. And it is interesting to see what a newspaper man, who probably didn't know that Ezekiel 37 existed, would have to say:

> The brightest promise you can make in this promised land is "I'll get you a hotel room tomorrow." We flew over from Athens—two hours above the moonlit Mediterranean by jet. It took three hotel moves before Swiss Air could settle us at the Garden Raamat Aviv. Each time we turn in the room key the tourists stir hopefully among the luggage in the lobby. However Israel is building more new hotels than any other country. It is a most amazing nation, and well worth the trip. From one end to the other it is four hundred miles if you measure on a bias, seventeen miles wide at the narrowest point. The new Israel looks like an incomplete housing project. Apartment houses are building in every town. Resorts are arising on crusader ruins at the seashore. Cities spring up in the desert. You buy apartments in Israel on a time payment plan. Private housing is rare. The buildings are three-story concrete affairs, with a raw, unfinished look. The architecture is not distinguished. They all seem to come from the same mold. . . . In twelve years, the country has gone through a great deal. It fought two wars, one nearly extinguished them. It has grown from 620,000 people to 2,500,000. Israel, now twelve years old, has had little time or money for frills. There is a vast tree-planting project. In a few more years, a green fringe will soften these concrete communities. It is surrounded by hostile Arab nations. Defense takes 60 percent of the national budget. Israel gets no military aid from the United States. Such aid would jeopardize our oil holdings in Saudi Arabia.

So here is the estimation of a newspaper man who traveled about in that land and saw something remarkable taking place.

It is arresting to pick up the Word of God and see that twenty-five hundred years ago Ezekiel was carried in the Spirit of the Lord into a valley of dead bones. And God said to him, "Ezekiel, these bones are the whole house of Israel. They are scattered. But I intend to bring them back together, and I'll bring them first as a corpse."

Now they are back, but in unbelief. Unbelief is the condition of the nation. They, I believe, will eventually build a temple. They will receive an antichrist. They will go through the Great Tribulation period after God concludes His purposes in the church and the church is removed from the earth scene. After Israel has gone through this period of tribulation, then the Messiah will come. Christ Jesus Himself said He would send His angels to the four corners of the earth and gather His people back to their land.

That gathering has nothing to do with the gathering today. They're going back today in unbelief. But when Christ will bring them together, according to Ezekiel 37, they will be a living nation.

As God looks at this world today, He sees it as a death valley, filled with dead bones. Not just Israel, but the whole earth is a vast desolation, with men and women dead in trespasses and sins. Out of these nations, God says, "I'm going to bring my people back alive into their own land in that day." God will again move in mighty power.

And I will gather the remnant of my flock out of all countries to which I have driven them, and will bring them again to their folds; and they shall be fruitful and increase. . . . Behold, the days come, saith the LORD, that I will raise unto David a righteous Branch, and a King shall reign and prosper, and shall execute justice and righteousness in the earth. In his days Judah shall be saved, and Israel shall dwell safely; and this is his name whereby he shall be called, THE LORD OUR RIGHTEOUSNESS. Therefore, behold, the days come, saith the LORD, that they shall no more say, The LORD liveth, who brought up the children of Israel out of the land of Egypt, but, The LORD liveth, who brought up and who led the seed of the house of Israel out of the north country, and from all countries to which I had driven them, and they shall dwell in their own land. (Jeremiah 23:3, 5–8)

Such a great miracle will eclipse even the tremendous Exodus that took place in their redemption and deliverance out of the land of Egypt.

The nation still commemorates that event, for the oldest holiday and holy day in the history of the world is the Passover Feast. They remember the night when the death-angel went through the land of

Egypt and God redeemed them from slavery and led them out of Egypt.

But great as it was, the Passover will sink into insignificance, compared to the future miracle when Christ Himself will bring them from all over the earth back into their land. Then the nation will be alive, spiritually alive.

My friends, we are living in tremendous crisis days, and it is dark on the outside. But here is one of the paradoxes of the Christian faith. Did you know that the darker it gets on the outside, the brighter it gets for the Christian? I personally would rather be living right now than at any moment in the history of the world. I thank God every day that He let me live at this time. And oh, I thank Him every day that He permits us to be teaching His Word worldwide! I never cease to thank Him. These are great days in which to live, my Christian friend!

THREE STAGES FOR THE WORLD

May I say to you, I have God's program, the Word of God, right here in my hand. I don't know just where we are on His timetable, but He is moving right on schedule. We can be sure of that. To live in this hour is a tremendous, a wonderful thing. Although I cannot know for sure, I think I've seen the corpse of Ezekiel 37 yonder today, Israel in the second stage.

The third stage hasn't come yet because God has a purpose, and that purpose is with the world, both Jew and Gentile. He is saying in effect, "I put you into one class, all in stage one, dead in trespasses and sins. In that state I declare that you are sinners—because that's what you are—so I can save some of you. If you will hear Me and trust My Son who died for your sins, I'll save you." God today has a purpose, for both Jew and Gentile, of calling out a people to His name.

In application He says to me, as He said to Ezekiel, "McGee, do you think those dead bones can live?" And my answer to Him is, "No, they can't, and if you are going to leave it to McGee they'll never live." But I do know this: the Spirit of God can make them live. He can give them a will to believe. So God says to you and me,

"Go ahead and speak, give out My Word because some of the dead bones are going to hear."

He that hath the Son hath life; and he that hath not the Son of God hath not life. (1 John 5:12)

Chapter 5

WHEN GOD FLEXES HIS MUSCLES
Isaiah 53

The most familiar symbol in the world today is not the Stars and Stripes; it is not the hammer and the sickle; it is not the Union Jack; and it is not the dollar sign.

The royal banner of the cross "towering over the wrecks of time" is more widely known on every continent and every isle of the sea than any other symbol. It is associated with the death of Christ though there is a wide diversity and disparity of its interpretation. No religion has ever had a symbol or an emblem that has encompassed so much of the earth's surface, that has been familiar to so many people over so long a time. The crescent of Islam runs a poor second, and that may be the reason they try harder.

Yet no one fully knows the meaning of the cross. No one today can adequately interpret the suffering and the death of Christ. No theologian, no matter how profound he might be, has ever been able to plumb the depths of the meaning of the death of Christ. It is still a profound mystery.

THE MYSTERY OF THE CROSS

The apostle Paul, who had written most of the epistles that deal with the death and the resurrection of Christ, could say at the conclusion of his life, "That I may know him, and the power of his resurrection, and the fellowship of his sufferings, being made conformable unto his death" (Philippians 3:10).

I would suggest a twofold reason for the mystery of the cross. First of all, the cross has always been foolishness to the world. That is exactly what the Word of God says: "For the preaching of the cross is to them that perish foolishness . . ." (1 Corinthians 1:18). And then Paul goes on to say, "But the natural man receiveth not the things of the Spirit of God; for they are foolishness unto him . . ." (1 Corinthians 2:14). Therefore the cross is not quite what the world wants in the way of religion. They were looking for Him to come, even the first time, riding a white charger to bring victory and deliverance to the earth from the iron heel of Rome. But He came riding upon a little donkey, and He was on the way to a cross. That did not appeal then. It does not appeal today.

Then there is a second reason for the mystery of the cross. God has drawn a veil of silence and a curtain of darkness over it. None of the four Gospels—neither Matthew, Mark, Luke nor John—actually records the events of the crucifixion itself. If you will read them again, you will see that they state that He was crucified and give some isolated and unrelated events which are connected with the death of Christ, but they do not describe the crucifixion itself. Today we are not permitted to sit down with that religious crowd of whom it was said, "And sitting down they watched him there" (Matthew 27:36). Even this crowd was shut out, in that they were denied the right to see the sad spectacle of the death of the Son of God. God drew the curtain of night over the cross. At high noon He blotted out the sun, and our Lord died in the darkness of those three hours. Artists through the centuries have attempted to place on canvas the horrendous death of the Savior of the world. Man has attempted to describe it in vivid verbiage, but none has done it justice. You and I will probably never know, even in eternity, the extent of His suffering.

> But none of the ransomed ever knew
>   How deep were the waters crossed,
> Nor how dark the night the Lord passed through,
>   Ere He found His sheep that was lost.
>
> —Elizabeth C. Clephane

THE SUFFERING CHRIST

Isaiah, seven hundred years before Christ was born in Bethlehem, lets you see something of the suffering of Christ that you will find nowhere else. Of course, the question immediately arises: How do you know that Isaiah was speaking of Christ? It is interesting that all of the rabbis, up to the early Christian centuries, said that Isaiah 53 spoke of the Messiah who was to come. But when they found that Christians were interpreting it in reference to the Lord Jesus, they immediately changed their view. However, the New Testament has too many references to Isaiah 53 to discount it.

We find that John in his Gospel told about the rejection of the Lord Jesus:

But though he had done so many miracles before them, yet they believed not on him; that the saying of Isaiah, the prophet, might be fulfilled, which he spoke, Lord, who hath believed our report? And to whom hath the arm of the Lord been revealed? (John 12:37, 38)

This is a quotation of Isaiah 53:1.

Paul does the same thing in Romans 10:16. In describing the gospel of the death and the resurrection of Christ, he writes, ". . . For Isaiah saith, Lord, who hath believed our report?"

Then there was that Ethiopian eunuch riding across the desert, having left Jerusalem, the religious capital of the world, but still in spiritual darkness. He was reading Isaiah 53 (though in his day the Scripture was not divided into chapters). And Philip, guided by the Holy Spirit, was led to join himself to that chariot as a hitchhiker. When he got up into the chariot, immediately this Ethiopian eunuch said to him, "Look, here is where I'm reading, and here is what it says":

. . . He was led as a sheep to the slaughter; and like a lamb dumb before his shearer, so opened he not his mouth; in his humiliation his judgment was taken away, and who shall declare his generation? For his life is taken from the earth. (Acts 8:32, 33)

Then the Ethiopian asked Philip, "Was the prophet speaking of himself or of another man?" The very interesting thing is Philip's response: "Then Philip opened his mouth, and began at the same scripture, and preached unto him Jesus." May I say to you, Jesus is the subject of the fifty-third chapter of Isaiah. The theme here is the suffering Savior, and it reveals the humanity of Christ in a wonderful, wonderful way. It tells why He took upon Himself humanity. Anselm, one of the great theologians of the Middle Ages, in his book entitled, *Cur Deus Homo—Why God Became Man,* offered one explanation: "Isaiah 53, He came to redeem lost mankind." That is the picture that is here. I say reverently that here you have His life all the way from the cradle to the grave and beyond.

"HIS VISAGE . . . SO MARRED"

Isaiah 53 actually begins in the chapter that precedes it. I want to lift out just one verse, Isaiah 52:14. Think about this:

As many were astounded at thee—his visage was so marred more than any man, and his form more than the sons of men.

No one—and I don't care who it is—has ever been marred more than Jesus was on the cross. This is a startling and shocking statement. I am of the opinion that after the three hours of darkness, when the light broke on the cross, the crowd looked up at the One hanging there and they gasped in horror. At that time He was probably little more than a quivering mass of human flesh. He had borne hell for you and me. He had paid the penalty for the sins of the world.

This was made real in my own heart during my first pastorate. I had a call from the hospital early one morning, about 4:30, requesting me to come there. One of my elders was captain of the fire department, and they sketched his accident rather briefly. His company had been called out early that morning, and he had gone out riding on the ladder truck. The driver of a milk truck, not hearing the siren, drove right out in the way. The fire engine driver, attempting to miss the truck, caused the entire rig to flip over, and these men who were riding on the back were dragged over that rough asphalt. When I got to the hospital his father was sitting at the bedside. I walked in, looked down at Will Norris and became deathly sick. I had to leave. I could not even tell where his face was. All you could see was a mass of flesh that was breathing, and he didn't breathe long. In less than an hour he was gone. As I drove home I thought to myself, *That is the most horrible sight I have ever seen!* And up to this day it is still the most horrible sight I have ever seen.

But, my friend, as I drove home I thought about Isaiah 52:14, that my Lord was marred more than any man: "As many were astounded at thee—his visage was so marred more than any man, and his form more than the sons of men. . . ." Jesus looked worse than Will Norris!

"WHO HATH BELIEVED?"

Now will you notice that the fifty-third chapter of Isaiah opens with this enigmatic inquiry:

Who hath believed our report? And to whom is the arm of the LORD revealed? (Isaiah 53:1)

This is still not a popular message, as we have indicated. The thing that is popular today is some freak or weird interpretation of the Bible that actually contradicts the Scripture. Way-out theology gets all the publicity.

I have been watching this trend on TV now for some time and also see it in our magazines. They have had nothing that represents fundamentalism in an objective, sympathetic, fair manner in years. In other words, they start with the premise that evangelical Christians are "intellectual obscurantists," which means we don't know nothin'. Well, this is the picture that they have attempted to draw of us. The "report" that Isaiah 53 presents is still not the popular report today. I frankly believe that the way liberalism came into the church was through weak preachers and weak laymen attempting to appeal to the crowd by presenting that which was not the gospel. It can still be said, "Who has believed our report, and to whom is the arm of the Lord revealed?"

That word *arm* in the Hebrew language is a vivid and picturesque word, meaning that God has *bared* His arm by rolling up His sleeve, symbolic of a tremendous undertaking. This is when God flexed His muscles.

God created the heavens and the earth, and Psalm 19 says, "The heavens declare the glory of God, and the firmament showeth his handiwork." That word *handiwork* is literally *fingerwork*, like a woman tatting or knitting. Creation didn't require any effort at all for God. He merely spoke the universe into existence. But when God was ready to redeem sinners, the work required His bared arm. When you are talking about power which is infinite to begin with, it is difficult to make the distinction, but God wants us to see that it was with a greater expenditure of power and of wisdom and of sacrifice to redeem man than it was to create universes. God wants us to know that He attaches much more importance to the redemption of sinners than He does to all the rest of His creation.

"LIKE A TENDER PLANT"

Now will you notice that Isaiah 53 immediately harks back to the boyhood of Jesus:

For he shall grow up before him like a tender plant, and like a root out of a dry ground. . . . (Isaiah 53:2)

Here we have the birth and the boyhood of our Lord. It says that He was like a root out of a dry ground. Isaiah had said previously (11:1) that a stem, a branch, a living branch would come out of Jesse. Jesse, you recall, was the father of King David. Why was Jesse named, since the Lord Jesus is presented in the New Testament as the King coming from David? Well, by the time you get to the period when our Lord came into the world, it was in "the fullness of time," as far as God was concerned. The family of David had returned to peasantry, no longer princes but peasants. The One in the royal line happened to be a carpenter in Nazareth.

He is a root out of a dry ground. If you want to know how dry it was, look at the nation into which He came at that time. It was dead spiritually. The religious rulers had reduced the Old Testament to a dead ritual, and they were far from God. They followed the letter of the Mosaic Law, but they had more ways of getting around it than modern man has in getting around the civil law.

Israel was not only a *dead* nation spiritually, but it was also under the iron heel of Rome. The people of Israel were not free. The Roman Empire produced no great civilization. They merely were good imitators of great civilizations. There was mediocre achievement and pseudoculture. The moral foundation was gone. A virile manhood and a virtuous womanhood were supplanted by a debauched and pleasure-loving citizenry.

The reason that the apostles' message of the grace of God fell on so many receptive ears was that people were tired of law. They had been taught to follow little, meticulously detailed programs in order to be saved rather than having a personal relationship with God. There was deadness everywhere.

Into such a situation Christ came. He came from a noble family that had been cut off, from a nation that had become a vassal to Rome, in a day and age that was decadent. The loveliest flower of humanity came from the driest spot and period of the world's history. It was humanly impossible for His day and generation to produce Him, but He came nevertheless, for He came forth from God.

You see, evolutionists have always had a problem with Him—actually two problems. Evolution wasn't supposed to produce Him for a few more million years. But then having "produced" Him about two thousand years ago, why hasn't there been another one like Him? May I say to you, He is a root out of a dry ground.

If you should go out and start walking across this Southern California desert without a green sprig anywhere, and suddenly you come upon a great big lovely head of iceberg lettuce growing out of that dry, dusty soil, you would be startled. You'd stop dead in your tracks and say, "Where in the world did this come from?" That is how amazing Christ's coming into the world was. There was *nothing* in the world to produce Him, my friend. He is a root out of a dry ground.

"THERE IS NO BEAUTY . . ."

Then Isaiah continues,

> . . . **He hath no form nor comeliness, and when we shall see him, there is no beauty that we should desire him.** (Isaiah 53:2)

This has led some people to draw a wrong conclusion, supposing that as a man our Lord was misshapen or diseased. May I say to you, Jesus was the perfect man. He could never have been the sacrifice for the sins of the world if He had not been perfect in every way—we know this from the Levitical requirements for a sacrificial lamb.

What is being said here is that on the *cross* there was no comeliness, nothing beautiful. Now I know today that the cross is a symbol that is popular. It is put up on churches, both Catholic and Protestant. They are beautiful crosses. I'm going this afternoon to dedicate a church and, although I do not know, I have a notion there will be a cross around there somewhere, and it will be a pretty one. They all are pretty now. But, my friend, the cross on which our Savior died was not pretty. "There is no beauty that we should desire him" is speaking of Him when He hung on that cross.

"DESPISED AND REJECTED"

Now will you notice verse 3,

He is despised and rejected of men, a man of sorrows, and acquainted with grief, and we hid as it were our faces from him; he was despised, and we esteemed him not.

This speaks of His total life. It doesn't mean that Christ was rejected only when He was crucified. Go back and read the sixty-ninth Psalm regarding the days that fill in those silent years. You'll find that from the time He was born He was rejected. Where was He born? He was born in a *stable!* As an adult, He could say, "The foxes have holes, and the birds of the air have nests, but the Son of man hath not where to lay his head" (Matthew 8:20). He went through this world rejected.

Then of His ministry when He walked the dusty roads of earth, we read,

Surely he hath borne our griefs, and carried our sorrows; yet we did esteem him stricken, smitten of God, and afflicted. But he was wounded for our transgressions, he was bruised for our iniquities; the chastisement of our peace was upon him, and with his stripes we are healed. (Isaiah 53:4, 5)

Healed of what? This passage has caused some to assume that there is physical healing in the atonement. But, as I said to a friend of mine who is head of a Pentecostal theological school, "If you want to include healing in the atonement, remember that there is also a new body in the atonement, and we know that there is a new earth in the atonement, but we don't have these blessings yet." Certainly this passage is not referring to physical healing in the atonement. There is a very excellent note in *The New Scofield Reference Bible* that I highly recommend. Allow me to quote it, as it expresses it better than I can.

> Because Matthew quotes this passage and applies it to physical disease (cp. Mt. 8:17 with context) it has been conjectured by some that disease as well as sin was included in the atoning death of Christ. But Matthew asserts that the Lord fulfilled the first part of Isaiah 53:4 during the healing ministry of His service on earth. Matthew 8:17 makes no reference to Christ's atoning death for sin. (p. 759)

Now let's examine that passage in Matthew and see what it means:

> **When the evening was come, they brought unto him many that were possessed with demons; and he cast out the spirits with his word, and healed all that were sick, that it might be fulfilled which was spoken by Isaiah, the prophet, saying, He himself took our infirmities, and bore our sicknesses.** (Matthew 8:16, 17)

Notice that it doesn't say that He bore our sicknesses on the cross. He bore them when He walked through this earth, my friend, during those three years of His healing ministry. He was *moved* by the suffering of the human family. His heart went out to them. *Disease* is not sin; rather, it is the result of the entrance of sin way back in the Garden of Eden. When He would walk by and see the blind and see the lame, He was moved with compassion. Obviously, we have only a very sketchy account of the miracles He performed. The Gospel of John says He healed *many*. Luke says He healed the *multitudes*. I believe that one of the reasons the Pharisees could not contradict the fact He was performing miracles—and they never did—was because there were literally thousands, yes, thousands of people He had healed who were walking about everywhere. Why? Because as the Son of God, He is moved by the suffering of humanity. Ending suffering was part of His ministry during His life on earth. The Bible doesn't say that in His *death* He heals disease.

Now let me make this very clear. The other passage of Scripture that ought always to be quoted with Isaiah 53 is 1 Peter 2:24:

**Who his own self bore our sins in his own body on the tree, that
we, being dead to sins, should live unto righteousness; by whose
stripes ye were healed.**

Healed of what? "Who his own self bore our *sins* in His own body."
When He died on the cross, He died for sin, my beloved.

Now let's look at that death.

**All we like sheep have gone astray; we have turned every one to
his own way, and the LORD hath laid on him the iniquity of us
all.** (Isaiah 53:6)

Three things in this verse are important to understand. It opens with
all, and it closes with *all*. "All we like sheep have gone astray." It
closes with "the LORD hath laid on him the iniquity of us all." When
Christ died on the cross, He took upon Himself the sins of the world.
Why? Because "we have turned every one to *his own way*"—expressed
here in those three words is the basic problem with the human family
today. We are like Adam going out of the Garden of Eden. I would
like to have said to him,

"Adam, where are you going?"

"I'm getting away from God."

"I thought you had fellowship with Him every day?"

"I did, but no longer."

He was going *his* own way, and from that day to this every man
goes his own way.

The Scripture says, "There is a *way* which seemeth right unto a
man, but the end thereof are the ways of death" (Proverbs 14:12).
The Lord Jesus said, "I am the *way*, the truth, and the life; no man
cometh unto the Father, but by me" (John 14:6). When the human
family turned away from God, it was *then* that Christ became the
sacrifice for the sins of the world: "The LORD hath laid on him the
iniquity of us all." At the crucifixion of our Lord it wasn't His
suffering at the hands of man during those first three hours, but it
was His suffering during those last three hours in the darkness, that
the cross became the altar on which the Lamb of God who takes away
the sin of the world was offered.

Three times we are told in Isaiah 53 that it was *God* who smote
Him: In verse 4 "smitten of God, and afflicted"; in verse 6 "the

LORD hath laid on him the iniquity of us all"; and verse 10 "yet it pleased the LORD to bruise him."

"The LORD hath laid on him the iniquity of us all." Consternation fills our souls when we recognize that it was God the Father who did it! "It pleased the LORD to bruise him."

Look again at the cross.

Christ was on the cross six hours, hanging between heaven and earth from nine o'clock in the morning until three o'clock in the afternoon. In the first three hours man did his worst. He heaped ridicule and insult upon Him, spit upon Him, nailed Him without mercy to the cruel cross, and then sat down to watch Him die. At twelve o'clock noon, after Jesus had hung there for three hours in agony, God drew a veil over the sun, and darkness covered that scene, shutting out from human eye the transaction between the Father and the Son. Christ became the sacrifice for the sin of the world. God made His Son's soul an offering for sin. Christ Jesus was treated as *sin*, for we are told in 2 Corinthians 5:21 that He was made sin for us—He who knew no sin.

Why did He do it? He did it because He loves you. God so *loved* the world that He *gave* His Son. God made the soul of Jesus Christ an offering for your sin!

If you want to know if God hates sin, look at the cross. If you want to know if God will punish sin, look at the Beloved of His heart enduring the tortures of its penalty. That cross became an altar where we behold the Lamb of God taking away the sin of the world. He was dying for somebody else—He was dying for you and me.

My friend, if God didn't spare His own Son, what do *you* expect at the hands of God when you stand before Him someday? Do you think that *you* can escape? The writer to the Hebrews asks the question. This is a question you cannot answer, I cannot answer, and even God cannot answer. I'm not being irreverent in saying that God can't answer this one, because the question is: "How shall we escape, if we neglect so great salvation . . .?" (Hebrews 2:3). Do you know how to escape? There is no way because Christ has taken the only route and has paid the tremendous price that you and I might be saved.

"A LAMB TO THE SLAUGHTER"

Notice how Isaiah uses the figure of the lamb:

**He was oppressed, and he was afflicted, yet he opened not his
mouth; he is brought as a lamb to the slaughter, and as a sheep
before her shearers is dumb, so he openeth not his mouth.** (Isaiah
53:7)

All the way from Abel to John the Baptist, Scripture uses the figure
of the lamb. This was the verse which the Ethiopian eunuch was
reading when Philip climbed up into his chariot: "He was led as a
sheep to the slaughter; and like a lamb dumb before his shearer, so
opened he not his mouth; in his humiliation his judgment was taken
away, and who shall declare his generation? For his life is taken from
the earth" (Acts 8:32, 33).

The Ethiopian asked Philip, "Who is the prophet talking about,
himself or another?" Philip said it was Another who was yet to come,
and he told him about Jesus who had come as the Lamb led to the
slaughter.

When Abel, you recall, brought that sacrifice to the Lord, it was
a *lamb*. Abel was no caveman, but an intelligent human being. I think
that he could meet anyone living today on an intellectual basis. After
all, we are descended from that line, and what we have is inherited
from him. If you had said to Abel, "Abel, I see you are offering a
little lamb. Do you think a little lamb will take away your sin?"

He would have answered, "No."

"Then why are you doing it?"

His reason would have been something like this: "God has asked
us to do it. He promised my mother that there is coming One who
will be our Savior. This little lamb is depicting Him, and I offer it as
a substitute. But there is coming One who will give Himself in volun-
tary, vicarious death. I don't know much about it yet, but I trust
God that He is coming."

Centuries passed, and at last one day John the Baptist marked out
Jesus and said, "Behold the Lamb of God, who taketh away the sin
of the world" (John 1:29). This is *God's* Lamb. This is the One to
pay the penalty for the sins of the world—your sin and my sin. With

the apostle Paul we can look back at that cross and say, "He loved me, and gave Himself for me."

Jesus didn't die to win your sympathy. Remember that when Jesus was on His way to the cross and the women of Jerusalem were weeping for Him, He said, ". . . Weep not for me, but weep for yourselves, and for your children. . . . For if they do these things in a green tree, what shall be done in the dry?" (Luke 23:28, 31). He did not want their sympathy, and He does not want ours. Oh, I think we would be cold-blooded indeed to read the story of the crucifixion of Christ and not be moved. When Clovis, leader of the Franks, first heard about the crucifixion of Christ, he was so moved that he leaped to his feet, drew his sword and exclaimed, "If I had only been there with my Franks!" But our Lord didn't want Clovis and his army. He told His own disciple to put up his sword. He could have the protection of legions of angels, but He was not here to be delivered—except to death for you and me. He did not die to beget sympathy in your heart; He doesn't want it. His was not a martyr's death. He did not die as did the martyrs who died singing praises, conscious of God's presence with them. Rather, Jesus cried out in that awful moment, "My God, my God, why hast thou forsaken me?" He was forsaken of God!

He died because "all we like sheep have gone astray . . . and the LORD hath laid on him the iniquity of us all." That's the reason He died. He had to do it to *save* you, my friend!

"HE SHALL BE SATISFIED"

I do not want to close on that note. This wonderful fifty-third chapter does not stop there. It opens with suffering, but it closes with satisfaction. Note now verse 11:

> **He shall see of the travail of his soul, and shall be satisfied; by his knowledge shall my righteous servant justify many; for he shall bear their iniquities.** (Isaiah 53:11)

Satisfaction.

Don't feel sorry for Him. If you think He was caught between the upper millstone of Roman power and the nether millstone of religious cupidity, forget it. He was not. He says, "No man taketh it [my life] from me, but I lay it down of myself. I have power to lay it down, and I have power to take it again. This commandment have I received of my Father" (John 10:18). The Book of Hebrews says, "Looking unto Jesus, the author and finisher of our faith, who for the joy that was set before him endured the cross, despising the shame, and is set down at the right hand of the throne of God" (Hebrews 12:2). He made adequate provision for the sin of the world. He is satisfied.

The cross is not an ambulance sent to a wreck. It is not first aid. It is not a temporary arrangement. The Lord Jesus is "the Lamb slain from the foundation of the world." And when you look into eternity you see what John describes, "And I beheld and, lo, in the midst of the throne . . . stood a Lamb as though it had been slain . . ." (Revelation 5:6). Scripture tells us that He sat down at God's right hand, and do you know why? For the same reason it says that God rested on the seventh day after He had created the heavens and the earth. He wasn't tired. He sat down because He had finished the job. I am sorry to have to report that I don't seem to finish anything; I always leave my desk covered with work to be done. But when Jesus went back to heaven He had finished everything that was necessary for your salvation and mine. Everything.

God in our day is satisfied with what Jesus did for you. Are you satisfied? "He shall see of the travail of his soul, and shall be satisfied." Oh, the restlessness today! How busy people are! My friend, rest in Him. He paid a tremendous price for you.

How shall we escape if we neglect so great salvation? Do you have the answer to that? Are you going to try to escape by neglecting that salvation? My friend, I do not know who is the worst sinner in your town, but if you are rejecting God's salvation for you, you are as guilty as the worst sinner in your town.

God has a remedy for every sin, except the sin of rejecting the Remedy. The Remedy is His Son.

Chapter 6

THE RAPTURE COMES NEXT

Why do we believe the Rapture comes next?

If you are a believer today and are trusting Christ, you are next on the program of God—as far as prophecy is concerned.

Now this does not mean we know *when* He is coming, because that is something which the Scriptures absolutely do not reveal. We cannot know the day, the hour, or the minute, or the twinkling of an eye when this event will take place.

But our attitude should be that of looking for that blessed hope. The word "looking for" is from a Greek word meaning "entertaining." It is a glorious and delightful prospect that one would look forward to in the future. I believe it is tissue-thin between where we stand today and the Rapture of the church. There are no signs, no Tribulation, no anything to be fulfilled before Jesus takes the church out of the world.

First of all I want to define our terms. What do we mean by Rapture? We are not going to resort to the dictionary at this point. But to define the word very briefly, the *Rapture* is the moment when Christ takes believers, which we shall call the church, out of the world. And that fits into a time program that God has put down, because God moves in a very orderly manner in every direction. So we can be sure this is a very orderly procedure. We believe that next on the program of God comes the Rapture when He takes the church out of the world.

Then after that we believe there will be a time of Great Tribulation, which is concluded with the return of Christ to the earth to set up His Kingdom. This has been labeled "the Revelation"—and I feel accurately so, because the Book of Revelation deals with the Great Tribulation and the coming of Christ at the end of the Great Tribulation to establish His Kingdom. You can see that this is a very orderly program that God is following.

There are those today who deny the Rapture because they say it is a term that is not used in the Bible. Their argument is that the Bible does not teach the Rapture. Well, I must categorically deny that, because in 1 Thessalonians 4:17 he says, "Then we which are alive and remain shall be caught up together with them in the clouds, to meet the Lord in the air: and so shall we ever be with the Lord." Now the word "caught up" is the Greek word *harpazo* which means "to lift, to snatch up, to draw up, to transport." It has several meanings, and one meaning is "to rapture." So you can exchange the translation of *harpazo* from "caught up" to rapture—"Then we which are alive and remain shall be raptured together with them in the clouds," and your translation would be as good as the one we have in the Authorized Version. I confess that I prefer the translation "caught up," but let's understand that the word *rapture* is in the Bible, and there is no ambiguity here. When one denies that the Bible teaches the Rapture, he is arguing semantics and not eschatology. And, candidly, I am not interested in going into the field of semantics.

There is another fallacy that is exploited by those who like to dismiss the Rapture. They maintain that when we say Christ is coming to take the church out of the world and that He will not return until the end of the Great Tribulation period (which obviously is the future seven-year period outlined in the Book of Daniel), we are saying that we believe in a second and *third* coming of Christ. They accuse us of believing that the Rapture is the second coming and the Revelation is the third coming of Christ. Well, that type of argument is, to my judgment, not dealing with the subject at all.

First, let me remind you that at the Rapture Christ does not return to the earth. Rather, He takes His own away from the earth. He does not come to it. In that sense it is not a return to the earth at all. However, at the Revelation Christ does come to the earth, which is the second coming. We call this the Revelation. He is coming at that time to set up His Kingdom.

Now let's make a comparison. At Christmas time we celebrate the birth of Christ. At Easter we commemorate the death and resurrection of Christ. At the incarnation the emphasis is put upon a baby. The Israelites hadn't been looking for Him to come that way. As George MacDonald put it, "They were looking for a king to lift them high. He came a little baby thing that made a woman cry." Christ came into the world as a baby.

After Jesus' birth, Scripture is silent. We have no other report until about thirty years later. There is one isolated reference that Dr. Luke gives us, but for thirty years there is a period called the silent years in the life of Christ. That is a very important period, yet we are told almost nothing about it.

Then thirty years later Jesus steps out into public view. He had lived a life of obscurity in that little town of Nazareth. Now He moves out and teaches publicly for three years, then goes to the cross at the end of that three-year period. He is buried and resurrected. This coming of Christ is for redemption. The first aspect or appearance was incarnation; the second aspect or appearance was redemption. Now there is a wide difference between the two—a little Baby (incarnation) and a Man on a cross (redemption). Anyone, I am sure, would recognize the difference. But we do not call that the first and second coming of Christ. We package it up in one coming, which is proper.

We do the same thing for His coming for the church, then later His coming to establish His Kingdom on the earth. We put both in one package—and I can see nothing wrong with that. There is a wide difference, though, between the Rapture and the Revelation. The difference is not only in time. At the Rapture, He comes as the Bridegroom to take His Bride, His church, out of the world. Remember that He does not come to the earth at that time at all. At the Revelation He comes as a King to the earth to establish His Kingdom.

Now as we look at the Rapture and the Revelation of Jesus Christ and the contrast between the two, I would like to deal with three different aspects of the subject:

(1) The *action* of each is different.
(2) The *attitude* toward each is different.
(3) The *anticipation* of each is different.

The *action* of the Rapture and the Revelation is different. There are certain physical factors that are connected with both of these events which bear no similarity at all. They are antipodes apart. In the *attitude* toward these there is a difference. There are certain psychological factors involved which are altogether different. Then in the *anticipation* there are several spiritual factors involved, and they likewise are quite different.

ACTION

Keep in mind that at the time of the Rapture Christ does not come to the earth. He does not touch down on the Mount of Olives. In fact He does not come to the earth proper.

The Lord Jesus was the first One to say anything about the Rapture. He mentions it the first time in John 14:2:

In my Father's house are many mansions: if it were not so, I would have told you. I go to prepare a place for you.

The "Father's house" is this vast universe in which we live. The "many mansions" are abiding places, in the Greek *moné*. Out yonder in space there are many abiding places. But Jesus said, "I go to prepare a place for you," that is, for His own.

It is quite obvious that the place He mentions is not on earth, because He left this earth when He ascended. Paul amplifies that statement, adding a great deal of detail.

For the Lord himself shall descend from heaven with a shout, with the voice of the archangel, and with the trump of God: and the dead in Christ shall rise first: then we which are alive and remain shall be caught up together with them in the clouds, to meet the Lord in the air: and so shall we ever be with the Lord.
(1 Thessalonians 4:16, 17)

The Lord Himself is coming and we (that is, those who are His own) are to meet Him in the air. So shall we ever be with the Lord. Now that is specific. There is no way that we can misunderstand that.

However, at the Revelation He will come to the earth. He will touch down on the earth. In Zechariah's prophecy we read:

And his feet shall stand in that day upon the mount of Olives, which is before Jerusalem on the east, and the mount of Olives shall cleave in the midst thereof toward the east and toward the

west, and there shall be a very great valley; and half of the mountain shall remove toward the north, and half of it toward the south. (Zechariah 14:4)

This is so specific, dealing with geographic places, that we are to take it literally. That is, when Christ comes the second time, His feet are to touch down on the Mount of Olives.

Let me illustrate with a familiar event in our day. In the first "moon shot," Borman and his crew went around the moon, but they did not touch down. To me, one of the most thrilling pulpits from which I ever heard the Bible read was on Christmas Eve 1968 when the astronauts in that little module that was going around the moon read Genesis 1. I don't know when I ever have been so thrilled to hear the Word of God read as I was that Christmas Eve. Now Frank Borman did not touch down on the moon, but he went to the moon. Then on the second moon shot, Neil Armstrong touched down on the moon, put his foot down. I suppose more than half the world saw him put his foot down on the moon. So we say that he was the first man who went to the moon, but actually Borman went around the moon. The parallel is quite similar. The Lord Jesus is coming but is not going to touch down. His church is going to meet Him in the air. Then we are told that He will come later and put His foot down— His foot shall touch the Mount of Olives. That, my friend, is going to be a far greater touchdown than when man touched down on the moon.

There is another contrast that is tremendous. At the Rapture *believers* are removed from the earth. At the Revelation—when Christ comes to the earth to establish His Kingdom—*unbelievers* are removed from the earth. This is something that is very important to observe.

At the Rapture, going back again to John 14, the Lord Jesus said:

In my Father's house are many mansions: if it were not so, I would have told you. I go to prepare a place for you. And if I go and prepare a place for you, I will come again, and receive you unto myself; that where I am, there ye may be also. (John 14:2, 3)

And Paul said, "The Lord himself shall descend from heaven" (1 Thessalonians 4:16). The Lord Jesus said, "I am going to come

myself and I am going to take you out of this world to be with Me."
This, I think, is quite clear. *Believers* are removed from the world at
the Rapture.

Now at the Revelation, *unbelievers* are removed from the earth.
Notice now Matthew 24, where Jesus is giving the discourse we call
the Olivet Discourse. The Olivet Discourse has nothing whatever to
do with the Rapture of the church because He is not talking about
the church. He simply is answering questions the apostles have put
to Him. In Matthew's account He is answering two of those questions:
(1) What is the sign of the end of the age? (2) What is the sign of His
coming? Now for the sign at the end of the age He gives this:

> **But as the days of Noe [Noah] were, so shall also the coming of
> the Son of man be. For as in the days that were before the flood
> they were eating and drinking, marrying and giving in marriage,
> until the day that Noe [Noah] entered the ark, and knew not until
> the flood came, and took them all away; so shall also the coming
> of the Son of man be. Then shall two be in the field; the one
> shall be taken, and the other left. Two women shall be grinding
> at the mill; the one shall be taken, and the other left. (Matthew
> 24:37–41)**

Now many folk think this refers to the Rapture, but He is not talking
about the Rapture in the Olivet Discourse. It is quite obvious what
He is saying if we will just let Him say it. He likens this to the days
of Noah, as to the conditions that will exist in the world. In the days
of Noah, we are told, when the flood came, it took them all away.
Whom did it take away? Noah and his family? No. Noah was left
here on the earth to continue the existence of the human race on the
earth. But it was that crowd of unbelievers, that crowd of great sinners, that were removed from the earth. They were the ones taken
away, and they were taken away in judgment.

Now he says here, "Just as it was in the days of Noah, so it will
be when the Son of Man comes." Comes where? To the earth. Who
will be taken away? Those who are judged. And He leaves those here
who will enter into the Kingdom and continue human life on this
earth.

Notice that it is altogether different. At the Rapture believers are
removed. At the Revelation unbelievers are removed.

Again notice another physical contrast here. At the Rapture there are no signs. At the Revelation there are many signs. In fact Matthew 24 answers the question as to the signs of His coming—coming to the earth to establish His Kingdom. For example, He says, "When ye therefore shall see the abomination of desolation, spoken of by Daniel the prophet, stand in the holy place," I know He is not talking to me because I don't have a holy place. The only people I know who ever had a holy place were the nation Israel. Apparently He is talking to them. The abomination of desolation, He says, will be there, and they are to look for that. Well, we are not looking for the abomination of desolation. Friend, I wouldn't even know an abomination of desolation if I met one on the street! Thank God, I am not looking for that; I am looking for Christ. There is a lot of difference between looking for Him and looking for an abomination!

In the Book of the Revelation, there is a marvelous division given. When I teach this great book, I keep in mind that the Book of the Revelation is not a hodge-podge. It is not a conglomerate of confusion, but it is the giving of the orderly steps by which Jesus Christ is going to become the ruler of this little earth on which we live. It deals with the past and the present and the future. They all are included in that wonderful Book of Revelation.

Then there is another distinction that we should properly make. It is the distinction that Paul called to our attention. He said,

Give none offence, neither to the Jews, nor to the Gentiles, nor to the church of God. (1 Corinthians 10:32)

This is the threefold division of the human family according to the Word of God: Jews, Gentiles, Church.

Now in the Book of the Revelation, after the church has been removed, we are told that before the great day of wrath comes, before the Great Tribulation breaks in all its fury on this earth, two companies are sealed. One is a company of 144,000 Israelites (this is one group Scripture recognizes—"Give none offence, neither to the *Jews* . . ."). Then there is a great company of Gentiles who are sealed, just as the Israelites were sealed. There were 144,000 Israelites sealed, but of Gentiles there was sealed a great company that no man could number. We see now two divisions of the human family that are sealed: Jews and Gentiles. But how about the third division, *the church of God?*

They are not sealed. And it would be frightful indeed if the church went through the Great Tribulation without being sealed. It would be bad enough to go through it sealed, but it would be tragic to go through it without some sort of protection. Remember that Christ in the Great Tribulation is no longer in the place of intercession, He is now in the place of Judge of all the earth. He is directing those events that will finally bring Him to the earth to assume power. The poor church—if it were in the world—is left out and would not be sealed during this period. Let me ask you, why wasn't the church sealed? Well, the church is with *Him* in the New Jerusalem. This is something to note.

Also we need to observe that at the Rapture there is no angel ministry. This may seem like a very unimportant detail, but it is a noticeable detail.

> **For the Lord himself shall descend from heaven with a shout, with the voice of the archangel, and with the trump of God: and the dead in Christ shall rise first.** (1 Thessalonians 4:16)

A common viewpoint is that we have a trio here who will join their voices together to bring in the Rapture, that the Lord will descend with a shout, but He will need a little help, so there is the voice of the archangel, and Gabriel will be there with a trumpet. To me that is utterly ridiculous and preposterous. The Lord's voice is the voice of the archangel in its majesty and in its dignity and in its authority. He is not going to need any archangel to help Him raise the dead and call His church to be with Him! I don't mean to be ridiculous, but can you imagine at the grave of Lazarus that the Lord Jesus would call Gabriel to help him raise Lazarus from the dead? Do you think Jesus, the Second Person of the Godhead, the One who is God Himself, would need any help? Neither will He need the angel Gabriel to blow a horn. It is *His* voice like the voice of an archangel, and it is like the sound of a trumpet. Someone asks me, "Do you *know* that?" Yes, I do know that. The Greek text is very clear at this point: "His voice is *like* the voice of an archangel, and it is *like* the sound of a trumpet." Also this is illustrated for us in John's vision on the Isle of Patmos in the first chapter of the Revelation. John said, "I heard behind me a great voice as of a trumpet . . . and I turned to see the voice that spake with me." Whom did he see? He did not see Gabriel blowing a trumpet, he saw the glorified Christ. Now, my friend, what you have at the Rapture is the Lord Jesus coming Himself to get His church, His bride. I don't know how that affects you, but it affects me a great deal. He will not send an angel to get us, He will come for us Himself!

However, at the Revelation there *is* an angel ministry. It is mentioned in the Olivet Discourse where it belongs:

And then shall appear the sign of the Son of man in heaven; and then shall the tribes of the earth mourn, and they shall see the Son of man coming in the clouds of heaven with power and great glory. And he shall send his angels with a great sound of a trumpet, and they shall gather together his elect from the four winds, from one end of heaven to the other. (Matthew 24:30, 31)

When He returns to the earth to establish His Kingdom, He sends out His angels. Now angels had ministered in the Old Testament to Israelites. The Law was given by the ministry of angels. So here at the end, He sends His angels to gather those who will enter into the Kingdom. It has nothing to do with the Rapture, you see. It is altogether different from the Rapture.

Now at the Rapture the Church is raised, and those in Christ— whether they be the living or the dead in Christ—are changed, and they enter the New Jerusalem. While at the Revelation the Old Testament saints and the Great Tribulation saints are raised to enter the Kingdom. The time is different. We need to recognize that. We are told in Matthew's record:

Then shall the King say unto them on his right hand, Come, ye blessed of my Father, inherit the kingdom prepared for you from the foundation of the world. (Matthew 25:34)

They are to enter into the Kingdom here upon this earth. And the Great Tribulation saints are going to be included. In the Book of Revelation John records:

And I saw thrones, and they sat upon them, and judgment was given unto them; and I saw the souls of them that were beheaded for the witness of Jesus, and for the word of God, and which had not worshipped the beast, neither his image, neither had

received his mark upon their foreheads, or in their hands; and
they lived and reigned with Christ a thousand years. (Revelation
20:4)

Where did they reign? Well, here on this earth.

But the rest of the dead lived not again until the thousand years
were finished. This is the first resurrection. Blessed and holy is
he that hath part in the first resurrection: on such the second
death hath no power, but they shall be priests of God and of
Christ, and shall reign with him a thousand years. (Revelation
20:5, 6)

This is a very important passage of Scripture, you see. It shows again
that the Rapture and the Revelation are quite different.

Also there is a symbol we need to note. When the Rapture is
mentioned, when He is talking about His church, He depicts Himself
not only as the offspring of David but also as the "bright and morning
star."

I Jesus have sent mine angel to testify unto you these things in
the churches. I am the root and the offspring of David, and the
bright and morning star. (Revelation 22:16)

Now when He is speaking to Israel, the symbol is altogether different.

But unto you that fear my name shall the Sun of righteousness
arise with healing in his wings; and ye shall go forth, and grow
up as calves of the stall. (Malachi 4:2)

To the church He is the "bright and morning star." To Israel and the
Gentile world during the Great Tribulation, He will be the "Sun of
righteousness."

In our world today the morning star appears shortly before the sun
comes up. I say shortly before, but sometimes it is quite awhile before
the sun comes up. Years ago, riding on the Super Chief train from
Los Angeles to Chicago, I was awakened in the morning by a flood
of light around the curtain of my roomette. I raised the curtain to see
what it was out there—I thought the sun was coming up. But it wasn't
the sun; it was the bright and morning star that had come up. Believe
me, it was bright! I assumed that the sun would be coming along in
the next few minutes, but it did not. It was awhile before the sun

appeared. I thought at the time that Christ to the church is the Bright and Morning Star who might appear at any time.

When he appears as the Bright and Morning Star, the signs will begin to take place on the earth that will bring the Sun of Righteousness to the new day that will be on this earth. That is the picture and the figure He was giving when He mentioned the fact that the Old Testament saints are to be raised at the end of the Great Tribulation period, together with the Tribulation saints. This brings to an end the first resurrection—that is, the resurrection of the saved. This concludes all of them: Christ the firstfruits, and those that are Christ's at His coming. Then we are told at the end of the Millennium the unsaved are to be raised for the Great White Throne judgment. So, you see, this naive idea that we are going to have a general judgment day when the dead will be raised, and the good will be put on one side and the bad on the other, does not fit Scripture. God does everything decently and in order. He has a system and a program that He generally follows, and He is certainly following it here.

Now this concludes our comparison of the action we see when we contrast the Rapture with the Revelation. The action is different, as we have seen in these physical factors.

ATTITUDE

The attitude is different because there are certain psychological factors that are altogether different.

At the Rapture there is deliverance and joy. It is a time of great joy which the believer anticipates. This is suggested in the following verse:

> **After this I looked, and, behold, a door was opened in heaven** [John, as a representative of the church was called up]: **and the first voice which I heard was as it were of a trumpet talking with me; which said, Come up hither [the Lord Jesus calling His own], and I will show thee things which must be hereafter.** (Revelation 4:1)

He doesn't say, "Come up here; I'm going to push you into the Great Tribulation—you need a little purifying." Of course the church needs purifying, but, my friend, the blood of Jesus Christ is what will cleanse us from all sin. You could stick me in a furnace for eternity and I don't think you would change this old nature of mine at all. What I need is mercy.

> **Keep yourselves in the love of God, looking for the mercy of our Lord Jesus Christ unto eternal life.** (Jude 21)

One of the wonderful things we can do in this day of apostasy is to look for the *mercy* of our Lord Jesus Christ. The *mercy* of God is what saved me. If God had not extended His mercy to me, I would not be saved. My friend, God's mercy is extended to me every day. Oh, how merciful He has been to me! And at the Rapture I am going out with the rest of you super-duper saints. Do you know why? Because of the mercy of God. He saved me by grace. He keeps me by His grace. And He is going to take me out at the Rapture by His grace. So I am looking for mercy. I hope you don't mind my looking for mercy, because I *need* it. And maybe you will need it also.

Now listen to this:

> **For they themselves show of us what manner of entering in we had unto you, and how ye turned to God from idols to serve the living and true God; and to wait for his Son from heaven, whom he raised from the dead, even Jesus, which delivered us from the wrath to come.** (1 Thessalonians 1:9, 10)

He delivered us from the *wrath* to come. Now the wrath to come in the Old Testament is that great day of wrath, the day of God's wrath, the Great Tribulation period. Paul, writing to the Thessalonian believers, says He has delivered us from the wrath to come and that we are to wait for His Son. Oh, what a comfortable, glorious feeling that gives!

There are those folk who say the church needs the Great Tribulation to purify it. Well, I agree that the church needs purifying. There is no question about that. But I have serious doubts that the Great Tribulation could purify us enough to enter into the presence of the Lord.

Also, these folk who say the church is to go through the Great Tribulation accuse us of looking for an escape mechanism. Friends, do you know that is absolutely accurate? Although I get a little tired of hearing it, I appreciate the plane stewardess going through that little ritual of demonstrating what to do in case of emergency. If something happens to the plane at high altitude, an oxygen mask will drop down. And in case the plane goes down in water, there will be boats and we have life preservers there. I feel it is a good thing to be prepared. I always have looked for an escape mechanism. In the past few years, I have had five major operations. And I am a coward. I don't like to go to a hospital. If there had been any way to escape, I would have escaped. And I thank God today that there is an escape mechanism from the Great Tribulation period! I do not know about these brave ones who want to go through the Great Tribulation. I think at the Rapture they will be going out with me—and they will be tickled to death that they missed the Tribulation. Let's not mind saying that. Paul said to a young preacher:

Looking for that blessed hope, and the glorious appearing of the great God and our Saviour Jesus Christ. (Titus 2:13)

What a glorious anticipation it is!

Paul, writing to the Roman believers, giving the benefits of justification by faith, mentions eight of them. The seventh one is this:

Much more then, being now justified by his blood, we shall be saved from wrath through him. (Romans 5:9)

What kind of wrath? Well, the only wrath that is coming is the great day of His wrath. It is mentioned again and again in the Book of Revelation, and it is what the Old Testament prophets had talked about. Imagine, friend, the joy the believers will experience at the time of the Rapture—delivered! Delivered from wrath!

Now at the time of the Revelation of Christ, the attitude will be entirely different.

Thou shalt break them with a rod of iron; thou shalt dash them in pieces like a potter's vessel. (Psalm 2:9)

I'm not looking for One who is going to treat me like that! This describes the Lord Jesus coming to this earth to put down rebellion. If you can think of a better way He could do it, then you suggest it to Him. Apparently even the infinite God was not able to come up with anything different from this. He intends to punish sinners. He intends to put down the rebellion on this earth. He intends to take the scepter of this universe. This is God's plan and purpose.

Now notice the attitude on earth when He comes in that role:

> **Behold, he cometh with clouds; and every eye shall see him, and they also which pierced him: and all kindreds of the earth shall wail because of him. Even so, Amen.** (Revelation 1:7)

They are wailing because of His coming. You see how different the attitude is from the attitude toward the Rapture.

> **And then shall appear the sign of the Son of man in heaven; and then shall all the tribes of the earth mourn, and they shall see the Son of man coming in the clouds of heaven with power and great glory.** (Matthew 24:30)

This is not speaking of the Rapture when He comes to take His church, His bride. Did you ever see a bride who went down to the altar crying? No, they go down smiling, my friend. If they do weep— and women do weep regardless of the way a situation goes—they are weeping for joy. Brides weep for joy. But here folk are mourning! This is something altogether different from the Rapture of the church.

We are given the order of procedure in the book of Daniel:

> **And at that time shall Michael stand up, the great prince which standeth for the children of thy people: and there shall be a time of trouble, such as never was since there was a nation even to that same time: and at that time thy people shall be delivered, every one that shall be found written in the book.** (Daniel 12:1)

He tells us that there is first to be a time of trouble followed by the resurrection of the Old Testament saints.

For the Rapture we are told to *wait.* For the Revelation the emphasis is upon the word *watch.* I don't mean to split hairs here, but the attitude is different. There is a different way to wait and watch. There are seventeen words in the Old Testament translated by the English words *watch* and *wait.* They don't mean the same. Though we may use the same word in English, it means something altogether different.

Friend, for the child of God, the Rapture is something for which we wait in happy anticipation. But not the unsaved—for them there is nothing but wrath ahead; nothing but judgment is coming. It is altogether different.

As we have looked at the Rapture and at the Revelation of Jesus Christ, we have seen many contrasts. We have seen that the *action* is different. We have seen that the *attitude* toward each is different. Now we shall see that in the *anticipation* of the Rapture and the anticipation of the Revelation there is a vast difference.

ANTICIPATION

Notice now the spiritual factor—the *anticipation* is different. At the Revelation of Jesus Christ, Israel will be back in the land of Israel. Israel is returning to their land, not for the Millennium, but for the Great Tribulation period. Even today they could be put out of that land again. The signs will take place during the Tribulation period, and the anticipation will be for the Great Tribulation to be over.

However, for the Rapture there are no signs. Oh, the church would enter the apostasy, I grant that, and John did say that the Antichrist would come, but before that there would be many antichrists. Paul said to young Timothy that there would be a falling away:

Now the Spirit speaketh expressly, that in the latter times some shall depart from the faith, giving heed to seducing spirits, and doctrines of demons; speaking lies in hypocrisy; having their conscience seared with a hot iron; forbidding to marry, and commanding to abstain from meats, which God hath created to be received with thanksgiving of them which believe and know the truth. (1 Timothy 4:1-3)

We are presently living in days of apostasy. One so-called theologian, who a few years ago espoused the "God-is-dead" movement, describes himself as a Christian atheist! My friend, that is quite a twist. How can one be a *Christian* atheist? Of course it is a contradiction of terms. It is utterly preposterous, and it does show how far we are into the apostasy.

But our hope today is not fixed, actually, upon the church. Our present hope is fixed on the Person of the Lord Jesus Christ.

At the time of the Revelation of Christ, there will be *signs*. And the signs are not good. They are signs of the coming of the terrible day of God's wrath. It is an anticipation of dread.

But we today are not looking for signs; we are looking for Him. This is the thing that Paul dealt with when he wrote to the believers in Thessalonica. You see, folk in the early church were looking for the Lord to come back in their lifetime. And when some of their loved ones died, they wondered if they had missed the Rapture. Paul, in 1 Thessalonians 4:13–17, assured them that they hadn't missed the Rapture. In fact, they are going to be raised first. Then the living will be caught up after them. And together they will meet the Lord in the air. "And so shall we ever be with the Lord." So the early believers called their cemetery where they buried their loved ones the *koimeterion*. We get our word *cemetery* from this Greek word *koimeterion*, but it didn't mean that then. A *koimeterion* was an inn where people came and spent the night. It was a *koimeterion* in Bethlehem that didn't have room for Mary and Joseph the night Jesus was born. So, you see, the thought of the folk in the early church was, *We are just putting our loved ones up for the night—until the day breaks.*

Oh, my friend, after all, most of the church has already missed the Great Tribulation. They have already gone through the doorway of death. They are already in the presence of Christ. And those who are alive are just going to bring up the end of the parade—the few that are left.

Death today means something entirely different for a believer from what it means to the unbeliever. For us death means that the body is put in the grave, the body is put to sleep—it is only the *body* that can be put to sleep. And that sleeping body is placed in the *koimeterion* (we call them today Holiday Inns, Ramada Inns, Hilton Hotels, etc.). It is just a temporary resting place. Because the day is coming when they are going to be raised from the grave.

Way back in the 1940s when I was a pastor in Pasadena, there was a wonderful couple in the church who celebrated their fiftieth wedding anniversary. They were kind enough to invite my wife and me to come and have part. And at the dinner that evening he did the most lovely thing any man could do who had been married to a woman for fifty years. He reached over and patted her on the hand and said to the group, "We are still on our honeymoon." Friend, you can't say anything nicer than that! In fact, that night going home, I said to my wife, "What in the world happened to our honeymoon?"

Well, it wasn't long after that when the man died. At the funeral a great company of friends came and they filed by the casket with tears in their eyes. He was much loved. Then the time came for the family to come out. They filed by. Then here came the widow. She came up to the casket where he was. She reached down and patted him on the hand, just as he had patted her on the hand. Then she bent down and kissed his forehead. And she said, "John, I'll see you in the morning." And she will. It will be some bright morning. But she is going to see him. She just put him in the *koimeterion* temporarily. The cemetery is only a place where you put your loved ones for a little while. We are looking for a great event—the Rapture. And the Rapture means we are going to see Christ. It means He is going to take us to be with Himself—to that place He has prepared for us.

My friend, that is the hope of the believer today.

What is your hope for the future?

If you have no hope for the future, you can look back to the past, to an historical event that took place over nineteen hundred years ago when Christ died on the cross for you and for me who were sinners. And you can trust Him as your Savior. Then you can turn your face to the sunrising because the Bright and Morning Star is going to appear one of these days.

Until then, may God richly bless you.

Chapter 7

DARKNESS AND LIGHT: THE DAY OF THE LORD

The Day of the Lord was the high hope and the far-off goal of the Old Testament. The entire Old Testament program was moving toward it. Everything in time and creation looked forward and moved toward that day. The Old Testament closed without its being realized, and up to today the Day of the Lord has not come.

The Old Testament closes with almost a sundown on the nation of Israel. The people were drugged to an unconsciousness of sin. They were in a spiritual stupor with no conviction, which is the lowest state of sin. The last word of the Old Testament is a curse, but it does not close with only a curse. It closes also with a great hope that although the sun has gone down and it is very dark, there is coming a new day, the Day of the Lord and the Sun of righteousness who ushers it in:

But unto you that fear my name shall the Sun of righteousness arise with healing in his wings. . . . (Malachi 4:2)

But when you come to the New Testament you do not find even there that the Day of the Lord had come. In Paul's first letter to the Thessalonians you read that this Day of the Lord was still in the future:

But of the times and the seasons, brethren, ye have no need that I write unto you. For yourselves know perfectly that the day of the Lord so cometh as a thief in the night. (1 Thessalonians 5:1, 2)

So when Paul wrote this in about A.D. 51, the Day of the Lord was still in the future, and after about two thousand years, it is yet future.

The expression "the Day of the Lord" occurs five times in the Book of Joel, a very brief prophecy. All the other Old Testament prophets also make reference to this momentous period of time, some using the terms "*the* day" or "the *great* day." You will find that references to the Day of the Lord occur seventy-five times in the Old Testament. This became such a familiar phrase and was such an understandable subject of the Old Testament that by the time of Zechariah, one of the last of the prophets, you will find that he could use the term "in *that* day" and it was understood that he meant the Day of the Lord. It was the great theme of the Old Testament.

Now when you get to the New Testament, you will find that it does not ignore the subject nor change it. And you'll find that both Paul (in 1 and 2 Thessalonians) and Peter address it. Now Paul and Simon Peter might have disagreed at Antioch about whether you are to eat certain meats or not, and on other minor points, but they did not disagree on this all-important subject: that the Day of the Lord was still a very important part of the program of God.

I believe that if you understand what the Day of the Lord is and get the picture that is set before us in the Word of God, you are well on the way to becoming a student of prophecy. In fact, you can become an authority in the field of eschatology.

WHEN WILL IT COME?

Now, the question arises: Is it possible to identify this period known as the Day of the Lord? Can we define it? Can we get it out of the realm of the nebulous and tenuous? Can we avoid thinking of it as a vague theory and a spurious theology, as is done today even in many seminaries? I find it interesting to note that this theme has not been treated in any of the Christian journals that have come to my desk during the past few years. They have almost ignored this subject altogether. Our young people are not being taught in many of our so-called Christian schools the fundamental truths such as what the Day of the Lord really means.

Now what about the boundaries to the Day of the Lord? Can we place it in the parenthesis of time? How can we fit it into the program of God?

The Day of the Lord has very definite reference to the return of Christ to the earth to establish His Kingdom. That is made very clear when you turn to Old Testament prophecy. I have already referred to the prophecy of Zechariah. Now let's read this important section of his prophecy. Note the language very carefully:

> **Behold, the day of the LORD cometh, and thy spoil shall be divided in the midst of thee. For I will gather all nations against Jerusalem to battle; and the city shall be taken, and the houses rifled, and the women ravished; and half of the city shall go forth into captivity, and the residue of the people shall not be cut off from the city. Then shall the LORD go forth, and fight against those nations, as when he fought in the day of battle.**

> **And his feet shall stand in that day upon the mount of Olives, which is before Jerusalem on the east, and the mount of Olives shall cleave in the midst thereof toward the east and toward the west, and there shall be a very great valley; and half of the mountain shall remove toward the north, and half of it toward the south.** (Zechariah 14:1–4)

Here is a very remarkable prophecy that says, "Behold, the day of the LORD cometh. . . ." Note it says in verse 4 that included in this day is the coming of the Lord Jesus Christ Himself. He is coming to the earth—it says specifically that His feet shall stand on the Mount of Olives.

These verses tell us this much: We know that the second coming of Christ to the earth to establish His Kingdom is part of the Day of the Lord. This great event is so important that actually many very fine expositors begin the Day of the Lord with this second coming of Christ to the earth at the end of the Tribulation period. The *Scofield Reference Bible* presents that viewpoint. The greatest teacher I ever sat under, Dr. Lewis Sperry Chafer, taught that. But there is one small change I will make in that view. It is that in my opinion the Day of the Lord begins *before* Christ's second coming, and I trust I'll be able to sustain that thesis.

The Day of the Lord is associated by the prophets with the Millennial Kingdom that is to be established on this earth. In fact, the

Kingdom is equally as great a theme of the Old Testament as the Day of the Lord is. Therefore the Day of the Lord includes the Kingdom. However, I think the Day of the Lord is the all-inclusive term, while the Kingdom is the smaller term.

And the LORD shall be king over all the earth: in that day shall there be one LORD, and his name one. (Zechariah 14:9)

Then the verses following give actual details as to where they will begin to measure the land in that day, and Jerusalem is to become the very center. Our Lord called it the city of the great king, and our Lord shall be king in Jerusalem in that day. So now we know that the Day of the Lord includes the second coming of Christ when He establishes His Kingdom, and it also includes His Kingdom.

Now we see that the New Testament confirms this. When you turn to 2 Peter, you will find a confirmation:

But the day of the Lord will come as a thief in the night; in the which the heavens shall pass away with a great noise, and the elements shall melt with fervent heat, the earth also and the works that are therein shall be burned up. (2 Peter 3:10)

Now the Day of the Lord includes the Millennial Kingdom up to the establishment of the new heavens and the new earth. It extends therefore to the new heavens, the very beginning of eternity future.

70TH WEEK OF DANIEL

When studying in the Book of Daniel, we find a great deal of information pertaining to the future of the nation Israel. Most significant is the "seventy weeks of Daniel"* in chapter 9. Daniel was one of the Jewish captives in Babylon, and to him God gave some specific information—including actual dating—as to the end of their captivity, their return to Israel, and their rebuilding of Jerusalem. That fits into secular history from 445 B.C. to 397 B.C. This was literally fulfilled.

---

*"70 weeks of Daniel." The Hebrew word *shabua* translated by our English word "week" literally means "seven." Therefore 70 weeks is 70 sevens. The context determines that "sevens" is being used as a unit of time and refers to years. Sir Robert Anderson, a brilliant and astute student of prophecy, worked out the dating of Daniel 9 in meticulous detail. It can be found in his classic work, *The Coming Prince*. See also Dr. McGee's books on Daniel.

Then the second period consisted of 430 years, from 397 B.C. until Christ came. And we find that the very day He rode into Jerusalem, presenting Himself as the Messiah, was the exact fulfillment of this. According to the lunar calendar which Israel followed, it was right up to the very minute!

After the 483 years there is a time break, and two events of utmost importance take place: "Messiah will be cut off"—this was the crucifixion of Christ. Also Jerusalem would be destroyed by the "people of the prince" who would come later on. This was fulfilled when the Romans under Titus destroyed Jerusalem in A.D. 70.

God's revelation to Daniel had nothing to say about the church age—it wasn't necessary to mention it. He was saying that there were 490 years that pertained to Daniel's people, which is the nation Israel. Today there are seven years (the seventieth week) of this period that have not yet taken place.

Now when you come to the New Testament, you'll find that something has been added, that the church is brought before us. We learn that after Messiah was cut off, He rose from the dead and ascended back to heaven. He sent the Holy Spirit on the day of Pentecost, and there took place something new: the calling out of a body of believers called "the church." And the calling out has been going on for about two thousand years.

The next thing on God's program we call the imminent coming of Christ for His church. We found out that Paul in substance said to the Thessalonian Christians who were weeping for their loved ones who had died, "Sorrow not, even as others which have no hope. Of course you sorrow, but you have a hope!" Why?

For the Lord himself shall descend from heaven with a shout, with the voice of the archangel, and with the trump of God: and the dead in Christ shall rise first: then we which are alive and remain shall be caught up together with them in the clouds, to meet the Lord in the air: and so shall we ever be with the Lord.
(1 Thessalonians 4:16, 17)

Those who believe that Jesus died and rose again (verse 14) will go with Him immediately to heaven. And in heaven there will take place the judgment for believers at the judgment seat of Christ to see whether they are to receive a reward or not (2 Corinthians 5:10).

But, you see, momentous things will be happening on the earth during that period. The Great Tribulation will take place, designated in the Old Testament as the "seventieth week of Daniel." It is the seven-year period yet to come which will complete the 490 years of the prophecy God gave to Daniel. It pertains to the nation Israel, and it will be concluded by the return of Christ to the earth as Zechariah says: "His feet shall stand on the Mount of Olives."

Now you can understand that when Christ calls His own out of the earth and into the air to meet Him, His feet won't be touching the Mount of Olives. His taking of His church out of the world is the event we call the Rapture of the church.

Then the Great Tribulation will take place here on earth, and at the end of that period Christ will return to establish His Kingdom on this earth. But during those seven years the earth will have been under a world dictator who will combine both religion and politics. He will bring the ecumenical movement under one head, and only he himself will be worshiped as God—2 Thessalonians reveals this fact, as does the Book of Revelation, and in the Old Testament Daniel confirms it. This world dictator, called Antichrist, will show himself as God in the temple of God. He also will be the political ruler, the dictator of the entire world. No one can break his rule on this earth except Christ at His second coming. The Lord Jesus Christ will come in judgment to establish His Kingdom, and that Kingdom will last for one thousand years. His coming to the earth is the Revelation of Jesus Christ.

The Rapture is the great theme of 1 Thessalonians, while the Revelation, meaning Christ's second coming to the earth, is the theme of 2 Thessalonians. And the interesting thing is that all of this is called in the Bible the Day of the Lord.

Now we have something else to look at here that is very important for us to see. We can now put down our pegs and say that the Day of the Lord does not begin with the return of Christ to the earth at His Revelation, but it begins at the Rapture when He takes His church out of the world. We're told very definitely that the Day of the Lord comes without warning at all. You see, the Bible has given signs to look for which will indicate the coming of Christ to the earth. But there are no signs for the Rapture of the church.

The Day of the Lord begins when the church leaves the earth, and that triggers the Great Tribulation period on the earth. The Day of the Lord does not begin therefore with the return of Christ to the earth; rather, it begins with the Rapture.

EVENING BEGINS THE DAY

Now I want you to notice something that is very interesting. The Hebrew day always began with sundown; it never began with sunup. Have you noticed even in Genesis, the very first chapter, how carefully that is given to us? It says, "The evening and the morning were the first day. . . . The evening and the morning were the second day. . . . The evening and the morning were the third day." The Day of the Lord also begins in darkness. It begins at sundown. That may change the thinking of some for this reason: A great many people think the Day of the Lord means the coming of Christ to establish His Kingdom. My beloved, the prophets make it very clear that this is *not* what they are talking about at all.

I turn now to the prophecy of Joel, and note this language very carefully:

Blow ye the trumpet in Zion, and sound an alarm in my holy mountain: let all the inhabitants of the land tremble: for the day of the LORD cometh, for it is nigh at hand; a day of darkness and of gloominess, a day of clouds and of thick darkness, as the morning spread upon the mountains: a great people and a strong; there hath not been ever the like, neither shall be any more after it, even to the years of many generations. (Joel 2:1, 2)

And our Lord Himself took that expression and called it the Great Tribulation. He said,

For then shall be great tribulation, such as was not since the beginning of the world to this time, no, nor ever shall be. And except those days should be shortened, there should no flesh be saved [that is, survive]. . . . (Matthew 24:21, 22)

There would be nothing like it before, nothing like it afterward. And Joel says that the Day of the Lord begins with *darkness* and *gloominess*. It begins with the Great Tribulation period, a time of darkness, just as the Hebrew day must begin.

Now this is the whole tenor of Scripture. You will find that all the references to the Day of the Lord identify it with judgment. Listen to this language in the Book of Ezekiel:

> **For the day is near, even the day of the LORD is near, a cloudy day; it shall be the time of the heathen.** (Ezekiel 30:3)

Do you notice what Ezekiel says? "The day is near . . . the day of the LORD is near, a *cloudy* day," if you please. He agrees with Joel. Now listen to the language used by Isaiah:

> **Howl ye; for the day of the LORD is at hand; it shall come as a destruction from the Almighty.** (Isaiah 13:6)

And then drop down to verse 9:

> **Behold, the day of the LORD cometh, cruel both with wrath and fierce anger, to lay the land desolate: and he shall destroy the sinners thereof out of it.**

The Day of the Lord, you see, is always associated with judgment. That is the way you find it in the Word of God.

Now I turn to what is probably one of the most remarkable prophecies that we have in the entire Bible on this subject. It is found in the first chapter of the little prophecy of Zephaniah:

> **The great day of the LORD is near, it is near, and hasteth greatly, even the voice of the day of the LORD: the mighty man shall cry there bitterly. That day is a day of wrath. . . .**

And the Great Tribulation is called a day of wrath.

> **That day is a day of wrath, a day of trouble and distress, a day of wasteness and desolation, a day of darkness and gloominess, a day of clouds and thick darkness, a day of the trumpet and alarm against the fenced cities, and against the high towers. And I will bring distress upon men, that they shall walk like blind men, because they have sinned against the LORD: and their blood shall be poured out as dust, and their flesh as the dung. Neither their silver nor their gold shall be able to deliver them in the day of the LORD's wrath; but the whole land shall be**

devoured by the fire of his jealousy: for he shall make even a speedy riddance of all them that dwell in the land. (Zephaniah 1:14–18)

You see, it is a time of judgment. The great day of His wrath is come, and it's the time of judgment upon the earth. This is the picture the Bible presents to us. Joel confirms it again:

And the LORD shall utter his voice before his army: for his camp is very great: for he is strong that executeth his word: for the day of the LORD is great and very terrible; and who can abide it? (Joel 2:11)

And then again in the third chapter:

Multitudes, multitudes in the valley of decision: for the day of the LORD is near in the valley of decision. (Joel 3:14)

Now, my beloved, all of these references relate the Day of the Lord to a period of judgment, and it would be very easy to give you cross-references that show the direct application to the Great Tribulation period, because in the Book of Revelation the Great Tribulation period has all of these things in it. Therefore the Day of the Lord will begin with night—the night of delusion, distress, and desolation.

But it is always God's plan to move from darkness to light—always. We find His first recorded words in the Book of Genesis when He moved into this earth after some great catastrophe took place. He said, "Let there be light." Where there is darkness, God moves in with light. Where there is sin, He moves in with salvation. It is His method. And though the great Day of the Lord opens with judgment, it leads to light, if you please. There is both darkness and light in the Day of the Lord.

Now I want to reaffirm this. The Day of the Lord comes without warning. We noted in all those passages the thought of its coming quickly. This doesn't mean it is coming soon, but when it comes it strikes suddenly! If the Lord Jesus took the church off this earth tonight (I say this to you very carefully), I am convinced that the Day of the Lord would break on this earth tomorrow. It would break suddenly!

You see, at the Rapture, God will remove the church which has lost much of its influence, though it does have some. He will also remove something else: a Restrainer. The Holy Spirit is the Restrainer, and He will still be in the world but not restraining evil. He today is holding back evil in order that the gospel might continue to go out, and He will do that up to the very moment the church leaves the world. Then when that takes place, evil will break like a great flood, like a dam giving way, and a flood of evil and of great judgment will come over this earth.

Now the return of Christ to this earth to establish His Kingdom has signs connected to it. However, at the time of the Rapture when He takes His own out of the world, which may be at any moment, there's not a sign given to us. It can take place at any time, and no man can set a date. We can't even say it may be soon. We do not know. Somebody said to me once, "Well, it may be this year that He will come." I said, "Don't say that, because the minute you begin to talk about dates, you contradict the Lord Jesus who said, '. . . In such an hour as ye think not the Son of man cometh'" (Matthew 24:44).

When He takes the church out of the world, that is called the Day of Christ. "Being confident of this very thing, that he which hath begun a good work in you will perform it until the day of Jesus Christ" (Philippians 1:6). So that is the great hope that is before the church.

As we have already seen, when Christ takes the church out of the world, then the Day of the Lord begins. And though it begins in darkness, it is certainly light for those who were taken out, that is, for the children of God. It is the end of the pilgrim pathway down here for them. The Day of Christ ends at the Rapture, and the Day of the Lord begins at that point.

In the prophecy of Hosea there are some very wonderful verses that speak of this period but are not identified as such. Note the picture that's given here:

> **For the children of Israel shall abide many days without a king, and without a prince, and without a sacrifice, and without an image, and without an ephod, and without teraphim.** (Hosea 3:4)

And that's the period we're living in today. For many years now, Israel has not had a place of sacrifice. Then God says,

> Afterward shall the children of Israel return, and seek the LORD
> their God, and David their king; and shall fear the LORD and
> his goodness in the latter days. (Hosea 3:5)

So that when Christ comes to this earth to establish His Kingdom, this verse will be fulfilled.

Now the Day of the Lord, I trust you can see, is a technical term, and it is also a theological term that embraces many momentous acts of God. You and I today are living in the day of salvation, and that doesn't mean a twenty-four-hour day. It doesn't really have reference to time but to a particular period. And this day of salvation for us ends when He takes the church out. Then the Day of the Lord begins. What a picture is presented to us here.

Let me give you someone else's very fine definition of the Day of the Lord. This is from Dr. J. Dwight Pentecost's book, *Things to Come:*

> It is thus concluded that the Day of the Lord is that extended
> period of time beginning with God's dealing with Israel after the
> rapture at the beginning of the tribulation period and extending
> through the second advent and the millennial age unto the creation
> of the new heavens and the new earth after the millennium.

GOD'S SCENARIO

The Day of the Lord, we see, begins with the Rapture which happens "in the twinkling of an eye," then the Great Tribulation. And the Day of the Lord extends through the seven years of the Great Tribulation period (Revelation 6–18) and the return of Christ to the earth to establish His Kingdom (Revelation 19). Then in Revelation 20, Satan is bound while Christ reigns a thousand years on the earth. Satan is then released for a little while—and don't ask me why, I don't know.

Someone asked the late Dr. Chafer, "Why in the world, when God gets Satan bound, does He release him for a little while?" And Dr. Chafer gave his characteristic answer, "You tell me why God released him in the beginning, and I'll tell you why God releases him again for a little while." Well, God has let him loose today, that's for sure.

And during that future day when Satan is loose for a brief period, he will lead a rebellion that God will put down.

The Great White Throne, the place of God's final judgment, is brought before us in Revelation 20:11-15. The Tribulation saints were resurrected and were with the Lord Jesus during His millennial reign. Now prior to the Great White Throne we see that the lost dead are resurrected, and they, "small and great," stand before God.

My friend, there are many people who say, "I'll take my chances before God." When I talked to a man in Altadena several years ago, he said to me, "McGee, you don't need to talk to me about these things. I've listened to you on the radio. I don't agree with you. I'll take my chances with God. I think He's merciful, and I'll take my chances. I'm a good man. I pay my honest debts." Well, that man is going to be there at the Great White Throne, and he's going to have an opportunity to tell the Lord that he paid his honest debts.

But I tell you, it's not going to be a pretty sight to stand before the One who has nail-pierced hands and hear Him say, "But I loved you so much I died for you. You, a sinner, lost, without hope. . . . I bore your sins in My own body to pay the penalty for *your* sin. Why did you reject Me?" May I say to you, friend, paying your honest debts is going to look mighty small in that day. If you've come to Christ and accepted Him as your Savior, of course you pay your honest debts! But just paying your honest debts won't get you into heaven—that's for sure.

All the lost appear there before the Great White Throne, and the curtain closes with these fateful words:

And whosoever was not found written in the book of life was cast into the lake of fire. (Revelation 20:15)

Then after that final judgment we find that eternity begins, the new heavens and the new earth come into view (Revelation 21, 22). Let me repeat: the Day of the Lord begins with the Rapture of the church and embraces everything from the Great Tribulation to the creation of the new heavens and the new earth. This is the tremendous picture that is presented to us in the Word of God.

You see, God makes it very clear that no Scripture, no prophecy, is to be interpreted by itself. Listen to what He says,

Knowing this first, that no prophecy of the scripture is of any private interpretation. (2 Peter 1:20)

In other words, Peter is saying this: You are not to lift out one little prophecy (the way many of the cults do it today) and build a doctrine on it. You are not to interpret it apart from other references to the same subject because no prophecy is of any private interpretation. You don't interpret it by itself. It has to fit into God's program of prophecy, you see. Therefore, the great Day of the Lord is one of the great terms of the Word of God. And when the Bible mentions it, you know it is speaking of this entire period, including all of it. We can put the boundaries on it: beginning at the Rapture of the church and what takes place on the earth, then ending with the beginning of eternity. Therefore you and I need today to interpret the present in terms of the future.

WATCH AND WAIT

I think that we're living in a day when the attitude toward the future is changing. There has never been a time when so much attention was given to the future. People years ago paid very little attention to the future, but now a great many of us are even waiting for the media to tell us who the man of the year is and why he was chosen! The future is important to us. We find the seriously thoughtful of the world pondering and speculating in terms of the future. Should not *God's* people also think in terms of the future? Our Lord urged us to do so.

The fact of the matter is, one of the great injunctions that He has given us is to stay alert and watch. I want you to notice what He has to say in the Olivet Discourse as He is speaking of His coming to the earth to establish His Kingdom.

Watch therefore: for ye know not what hour your Lord doth come. But know this, that if the goodman of the house had known in what watch the thief would come, he would have watched, and would not have suffered his house to be broken up. (Matthew 24:42, 43)

Is the Lord Jesus coming as a thief for the church? No. The thief is one you're not looking for. We're "looking for that blessed hope, and the glorious appearing of the great God and our Savior Jesus Christ" (Titus 2:13).

And you'll notice that this is the very thing Paul deals with when writing to the Thessalonian believers:

> **For yourselves know perfectly that the day of the Lord so cometh as a thief in the night. For when they shall say, Peace and safety; then sudden destruction cometh upon them, as travail upon a woman with child; and they shall not escape. But ye, brethren, are not in darkness, that that day should overtake you as a thief.** (1 Thessalonians 5:2–4)

My beloved, our Lord will not come for His church as a thief. But when He comes to the earth to establish His Kingdom, He *will* come as a thief, breaking into this world, interfering with men's little plans and programs.

Several years ago I decided to make a study of the Hebrew word for "watch and wait." I thought it was a single word, but I found out there are seventeen words in the Hebrew that are translated by the English words *watch* and *wait*. It's amazing how many ways you can watch and wait. Let me illustrate.

At the beginning of hunting season, a man gets a deer license. He goes up into Utah, goes out into the woods, climbs up on a mountain, and he waits there and watches. At every sound of movement he hears out there in the woods, he raises his gun—and it better not be another hunter because he's apt to shoot him too—but he's waiting there for a deer to appear. That's one way to wait and watch.

Then later you can see him down at the airport, pacing up and down. And you say, "I see you're waiting and watching again." He says, "Yes, but differently. I'm waiting for the plane to come in. My mother-in-law's coming out from Iowa to visit us for the holidays. The plane is two hours late, and I do not have time to waste down here waiting for her!" So he paces up and down. That's another way to wait and watch, isn't it?

Then you meet him a couple of days later, during the Christmas rush, down at the corner of Seventh and Hope Streets. And you see him again pacing up and down and looking at his watch. He's waiting.

You step up to him and say, "What in the world is the matter?" He says, "Well, I'm waiting for my wife. She's already forty-five minutes late, and I'm waiting for her."

Now that is different from waiting up yonder in the mountains with a gun for a deer, although he may wish he had his gun with him down there at Seventh and Hope Streets! He's waiting differently again. My friend, you can wait in many different ways.

Now the world is not wanting Christ to come. They're in rebellion against Him. But He's going to break through one of these days. Before He breaks through into the world, He's going to take His own out of the world, and they are watching; they are waiting, "Looking for that blessed hope, and the glorious appearing of the great God and our Savior Jesus Christ" (Titus 2:13).

The minute that Christ takes His church out of the world, the Day of Christ, the period of His grace, ends. No longer will He be calling the church out of the world because the church shall be with Him.

Then finally His wrath comes. The great Day of the Lord is darkness, not light, as the Great Tribulation breaks on the earth with a world dictator who will establish an ecumenical movement and a world political movement. Nothing can deter it except the return of Christ, and He will break through like a thief, intruding into this world, establishing His Kingdom on this earth. He will reign on this earth for a thousand years. The period ends with the establishment of the new heavens and the new earth and with those who are His own living in the New Jerusalem.

This is God's program, my beloved. The Word of God tells us that we know not what a day will bring forth, but every child of God knows that we have a wonderful Shepherd and that we can never be taken out of our Shepherd's hands—either in time or in eternity. It is reassuring to know that our Shepherd has a program for the future. This gives hope; it gives purpose and direction to life. I do not know about you, but for me it adds a great deal of color to the drabness of living down here on this earth. It is an incentive today for living for God.

What about the future for you? Suppose Christ does come this year. Unless you are trusting Him as your Savior, there is nothing ahead of you but the Day of Judgment that will take place on this earth.

For God so loved the world, that he gave his only begotten Son, that whosoever believeth in him should not perish, but have everlasting life. For God sent not his son into the world to condemn the world; but that the world through him might be saved. (John 3:16, 17)

My beloved, today is the day of salvation.

Chapter 8

FROM THE TOP OF THE MOUNT OF OLIVES YOU CAN SEE FOREVER

A great many thoughtful and knowledgeable people are wondering if we are approaching the end of this civilization as we know it. At the present time there is an unusual interest in what the Bible has to say about the conclusion of man's little day upon this earth. Any study which deals with these final events is incomplete without a careful examination of the words of the Lord Jesus Christ Himself during His earthly life. These are recorded in Matthew 24 and 25. We call these two chapters the Olivet Discourse simply because they were spoken by our Lord to His disciples while they were together on the Mount of Olives.

Now as we approach this study, it will help us to keep in mind that in the four Gospels we have the Lord Jesus Christ presented in the fourfold aspect of His glorious coming to this earth, and it takes four Gospels to present Him. The first Gospel, the Gospel of Matthew, presents Him as King. He was born a King and He is a King. In the Gospel of Mark, Jesus is presented as the Servant. Then in the Gospel of Luke He is presented as the Son of Man, and in the Gospel of John He is presented as the Son of God. So you have Him presented in this fourfold way. Therefore, when you are reading any one of these Gospel records, it is well to remember what the writer is attempting to emphasize.

Now in the Olivet Discourse Jesus is speaking of last things, events that have to do with His Kingship. It has nothing in the world to do with the church. Unfortunately, men have been attempting to read some nineteen hundred years of church history into the Olivet Discourse. They have been superimposing the church upon a discourse in which the church is not even mentioned and has no place at all. If you keep that in mind it will be helpful to you indeed. (See chart, p. 142 .)

Moses mentioned the fact that God was going to raise up a prophet like himself. He said:

> **The LORD thy God will raise up unto thee a Prophet from the midst of thee, of thy brethren, like unto me; unto him ye shall hearken.** (Deuteronomy 18:15)

And God repeated it:

> **I will raise them up a Prophet from among their brethren, like unto thee, and will put my words in his mouth; and he shall speak unto them all that I shall command him.** (Deuteronomy 18:18)

The Lord Jesus Christ is the fulfillment of this prophecy. He is that Prophet, and Matthew 24 and 25 is His prophecy.

In Matthew 23 and 24 Jesus denounced the religious rulers, then He went out and wept over the city of Jerusalem. He had denounced them in scathing terms. He had censured them in a fashion that absolutely blanches your soul when you read the account. But this One who had spoken like that is the King, and He had exposed them with a broken heart. Now He says:

> **O Jerusalem, Jerusalem, thou that killest the prophets, and stonest them which are sent unto thee, how often would I have gathered thy children together, even as a hen gathereth her chickens under her wings, and ye would not! Behold, your house is left unto you desolate. For I say unto you, Ye shall not see me henceforth, till ye shall say, Blessed is he that cometh in the name of the Lord.** (Matthew 23:37–39)

You and I have no notion how literally that was fulfilled in A.D. 70. Clouds were hanging over the city of Jerusalem, and the Roman army made its attack on the city and destroyed it. The prophecy was literally fulfilled, fulfilled in such a way that the words of our Lord were carried out to the very letter.

Then our Lord turned His back on Jerusalem, and we pick up our study at this point.

And Jesus went out, and departed from the temple: and his disciples came to him for to show him the buildings of the temple. (Matthew 24:1)

The Lord Jesus has just told His disciples that His Kingdom would be postponed and that the temple would be left desolate. The temple was made up of many buildings. This was the temple that Herod was having built, and the construction was still in progress. It was made of white marble, and at this time it was very large and very beautiful. The disciples are disturbed at the statement of Jesus that it is to be left desolate. So the disciples come to Him, wanting to show Him around the buildings.

And Jesus said unto them, See ye not all these things? verily I say unto you, There shall not be left here one stone upon another, that shall not be thrown down. (Matthew 24:2)

"See ye not all these things?" The disciples think they see it, and they ask Him to take a look. So He says to them, "Do you really *see* it?" In our contemporary society, this is a good question for us to consider. Do we really *see* the world around us?

When my wife and I first came to Southern California, we spent every Monday, which was my day off, riding around looking at this fantastic place. And it *was* fantastic in those days before everybody in the world tried to settle here! As we marveled at one beautiful spot after another, I would say to my wife, "But we really don't see it as it is. All of this is under God's judgment. It all will pass away." My friend, all these cultural centers, these great schools, these skyscrapers, these great cities which we see are going to pass away someday. It doesn't seem possible, and that is how the disciples felt.

Jesus continued by saying, "There shall not be left here one stone upon another, that shall not be thrown down." If His first statement put them in shock, this must have traumatized them.

When I was at the wailing wall in Jerusalem several years ago, the tour director tried to call my attention to the way the stones had been worn away by the people who had come there over the years to weep. That was certainly worth noting, but the thing that impressed me was that the wall was constructed of many kinds of stones. History tells us that the wailing wall was made up of stones which came from different buildings in different periods. At the pinnacle of the temple, which evidently was the corner of the temple area, recent excavations reveal the same thing—there are all kinds of stones from different periods. What does that mean? My friend, that means that not one stone was left upon another—the builders had to go and pick up stones from different places because in A.D. 70 the Roman army under Titus really destroyed that city!

Although this is ancient history to us, it was a shocking revelation to the disciples. They talked it over, I am sure, then came to Him with three questions.

And as he sat upon the mount of Olives, the disciples came unto him privately, saying, Tell us, when shall these things be? and what shall be the sign of thy coming, and of the end of the world? (Matthew 24:3)

(1) "When shall these things be?"—when one stone would not be left upon another.
(2) "What shall be the sign of thy coming?" The answer to this question is found in verses 23–51.
(3) "What shall be the sign of the completion of the age?" The answer to this question is found in verses 9–22.

The Lord Jesus is going to answer these three questions, and we call His answers the Olivet Discourse because it took place on the Mount of Olives.

JESUS ANSWERS THE DISCIPLES' QUESTIONS

The first question, "When shall these things be?"—when one stone shall not be left upon another—is not answered in the Gospel of Matthew. We find it in the Gospel of Luke, and we find segments of it in the Gospel of Mark. Why is it not included in Matthew's Gospel? Because Matthew is the Gospel of the Kingdom; it presents the King. The destruction of Jerusalem in A.D. 70 has something to do with this age in which we live, but it has nothing to do with the distant future when the King is coming. Therefore, Matthew does not carry that part of the Olivet Discourse.

Let's look at our Lord's answer to the first question, as recorded in Luke's Gospel:

> **And when ye shall see Jerusalem compassed with armies, then know that the desolation thereof is nigh. Then let them which are in Judea flee to the mountains; and let them which are in the midst of it depart out; and let not them that are in the countries enter thereinto. For these be the days of vengeance, that all things which are written may be fulfilled. But woe unto them that are with child, and to them that give suck, in those days! for there shall be great distress in the land, and wrath upon this people. And they shall fall by the edge of the sword, and shall be led away captive into all nations: and Jerusalem shall be trodden down of the Gentiles, until the times of the Gentiles be fulfilled.** (Luke 21:20–24)

Undoubtedly, many of those who heard the Lord Jesus say these things were present in A.D. 70 when the Roman armies surrounded the city, laid siege to it, cut it off from the rest of the world, then finally breached the wall and got in. What the Romans did was terrible. They demolished the city. It was the worst destruction in its history, more devastating than that conducted by Nebuchadnezzar over six centuries earlier. When the Romans destroyed Jerusalem in A.D. 70, the first part of the Olivet Discourse was fulfilled.

The next two questions asked by the disciples were these: "What shall be the sign of thy coming, and of the end of the world [age]?"

The Lord is going to answer the disciples' questions in their chronological and logical order. He will answer their last question first and their second question last. The first thing the Lord deals with is the sign of the end of the world, or more accurately, the end of the age. The world will never come to an end. The old world will pass away and a new earth will be brought on the scene. It will be similar to trading in your old car for a new one. You don't say, "This is the end of the car age for me. I don't have a car anymore." You *do* have a car because you traded your old one in and got a new one. And the Lord is going to trade the old world in for a new one. The world will never come to an end. But it will be the end of an age, and that is the word the disciples are using in their question to the Lord Jesus.

In this Olivet Discourse when Christ speaks of His coming, He is referring to His return to the earth to establish His Kingdom. The church is not in the picture at all. In fact, by the end of the age the church will have been removed, and it will be the last days of the nation Israel. He is speaking about the Great Tribulation period and so labels it in this discourse.

JESUS TRACES THE CHARACTERISTICS OF THIS AGE

And Jesus answered and said unto them, Take heed that no man deceive you. (Matthew 24:4)

The phrase "take heed that no man deceive you" is characteristic of this entire age. The Lord gives this word of caution because there will be much deception, especially during the Tribulation period when the Antichrist will appear. Peter warns us in 2 Peter 2:1,

But there were false prophets also among the people, even as there shall be false teachers among you, who privily shall bring in damnable heresies, even denying the Lord that bought them, and bring upon themselves swift destruction.

We don't have to worry about false prophets because if anybody starts prophesying in our day, we Christians can pooh-pooh him right off the scene because prophets are not for this period. However, we are to beware of false teachers, and there are a great many of those around. We must test them by Scripture.

I received a letter once which illustrates this fact. It came from a woman who apparently had an important position in an insurance company, and she told of a well-meaning friend who introduced her to a cult. After going to her friend's church for one year, she heard our Bible-teaching radio program, and the Scripture alerted her to the error of the cult. Then she told how she and her entire family went to a good church in her area. My friend, we need to beware of false teaching. There is a lot of it around in our day. Our Lord warns, "Take heed that no man deceive you."

For many shall come in my name, saying, I am Christ; and shall deceive many. (Matthew 24:5)

Near the end of the age many people will claim to be Christ. We have such people present with us now. One man established a "holy city" in Northern California and expected any minute to be called to Washington, D.C., to solve the problems of the world. There are no "holy cities" on the face of the earth, but someday the Lord will come from the Holy of Holies in heaven to earth and solve the problems. It should be remembered that even now there are many antichrists, but at the end of the age there will come *one* Antichrist who will oppose Christ and set himself up as the only authority.

I believe that our Lord, up there on the Mount of Olives, looked down to the end of the age and to the Great Tribulation period. But at the beginning of His discourse, He bridged the gap by giving us a picture of the present age of the church. I recognize that there are many good Bible teachers, much better than I am, who take the position that in verses 5–8 He is speaking of the Tribulation period also; so if you want to disagree with me you will be in very good company. However, it is my view that our Lord is not referring to the Great Tribulation until we reach verse 9 of this chapter.

And ye shall hear of wars and rumours of wars: see that ye be not troubled: for all these things must come to pass, but the end is not yet. (Matthew 24:6)

Wars and rumors of wars are not the sign that we are at the end of the age, by any means. The Lord is bridging the gap from where the disciples are to the end of the age. It is easy to think of major wars as indicative of the fact that we are at the end of the age. They are not! There have been many major wars in the past few thousand years and only about two hundred years of peace. When I was a little boy at the end of World War I, I remember hearing my Dad and others talking about the books being printed declaring it was the end of the world. World War I caused this type of thinking. But after the war, we had a worldwide depression, World War II, and the atom bomb. By this time I was a pastor in Pasadena, and I told my congregation that a wheelbarrow load of books would come out saying that we were at the end of the world because of World War II. You know something?

I was wrong! *Two* wheelbarrow loads of books were printed, and they
were sensational.

We have come a long way from World War II, and the end of the
age still has not come. We should listen to the Lord and stop listening
to false teachers. We will hear about wars and rumors of wars, but
we should not be troubled because all these things will come to pass,
and still it will not be the end of the age. Friend, we should also keep
in mind that man will never solve the problem of war. The League
of Nations could not solve this problem, and the United Nations will
not be able to solve it either. There will be no peace until the Prince
of Peace comes.

> **For nation shall rise against nation, and kingdom against king-
> dom: and there shall be famines, and pestilences, and earth-
> quakes, in divers places. All these are the beginning of sorrows.**
> (Matthew 24:7, 8)

These are characteristics of the entire age and are therefore not signs
of the end of the age, "but the end is not yet" (verse 6).

False christs, rumors of wars, famines, pestilences, and earth-
quakes characterize the entire church age, but they will apparently
be intensified as we draw near to the end of the age. Right now the
population explosion has the world frightened and rightly so. People
are starving to death by the thousands and the millions. And this
situation is going to increase. But the old black horse of famine (see
Revelation 6:5, 6) hasn't appeared yet, but at the end of the age the
black horse and its rider will come forth. What we see today is just
the beginning of sorrows.

The next verse begins with our first *time* word—"then."

THE BEGINNING OF THE TRIBULATION
WITH ITS SIGNS

Now the Lord begins to speak of the time of Tribulation. You and
I are living in the "age of the church" or the "age of the Holy Spirit,"
as some people like to speak of it. The Bible divides the world today
into three groups of people: the Jews, the Gentiles, and the church
of God (see 1 Corinthians 10:32). In this age God is calling out a
people to His name from both Jews and Gentiles to comprise the third

group, the church. It is this third group which will be taken out of the world at the time of the Rapture. Then the Great Tribulation will begin, and I believe that verse 9 speaks of this beginning—

Then shall they deliver you up to be afflicted, and shall kill you: and ye shall be hated of all nations for my name's sake. (Matthew 24:9)

"Then shall they deliver you up to be afflicted"—who is the *you?* Obviously, He is not addressing the church but the nation Israel. The affliction He is talking about is anti-Semitism on a worldwide scale.

At this point let me inject an important fact for Christians in our day. As long as the true church is in the world, there could not be worldwide anti-Semitism because the church would resist it. No genuine believer in the Lord Jesus could hate the Jews; it is an impossibility. It is my feeling that the liberal wing of the church is presenting a false front to the Jews and that in the final analysis will turn against them. But as long as the true church is in the world, there won't be worldwide anti-Semitism; it will break out *after* the church has been removed at the Rapture.

And then shall many be offended, and shall betray one another, and shall hate one another. And many false prophets shall rise, and shall deceive many. (Matthew 24:10, 11)

As we saw earlier, the church is warned against false teachers while Israel is warned against false prophets. So here, after the church has been removed, again the warning is against false prophets.

And because iniquity shall abound, the love of many shall wax cold. (Matthew 24:12)

This is a *principle,* and there are many principles in this Olivet Discourse which we can apply to our own day. Not long ago I met a preacher who had been a schoolmate of mine. He has become liberal in his theology; he drinks his cocktails, smokes his cigarettes, and lives just like the rest of the world lives. He told me, "McGee, you don't fight city hall; you join it!" He told me about how sinful practices had gotten into his church and how he is not planning to fight them. When iniquity abounds, the love of many grows cold, and this will be even more true at the end of the age.

This next verse is very startling to some folk—

But he that shall endure unto the end, the same shall be saved.
(Matthew 24:13)

The question is: who endures to the end? Well, when I study the Book of Revelation, I find that God will stop all the forces of nature and of evil and even the forces of good while He seals a certain number of folk. So who is going to endure to the end? Those whom He seals at the beginning, of course. The Good Shepherd—in all ages—will bring His sheep through to the end. When He starts with one hundred sheep, He comes through with one hundred sheep.

When someone says to me, "So-and-so was very active in the church and has gone into sin. Is he saved?" I can only reply that I do not know. We will have to wait to see what happens. I tell people that the pigs will eventually end up in the pigpen, and the prodigal sons will all find their way back to the Father's house. It *is* confusing to find a son in a pigpen and a pig in the Father's house. Peter says, ". . . The sow that was washed [has returned] to her wallowing in the mire" (2 Peter 2:22). Let's say that one of the little pigs went with the prodigal son to the father's house, that he was scrubbed clean, his teeth brushed with Pepsodent, and that a pink ribbon was tied around his neck. But he wouldn't stay in the father's house. Sooner or later he would go back to the pigpen where he belonged. "He that shall endure unto the end, the same shall be saved." You'll just have to wait and see. Sometimes a son, a Christian, will get into a pigpen, but since he is a son, he will get out someday. Why? Because he has a wonderful Shepherd. "The same shall be saved."

And this gospel of the kingdom shall be preached in all the world for a witness unto all nations; and then shall the end come.
(Matthew 24:14)

The gospel of the Kingdom is what John the Baptist preached— "Repent ye: for the kingdom of heaven is at hand" (Matthew 3:2). The Lord Jesus began His ministry with that message—"From that time Jesus began to preach, and to say, Repent: for the kingdom of heaven is at hand" (Matthew 4:17). Also, He sent His apostles out with that message (Matthew 10). But in Matthew 11 we see that our Lord's message changed to, "Come unto me, all ye that labour and are heavy laden, and I will give you rest." In Matthew 20:28 He said that He had come to give His life a ransom for many. But during the Tribulation period, the gospel of the Kingdom will again be preached. It is not for our day because we are to preach the gospel of the grace of God.

Is the gospel of the Kingdom another gospel? No, my friend, it is not. It is the same gospel with a different emphasis. We have no right to say that the Kingdom of heaven is at hand because we don't know. But when the Great Tribulation period begins, the people will know that they are close to the end, although they will not know the day nor the hour. Therefore, the message will be, "Repent: for the kingdom of heaven is at hand."

Now let me answer our critics who say that we who hold the dispensational view of Scripture teach that there are two or more ways of being saved. No, God has never had more than one basis on which He saves men, and that basis is the cross of Christ. Every offering before Christ came looked forward to the cross of Christ, and every commemoration since He has come looks back to the cross of Christ.

To illustrate this, let's go back to Genesis 4 and look at the offering which Abel brought to God. He brought a little lamb. If you had been there, you could have asked Abel, "Why are you bringing this little lamb? Do you think that a little lamb will take away your sins?" He would have said, "Of course not! I'm bringing this little lamb because God told me to do so. I am bringing it by faith." Then you could have asked him, "Well, if it won't take away your sins, why would He ask you to bring it?" Abel's answer would have been something like this: "This little lamb is pointing to One who is coming later, the seed of the woman, my mother. That One will take away our sins. I bring this little lamb by faith, recognizing that I am a sinner and need a substitute." You see, Abel was looking forward to the One who was coming.

John the Baptist not only said, "Repent ye: for the kingdom of heaven is at hand," but he also said, "Behold the Lamb of God, which taketh away the sin of the world" (John 1:29). John identified Him. Before the coming of Christ everyone who had come to God on His terms was saved by *credit*. And they were forgiven on the basis of the death of Christ. In the Old Testament God never saved anyone by Law. At the heart of the Mosaic system was the sacrificial system.

They brought a lamb to God because the Law revealed that they were lawbreakers, that they were not obeying God, and that they needed to have a substitute to pay the penalty of their sins. The Law was given "that every mouth may be stopped, and all the world may become guilty before God" (Romans 3:19). My friend, you and I are lawbreakers; we are sinners needing a Savior. The thing to do is to receive Christ as your *Savior* before He comes as the Sovereign of this universe when He will be your *Judge*.

Now, going back to the verse we have been considering, "This gospel of the kingdom shall be preached in all the world for a witness unto all nations; and then shall the end come." This does not mean that while the church is here in the world the end can't come until the gospel of the grace of God is preached worldwide. I know there are those who use this verse to promote their Bible-teaching programs. While it is laudable to want to get the gospel to the ends of the earth, this is not the verse to use to promote it. You see, my friend, it is important to interpret Scripture in its context. Remember that our Lord is answering the question, "What is the sign of the end of the age?" He is speaking of that end time.

THE GREAT TRIBULATION
WITH ITS TROUBLE AND SORROWS

Now Jesus gives the sign that will identify this period of time.

When ye therefore shall see the abomination of desolation, spoken of by Daniel the prophet, stand in the holy place, (whoso readeth, let him understand). (Matthew 24:15)

What is the abomination of desolation? Well, Daniel tells us about two of them. One of them was Antiochus Epiphanes, the Syrian, who came down and destroyed Jerusalem. In Daniel 11:31 we read: "And arms shall stand on his part, and they shall pollute the sanctuary of strength, and shall take away the daily sacrifice, and they shall place the abomination that maketh desolate." History bears out the fact that Antiochus Epiphanes came against Jerusalem in 170 B.C., at which time over 100,000 Jews were slain. He took away the daily sacrifice from the temple, offered the blood and broth of a swine upon the altar, and set up an image of Jupiter to be worshiped in the Holy Place.

However, our Lord is undoubtedly referring to the second abomination of desolation to which Daniel alludes (Daniel 12:11), and I believe that it will be an image of Antichrist which will be set up in the temple. During the Tribulation, the temple will be rebuilt and the nation of Israel will be back in Palestine. Obviously, our Lord is speaking of the temple rather than the church, because the church has no holy place. However, we cannot be certain that this is the abomination of desolation to which our Lord refers in the passage before us. This is just our surmising.

I am not looking for the abomination of desolation—I wouldn't know it if I met it on the street. But the people in the last days will be looking for it because it will be the sign to prove that they are in the Great Tribulation period. Instead of our looking for Antichrist and his abominations, we are told to be "looking for that blessed hope, and the glorious appearing of the great God and our Saviour Jesus Christ" (Titus 2:13).

Our Lord says, "Whoso readeth, let him understand," which means the people who are living at that time *will* understand. Since you and I won't be there, He hasn't given us many details.

Now we are given another *time* word. When the abomination of desolation appears, "then"—

Then let them which be in Judea flee into the mountains. (Matthew 24:16)

You and I are not expecting to flee to the mountains of Judea. I live very near the Sierra Madre mountains, and my neighbor tells me that if an atom bomb is dropped in Southern California, he is going to head for a certain canyon up there (and I may follow him!), but that will not fulfill this prophecy. In fact, it has nothing whatever to do with it. Rather, it has to do with people who are in Judea. Our Lord is giving that prophecy to those people, not to us.

Let him which is on the housetop not come down to take any thing out of his house. (Matthew 24:17)

The housetop in Palestine corresponds to our front porch or our patio. Again let me emphasize the fact that our Lord is speaking to the folk in Palestine, not to you and me. This warning is not applicable to us; we don't spend our time on our housetops!

Neither let him which is in the field return back to take his clothes. (Matthew 24:18)

This refers to people engaged in agriculture. If a worker in the fields leaves his cloak at the end of the row in the early morning when it is cool, and the word comes that the abomination of desolation has appeared, he is not to go back and get his cloak, but he is to start running.

And woe unto them that are with child, and to them that give suck in those days! (Matthew 24:19)

This reveals our Lord's great care and concern for mothers and little children. It will be a time when one should not have children.

It is believed that there will be a great population explosion at the beginning of the Great Tribulation. The fact that this earth is becoming overweighted with people in our day may be another evidence that we are approaching the end of the age.

But pray ye that your flight be not in the winter, neither on the sabbath day. (Matthew 24:20)

Again, these are people who are observing the Sabbath day, which is Saturday. This is another proof that Christ is speaking directly to the Jewish people. I don't go to church on the Sabbath but on Sunday because my Lord rose from the dead on that day.

For then shall be great tribulation, such as was not since the beginning of the world to this time, no, nor ever shall be. (Matthew 24:21)

"For then shall be great tribulation"—in Revelation 7:14 the literal translation is "the tribulation the great one," placing the article before both the noun and the adjective for emphasis. In other words, this Tribulation is unique; there has been nothing like it in the history of the world, and there will never again be anything like it. Notice that our Lord is the One who labels the end of the age as the Great Tribulation. (If you want to find fault with it, talk to Him, not to me.)

"Such as was not since the beginning of the world to this time, no, nor ever shall be." Since that is true, believe me, people will know it when it gets here! I hear people today talking about the church going through the Tribulation, and they don't seem to realize how severe it will be. In fact, some folk say that we are in the Great Tribulation at the present time! Well, things are bad in our day, I'll grant that, but this period can be matched with many other periods in history. When the Great Tribulation gets here, there will be nothing to match it with in the past or in the future.

And except those days should be shortened, there should no flesh be saved: but for the elect's sake those days shall be shortened. (Matthew 24:22)

We read in the Book of Revelation that during the Tribulation one-third of the population of the earth will be destroyed. On another occasion one-fourth of the population will be destroyed. It is absolutely unique. Using the simile given to us in Revelation 6, the red horse of war, the black horse of famine, and then the pale horse of death will ride during that period, and the population of the earth will be decimated. There was a time when this seemed to be an exaggeration. Even some good commentators considered it hyperbole. However, now that so many nations of the world have nuclear capabilities which could destroy the population of the world, it no longer appears to be exaggerated.

There is comfort in this verse—"But for the elect's sake those days shall be shortened." God will not let mankind commit suicide. That is the reason this will be such a brief period.

JESUS ASSURES THEM
CONCERNING HIS COMING AGAIN

Now we come to what will be the sign of His coming.

Then if any man shall say unto you, Lo, here is Christ, or there; believe it not. For there shall arise false Christs, and false prophets, and shall show great signs and wonders; insomuch that, if it were possible, they shall deceive the very elect. Behold, I have told you before. (Matthew 24:23–25)

Don't miss what He is saying here. The ability to work miracles in our day should be looked upon with suspicion because the next great miracle worker will not be Christ; he will be Antichrist and his false prophet.

"If it were possible, they shall deceive the very elect." Who are the elect? In the Scriptures there are two elect groups: the elect of the nation Israel and the elect of the church. We have to use common sense to determine which group is meant. Who has our Lord been talking about up to this point? Israel. All right, Israel is the elect in this verse also. Jesus is not talking about the church. You can fool some of the people all of the time. You can fool all of the people some of the time. But you cannot fool God's children all of the time. It just can't be done. I have read many letters which testify of this. A recent letter is from a woman who has come out of a religious cult. She listened to our Bible-teaching radio program for months before she could see the error of the cult's teaching. It isn't possible to fool God's children all the time. They will come out of a cult eventually.

> **Wherefore if they shall say unto you, Behold, he is in the desert; go not forth: behold, he is in the secret chambers; believe it not. For as the lightning cometh out of the east, and shineth even unto the west; so shall also the coming of the Son of man be.** (Matthew 24:26, 27)

When He comes, there will not be any John the Baptist to announce Him. But when He comes, the whole world will know and it will be as public as lightning. Those of you who live in the Middle West know that a lightning storm is a public affair. When it comes everybody knows about it, and sometimes it is a frightful experience. The Lord's second coming to the earth will be like that. No one will need to announce it. When our Lord comes the second time to establish His Kingdom on earth, everyone will know He is coming. And remember that His second coming to earth does not refer to the Rapture.

> **For wheresoever the carcase is, there will the eagles be gathered together.** (Matthew 24:28)

This is the most difficult verse to understand in the entire Olivet Discourse. After speaking of His coming in glory like lightning out of heaven, then to speak of carrion-eating birds seems strange indeed.

But I believe it refers to Christ's coming in judgment because Revelation 19 tells us about an invitation that went out to the birds to come together for a great banquet:

> **And I saw an angel standing in the sun; and he cried with a loud voice, saying to all the fowls that fly in the midst of heaven, Come and gather yourselves together unto the supper of the great God; that ye may eat the flesh of kings, and the flesh of captains, and the flesh of mighty men, and the flesh of horses, and of them that sit on them, and the flesh of all men, both free and bond, both small and great. And I saw the beast, and the kings of the earth, and their armies, gathered together to make war against him that sat on the horse, and against his army.** (Revelation 19:17–19)

The birds that feed on carrion seem to be agents of divine judgment. When the Lord comes again, He will come in judgment.

> **Immediately after the tribulation of those days shall the sun be darkened, and the moon shall not give her light, and the stars shall fall from heaven, and the powers of the heavens shall be shaken.** (Matthew 24:29)

Notice that this is to be "immediately *after* the tribulation of those days." My understanding is that all of these things will take place at Christ's second coming to the earth.

> **And then shall appear the sign of the Son of man in heaven: and then shall all the tribes of the earth mourn, and they shall see the Son of man coming in the clouds of heaven with power and great glory.** (Matthew 24:30)

"Then shall appear the sign of the Son of man in heaven." What is that sign? Again I will have to speculate. Back in the Old Testament the nation Israel was given the glory, the shekinah presence of God. No other nation or people has ever had that, nor does the church have it. The shekinah glory rested over the tabernacle and later the temple at Jerusalem. But because of Israel's sin, the shekinah glory left the nation. When Christ came the first time, He laid aside, not His deity, but His prerogative of deity, He laid aside His glory—although John says, "We beheld his glory" (John 1:14) because there were times when it broke through. However, at His second coming, I believe that the shekinah glory will hover over the earth before He breaks through, and that will be the "sign of the Son of man in heaven."

"They shall see the Son of man coming in the clouds of heaven with power and great glory." This is His return to earth to set up His Kingdom.

And he shall send his angels with a great sound of a trumpet, and they shall gather together his elect from the four winds, from one end of heaven to the other. (Matthew 24:31)

The "elect" spoken of in this verse is still the nation Israel. The prophets in the Old Testament foretold a miracle that would bring the Jews back into their land. This is not the church which is going to be caught up out of this world to meet the Lord in the air. Angels are not connected with the Rapture. The Lord will come in person to receive the church with the sound of a trumpet, and His voice will be like that of an archangel. He will not need any help to gather His church together. He died for the church, and He will bring it together. When He says that the "angels . . . shall gather together his elect from the four winds, from one end of heaven to the other," we can be sure that He is talking about the nation Israel—ministering angels have always been connected with Israel.

THE SIGN PARABLES

Now learn a parable of the fig tree; When his branch is yet tender, and putteth forth leaves, ye know that summer is nigh: so likewise ye, when ye shall see all these things, know that it is near, even at the doors. (Matthew 24:32, 33)

I do not see how the fig tree could represent anything other than the nation Israel (for example, see Jeremiah 24 and Hosea 9:10). There are certainly fig trees growing in abundance in Israel even in our day after all that has happened to that land. I was impressed with the fig orchards north of Jerusalem and the vineyards south of Jerusalem. The area south of Bethlehem is filled with vineyards. Fig trees and grapevines identify the land, and I believe that our Lord is using the fig tree as a symbol of that land.

Verily I say unto you, This generation shall not pass, till all these things be fulfilled. (Matthew 24:34)

"This generation"—the Greek word can mean race and refer to the nation Israel. Or it could refer to the generation that will be living at the time these predictions come to pass. A generation is reckoned to be about twenty years, and certainly the predicted events of this section will take place in a much briefer time than twenty years. My feeling is that it could refer to either one, but I much prefer the interpretation that it refers to the preservation of the Jewish race. Haman was not able to destroy them, neither was Pharaoh, nor did Hitler succeed in his attempts. And no dictator in our day will be able to exterminate these people—God will see to that.

Heaven and earth shall pass away, but my words shall not pass away. (Matthew 24:35)

He says, "You can just underscore what I've said, because heaven and earth will pass away, but My words will not." Heaven and earth will pass away and there will be a new heaven and a new earth (Revelation 21:1), but He will not change His Word. It will stand throughout the eternal ages.

But of that day and hour knoweth no man, no, not the angels of heaven, but my Father only. (Matthew 24:36)

Although they will know that this period is drawing near, they will not know the day nor the hour. Since there have been so many folk in our day who have tried to pinpoint the time of Christ's return, I'm of the opinion that in that future day there will be some folk who will try to figure it down to the very hour. But no one will know either the day or the hour. And He will use the illustration of Noah—

But as the days of Noe [Noah] were, so shall also the coming of the Son of man be. (Matthew 24:37)

Christ will come in a day which will be like the days of Noah.

For as in the days that were before the flood they were eating and drinking, marrying and giving in marriage, until the day that

> **Noe [Noah] entered into the ark, and knew not until the flood came, and took them all away; so shall also the coming of the Son of man be.** (Matthew 24:38, 39)

Now, the days of Noah were characterized by gross immorality—every thought and imagination of man's heart was only evil continually (see Genesis 6:5). But our Lord says that His coming will be in days like the days of Noah, and He mentions that they were eating and drinking. Is there anything wrong with eating and drinking? No, we are told that whatever we do—whether we eat or drink, or whatsoever we do—we are to do all to the glory of God (see 1 Corinthians 10:31). However, the people in Noah's day were not eating and drinking to the glory of God. In fact, they were living as though God did not exist.

A little boy was invited out to dinner for the first time in his life. He was just going next door, but to him it was a big event. So when the time came to go, he made a beeline for the house next door. When they sat down to the table to eat, the boy automatically bowed his head to offer thanks for the food because he came from a Christian home. Suddenly he realized he was the only one with a bowed head and the rest of the folks were passing food back and forth. He opened his eyes and, not having any inhibitions, said, "Don't you thank God for your food?" There was embarrassing silence for a moment, and then the lady of the house said, "No, we don't." The little fellow thought for a moment and then said, "You're just like my dog—he just starts right in!"

In our day, while millions are starving to death, multitudes of people receive a meal that comes from the hand of God three times a day, and they never think of thanking God. And in that future day they will be right on the verge of the coming of Christ, and they will be living as though it will never take place.

Also, the people of Noah's day were "marrying and giving in marriage." Certainly our Lord is not saying that marriage is wrong. His point is that they rejected so completely God's warning through Noah that they went ahead and had their weddings—maybe even "church" weddings—right up to the day that Noah entered into the ark. They lived as though God did not exist. They did not believe that He would judge them and scorned the warning that a flood was imminent. "And knew not until the flood came, and took them all away; so shall also the coming of the Son of man be."

Then shall two be in the field; the one shall be taken, and the other left. Two women shall be grinding at the mill; the one shall be taken, and the other left. (Matthew 24:40, 41)

I can hear someone saying to me, "Well, preacher, you have finally painted yourself into a corner. You said the church and the Rapture are not in the Olivet Discourse, but here they are. Two shall be in the field; one shall be taken, and the other shall be left."

Well, my friend, He still is not talking about the Rapture. After all, what is our Lord talking about here? "As it was in the days of Noah." Who was taken away in the days of Noah? "They knew not until the flood came, and took them *all* away." They perished in the flood. This is not referring to the Rapture when the church will be taken out of the world. Rather, this pictures the removing from the earth by judgment those who are not going to enter the millennial Kingdom.

Watch therefore; for ye know not what hour your Lord doth come. (Matthew 24:42)

"Watch" is the important word, and it has a little different meaning from the watching that a child of God does now in waiting for the Rapture. Today we have a comforting hope. In that future day, it will be watching with fear and anxiety. In the night they will say, "Would God it were morning," and in the morning they will say, "Would God it were evening." Today we are to wait and long for His coming. In that future day they will watch with anxiety for His return.

You may think that I am splitting hairs, but I'm not. I looked up the Hebrew word for *watch* and found that it had about seventeen different meanings. Although in English we have only the one word, it has several different meanings also.

Let me illustrate this by a man who goes deer hunting. Every year this man goes into the woods and to about the same spot. He puts up camp, and early in the morning he goes over the hogback on the hill and sits down by the trunk of an old tree and waits. After a while he hears a noise in the brush and thinks it might be a deer. He lifts his rifle and waits. He is watching for a deer.

Two weeks later you meet this same man down on the main street corner of town, and you see that he is looking intently down the street. You know that he is waiting for someone. You walk up to him and say, "Who are you watching for?" He replies, "I'm waiting for my wife; she is forty-five minutes late." He is watching for a dear again, but it is a different dear and he is watching in a little different way.

A month or two later you go to the hospital and you pass a room and see this man and his wife sitting by the bedside of a little child. The child has a burning fever, and the doctor has told them that the crisis will come about midnight. They are watching. My friend, that is a different type of watching than watching for a deer or waiting for a wife on the corner. This is watching with anxiety. And I think it will be somewhat with the same feeling that folk will watch for our Lord's second coming.

But know this, that if the goodman of the house had known in what watch the thief would come, he would have watched, and would not have suffered his house to be broken up. Therefore be ye also ready: for in such an hour as ye think not the Son of man cometh. Who then is a faithful and wise servant, whom his lord hath made ruler over his household, to give them meat in due season? (Matthew 24:43–45)

What our Lord does in the remainder of the Olivet Discourse is to give parables to illustrate the attitude of folk to His coming and what will happen when He does come.

Blessed is that servant, whom his lord when he cometh shall find so doing. Verily I say unto you, That he shall make him ruler over all his goods. But and if that evil servant shall say in his heart, My lord delayeth his coming; and shall begin to smite his fellow-servants, and to eat and drink with the drunken; the lord of that servant shall come in a day when he looketh not for him, and in an hour that he is not aware of, and shall cut him asunder, and appoint him his portion with the hypocrites: there shall be weeping and gnashing of teeth. (Matthew 24:46–51)

This parable reflects the attitude of some folk in that future day. They shall say, "Well, the Lord delays His coming—so I'll just go on living carelessly." When Christ returns, He will judge that person.

This is a great principle which is applicable to every age. You and I ought to live our lives in the light of the fact that we are to stand in the presence of Christ. Note that I didn't say in the light of the *coming* of Christ but in the light of the *presence* of Christ. Regardless of whether Christ comes one hundred years from today or a thousand years, you and I will stand in His presence. Whether you are saved or lost, you will stand in His presence. If you are saved, you will have to give Him an account of your life to see if you receive a reward. If you are lost, you will stand there to be judged. Therefore, every person should live his life in light of the fact that he is to stand in the presence of the Lord. This is the great emphasis in the Olivet Discourse. Therefore, it has applications to us, although the interpretation is specifically to folk living at the time of Christ's return as King.

Now chapter 25 enlarges upon the answer of Jesus to the question, "What shall be the sign of thy coming?" There is the parable of the ten virgins, which tests the genuineness of the faith of Israel; the parable of the talents, which tests the faithfulness of His servants; and the judgment of the gentile nations, which tests their right of admission into the Kingdom. This chapter shows the significance of the coming of Christ as it relates to these groups that shall then be in the world. A close analysis of each group will reveal that it can be stripped down to a personal attitude and relationship to Jesus Christ.

PARABLE OF THE TEN VIRGINS

The parable of the ten virgins is the basis for those who believe in what is known as the partial Rapture, where only some will be taken out of the world. The "partial Rapture" group is made up of very fine people. When I first became pastor in Nashville, Tennessee, there was a wonderful Bible class there, and they supported me in getting Bible conferences into Nashville. From the beginning, the class had been taught by a teacher who believed in a partial Rapture. Candidly, I feel that the partial Rapture theory ministers to spiritual snobbery. I never met one of that group who didn't think that he was with the five wise virgins. In fact, I have never in all my life met one who thought he was classed with the foolish virgins! I was a young preacher in those days, and as I worked with them I had the feeling that they were not sure that I was one of them. I suspected that they classified me as one of the foolish ones.

I thank God that when the Rapture takes place, every believer is going out. And we won't be going on the basis of merit. All of us will be leaving because of the grace of God. He saves us by grace; He keeps us by grace; He will take us out of this world by grace; and when we have been there for ten million years, it will be by the grace of God.

The ten virgins do not refer to the church; they refer to the nation Israel. My friend, we need to let our Lord answer the questions of these men who were His apostles. They had asked Him the questions. If we try to make out that He is talking to us about something altogether different, it is as though we are interrupting Him. Let's just listen and know that, although He is talking to someone else, we can make application of these wonderful parables to our own lives.

> **Then shall the kingdom of heaven be likened unto ten virgins, which took their lamps, and went forth to meet the bridegroom.** (Matthew 25:1)

To better understand the customs in Israel during the New Testament period, we refer to the Peshitta, which is a Syriac version of the Bible. Although it is not a text to be recommended, it does shed light on some of the customs of the day. The Peshitta translation of the verse before us indicates that the virgins went forth to meet the bridegroom *and the bride*, which means that the bridegroom is coming from the marriage to the marriage supper. It is my understanding that although the marriage of Christ and the church takes place in heaven, the marriage supper takes place on this earth. A passage in the Gospel of Luke substantiates this. As our Lord is giving warnings and parables, He says,

> **Let your loins be girded about, and your lights burning; and ye yourselves like unto men that wait for their lord, when he will return from the wedding; that when he cometh and knocketh, they may open unto him immediately.** (Luke 12:35, 36)

You see, the wedding has taken place, and if He is coming from the wedding, obviously the bride is with Him; no man ever went on a honeymoon by himself—if he did, it wasn't a honeymoon!

So here in the parable of the ten virgins, Christ, pictured as the bridegroom, is bringing the bride with Him, and the believers on earth are waiting for Him to come. While the Great Tribulation has been going on upon the earth, Christ has been yonder in heaven with His bride, the church. Then at the conclusion of the seven years of Tribulation, He comes back to earth with the church.

This, now, is the attitude toward His coming on the part of those on earth—

And five of them were wise, and five were foolish. They that were foolish took their lamps, and took no oil with them: but the wise took oil in their vessels with their lamps. (Matthew 25:2-4)

Oil is symbolic of the Spirit of God. In that day I think there will be phonies as there were at His first coming. Jesus called them hypocrites. They will have lamps but no oil.

While the bridegroom tarried, they all slumbered and slept. And at midnight there was a cry made, Behold, the bridegroom cometh; go ye out to meet him. Then all those virgins arose, and trimmed their lamps. (Matthew 25:5-7)

Notice that *both* the wise and the foolish virgins slept. The difference in them was that some had the Holy Spirit (represented by the oil) and some did not—because they were not genuine believers.

Our Lord concludes this parable with a warning—

Watch therefore, for ye know neither the day nor the hour wherein the Son of man cometh. (Matthew 25:13)

Notice that it is "the day nor the hour" rather than the century or the year, as His coming is from our perspective. The attitude for His own during this future period is to *watch*. That is the important thing for them to do.

PARABLE OF THE TALENTS

This is another parable for that future generation that will be waiting for our Lord's return to earth.

For the kingdom of heaven is as a man travelling into a far country, who called his own servants, and delivered unto them

his goods. And unto one he gave five talents, to another two,
and to another one; to every man according to his several ability;
and straightway took his journey. (Matthew 25:14, 15)

Notice that the master gave to his servants responsibilities according
to their individual abilities.

Then he that had received the five talents went and traded with
the same, and made them other five talents. And likewise he that
had received two, he also gained other two. (Matthew 25:16, 17)

The "talents" were sums of money. They do not represent "talents"
in the sense of the natural endowments of a person, such as a musical
talent. The application to us is that whatever God has given to us, we
are to use for Him.

But he that had received one went and digged in the earth, and
hid his lord's money. (Matthew 25:18)

All were given a certain sum of money and told to use it profitably.
But one buried the talent he had been given. He was not faithful to
his master.

After a long time the lord of those servants cometh, and recko-
neth with them. And so he that had received five talents came
and brought other five talents, saying, Lord, thou deliveredst
unto me five talents: behold, I have gained beside them five
talents more. His lord said unto him, Well done, thou good and
faithful servant: thou hast been faithful over a few things, I will
make thee ruler over many things: enter thou into the joy of thy
lord.

He also that had received two talents came and said, Lord, thou
deliveredst unto me two talents: behold, I have gained two other
talents beside them. His lord said unto him, Well done, good
and faithful servant; thou hast been faithful over a few things, I
will make thee ruler over many things: enter thou into the joy of
thy lord.

Then he which had received the one talent came and said, Lord,
I knew thee that thou art an hard man, reaping where thou hast
not sown, and gathering where thou hast not strawed: and I was

afraid, and went and hid thy talent in the earth: lo, there thou hast that is thine. (Matthew 25:19–25)

The response of his master was this—

His lord answered and said unto him, Thou wicked and slothful servant, thou knewest that I reap where I sowed not, and gather where I have not strawed: thou oughtest therefore to have put my money to the exchangers, and then at my coming I should have received mine own with usury.

Take therefore the talent from him, and give it unto him which hath ten talents. For unto every one that hath shall be given, and he shall have abundance: but from him that hath not shall be taken away even that which he hath. And cast ye the unprofitable servant into outer darkness: there shall be weeping and gnashing of teeth. (Matthew 25:26–30)

There is a great principle in this parable for us. And it was given in light of the fact that all of us—you and I included—are going to have to stand in the presence of God and give an account of how we have used what He has given to us. The Lord is not going to ask us how *much* we have done for Him but how *faithful* we have been to that which He wanted us to do.

For the child of God there are two important things: (1) find out what God wants us to do. We must determine what the talent is that He has given us, and then (2) be faithful in the use of it. To some of us God gives a very small ministry, and that may be upsetting to us, but if we are one-talent people, God expects us to be *faithful* with that.

JUDGMENT OF THE NATIONS

In this chapter our Lord is alerting God's people to the fact that we are to ready ourselves for His coming. This is certainly true in the next few verses.

During the Tribulation period all nations will have the opportunity to hear and receive God's message. The gospel of the Kingdom will be preached among all nations, we are told. But some will reject God's messengers, Christ's brethren, and thereby reject Christ.

When the Son of man shall come in his glory, and all the holy angels with him, then shall he sit upon the throne of his glory. (Matthew 25:31)

The polarization of all of the Olivet Discourse is moving toward the placing of Jesus Christ on the throne of this world. This is the message of the Gospel of Matthew—in fact, it is the message of the entire Word of God.

Now we will see that the nations will be judged. You may ask, "Doesn't it mean individuals?" Yes, you can consider it as individuals composing the nations. But nations are responsible to God.

And before him shall be gathered all nations: and he shall separate them one from another, as a shepherd divideth his sheep from the goats:

And he shall set the sheep on his right hand, but the goats on the left. (Matthew 25:32–33)

Now notice what the test is—

Then shall the King say unto them on his right hand, Come, ye blessed of my Father, inherit the kingdom prepared for you from the foundation of the world: for I was an hungered, and ye gave me meat: I was thirsty, and ye gave me drink: I was a stranger, and ye took me in: naked, and ye clothed me: I was sick, and ye visited me: I was in prison, and ye came unto me.

Then shall the righteous answer him, saying, Lord, when saw we thee an hungered, and fed thee? or thirsty, and gave thee drink? When saw we thee a stranger, and took thee in? or naked, and clothed thee? Or when saw we thee sick, or in prison, and came unto thee?

And the King shall answer and say unto them, Verily I say unto you, Inasmuch as he have done it unto one of the least of these my brethren, ye have done it unto me. (Matthew 25:34–40)

The 144,000 Jews sealed at the time of the Great Tribulation will go out over the entire world to preach the message of the gospel of the Kingdom, which is to receive Christ as the sacrifice for their sins and to be ready for His immediate coming. Some nations will reject Christ. Antichrist will have God's people butchered and slain, and anyone who would give them a cup of cold water will do so at the risk of his life. To hand out a cup of cold water has little value in our day, but in the Great Tribulation it will have tremendous value. It will mean taking a stand for Jesus Christ.

The basis on which the nations will be judged is their acceptance or rejection of Jesus Christ. Because the messengers were representing Him, He says "Inasmuch as ye have done it unto one of the least of these my brethren, ye have done it unto me." That will be the way people will evidence faith in the message that the Kingdom of Heaven is at hand and that they have repented and turned to Christ to be saved.

For those who reject Him there is only judgment:

Then shall he answer them, saying, Verily I say unto you, Inasmuch as ye did it not to one of the least of these, ye did it not to me. And these shall go away into everlasting punishment: but the righteous into life eternal. (Matthew 25:45, 46)

Entire nations will enter the millennial Kingdom. Out of these will be some individuals who will reject Christ. But the judgment of the nations at the second coming of Christ is to determine what nations are to enter the millennial Kingdom. This judgment is separate and distinct from all other judgments.

It is important to keep in mind that this judgment of the nations will take place at Christ's second coming to the earth when He will actually set up His Kingdom and bring to this war-weary world one thousand years of peace—which we call the Millennium.

"But," you say, "the reign of Christ on the earth is somewhere out there in the future. What about today? Can our nation or any nation bring peace to the world?"

Multitudes are thinking today that we can have peace if we could just meet around a conference table. That is the method that liberalism has been preaching for years, and it is the reason we are in such a muddle in this country. We are being told that if we could just get the heads of state to sit down together around a conference table, they could settle everything. Oh, my friend, they can't settle anything because men's hearts have to be made right. To think otherwise is just a pious wish that has no scriptural foundation at all. This is the reason the United Nations has proven to be such a miserable failure.

We cannot bring peace on the earth through that medium. God has a better plan. God's method is to *change* human hearts. The only thing in the world that can change the human heart is the Word of God, and by that Word we can be made new creatures in Christ. We can become children of God, and peace among men is possible only through that method in this present hour.

Christ is going to bring peace on this earth when He returns, coming in great power and great glory. As we have seen, all four of the Gospel writers set forth the Lord Jesus in some aspect of His character, and all of them see Him coming again. Matthew sees Him as the King and presents His coming as the King, which is the reason Matthew gives us this part of the Olivet Discourse. Mark shows Him as the suffering Servant, obedient to the Father; Luke sees Him as the Man, the Shepherd who went out and found the lost sheep; John sees Him as the Son of God, the Savior of the world. All see Him as the resurrected Christ, the ascended Christ, and coming again to this earth to establish His Kingdom.

There are those who are looking for Him in great anticipation. Also, there is the businessman, more interested in the stock report than he is in the coming of Christ; there is the student, more interested in his future than he is in the coming of Christ; there are those who have other absorbing interests. But there *are* those who are concerned about His coming for His own.

My friend, you could not possibly be interested in His coming for His own or His coming to establish His Kingdom unless you have a relationship with Him based on the fact that He came about two thousand years ago and died on a cross for our sins.

May I say that our business today is not to try to establish a kingdom, and our business is not to try to make this world a better place. As Dr. George Gill used to say, some men are trying to make this world a better place for men to go to hell in. Someone else said that our business is not to clean out the fish pond but to *fish* in it. We today are trying to get men and women to turn to Christ.

You may recall that after the luxury liner, the *Morro Castle*, burned at sea, the captain was accused and arrested, charged with negligence. He was tried and exonerated. The court found that he had done everything that he could have done. I was using this illustration in a message when I was speaking in either Michigan or Minnesota, and the nephew of that captain came to speak to me after the service. He told me that his uncle, the captain, was a wonderful Christian. He said to me, "I thank you for what you said about my uncle because there are many people even today who still think he was guilty." He was not guilty, friends; he did everything that a captain could possibly do.

But suppose that when that ship caught fire and it seemed sure that it was going down at sea, the captain had called the crew together and said, "Now, let's not wake up any of the passengers. We want them all to get as much sleep as they can tonight. I want you fellows to get out the mops and swab the decks and polish the brass. I hate to see a dirty ship go to the bottom of the ocean! I want it to go down polished and shined. And we certainly don't want to disturb the passengers." Had the captain said that, he would have been guilty of negligence. But he didn't do that. The facts came out that he immediately aroused the passengers and told them, "Your lives are in danger. This ship will either go down or it will be grounded. We have to put you in the lifeboats if you are going to be saved!" He tried to get them all to safety in lifeboats, never giving a thought about polishing the ship or swabbing the deck.

There are two types of churchmen in our contemporary society: those who are trying to polish up the old boat, and those who are trying to get the passengers into the Lifeboat, which is Christ.

God says that He has no intention of saving this civilization, marvelous though it is. It is godless, and God has judged it. The torch will be put to it one of these days.

Some of us believe that helping folk get into that Lifeboat is our business. We are not trying to straighten out the world. Rather, we beseech you in Christ's stead to accept the salvation which He has provided for you.

CHART OF OLIVET DISCOURSE

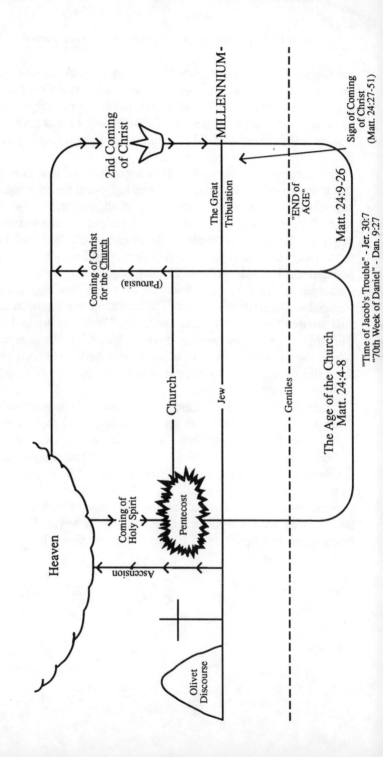

Chapter 9

THE AMAZING, ALARMING, AND AWFUL APOSTASY

Jude, the servant of Jesus Christ, and brother of James, to them that are sanctified by God, the Father, and preserved in Jesus Christ, and called: mercy unto you, and peace, and love be multiplied. Beloved, when I gave all diligence to write unto you of the common salvation, it was needful for me to write unto you, and exhort you that ye should earnestly contend for the faith which was once delivered unto the saints. For there are certain men crept in unawares, who were before of old ordained [written of beforehand] to this condemnation, ungodly men, turning the grace of our God into lasciviousness, and denying the only Lord God, and our Lord Jesus Christ. (Jude 1-4)

We are seeing in our day an amazing, an alarming, and an awful apostasy of the church. There has always been a question among students of prophecy about just how far the organized church would go into the apostasy before the Rapture occurs. That is, at what particular point in the apostasy would the true church, made up of those who were believers in the Lord Jesus Christ, be taken out of the world?

Now some of us did not believe that we would see the organized churches plunge this far into a departure from the faith before the true church—that is, the body of believers who actually trust in Christ as Savior, recognizing they are sinners and their only hope is in Him—would be taken out of the world. When Dr. William Culbertson was here in Los Angeles speaking at the Prophetic Conference, he said to some of us privately, "The things I am seeing today I thought would not take place until the Tribulation!" And I'm sure that this is the viewpoint of many students of prophecy today.

In this sense, therefore, it's an amazing apostasy that has come upon us. Suddenly the church has departed from the faith, and it has happened when many of us thought that by the time this happened the true church would be gone.

In view of some of the activities of the contemporary church, it's an alarming apostasy. Because of the present conditions in the church, and in this message I will merely touch the fringe of them, it is an awful apostasy. For this reason I think we can accurately say that we are right now in an amazing, alarming, and awful apostasy in the church.

Now when I say apostasy, I mean it in the Bible sense, a departure from the faith. The word in the original Greek is *aphistemi*. *Histemi* means "to stand" and *apo* means "away from." Let me illustrate it this way: It's my custom to stand at the pulpit to preach, but if I stood over by the piano, it would be *aphistemi*, standing away from the pulpit. And today there is an *aphistemi*, an apostasy in the church, which means that men who at one time professed to believe the great basic truths of the Christian faith have now denied those things. They have departed from them.

For that reason it might be well to take a second look at what the Scripture states about the apostasy in relationship to the Rapture of the true believers. In light of where we are at the present time we need to see what the Word of God actually says in this connection.

The question arises: Will these organized churches go into total apostasy? Will there be a total eclipse of the faith? The Lord Jesus made a statement in Luke 18:8 that has been difficult for many to accept, and I must confess that it was very difficult for *me* to accept years ago. He asked: ". . . When the Son of man cometh, shall He find *the* faith on the earth?" That is, will He find the body of truth that He left here some two thousand years ago? Will He find *the* faith upon the earth? This question is so couched in the Greek (we can't do this in English) that it demands a negative answer. So the answer to it is no, He will not find *the* faith upon the earth when He returns.

And so we draw from this that there will be a total apostasy of the organized church.

We have this confirmed, I think, in the seven churches of Asia Minor (see Revelation 2 and 3). You find that the church in Ephesus represents the apostolic church, the church at its best. And it's true that after the apostolic era the church grew numerically, and it did spread over the earth. But never has the church been as strong spiritually as it was back then. Today it's like that little mustard seed that got hold of the Vigoro—my, it just blossomed up and outdid itself. That little mustard seed should have been a plant but it became a tree. And that is exactly what has happened to the church which has gone in for numbers and buildings and programs and those things that you see from the outside. But I think it can be said of the church today what the Lord Jesus said of the Pharisees: "Outside you're a beautiful sepulchre, all white marble. But inside—dead men's bones." That's an awful, frightful picture He gave of religion in His day, and He said that those conditions would prevail at the end of the age.

Now the church of Laodicea is the seventh and the last of the churches mentioned in Revelation. It represents that last period, the last death struggle of the church. The question is asked again: Why is not the Rapture mentioned at the end of the Laodicean period? And I must confess that I've had the post-tribulationists and the amillennialists taunt me with that question. It has been difficult to answer them. What exactly do we mean by insisting upon a Rapture at the end of the Laodicean period? The fact of the matter is, it doesn't take place, apparently, at the end of the Laodicean period. John was caught up to heaven at the beginning of chapter 4, and chapter 3 ended the Laodicean period. We always think of John as being representative of the church. But when he gets caught up to heaven he finds the twenty-four elders, who actually represent the church, and the church is already there! So at some time during the Laodicean period the true church leaves the earth, and the organized church goes right on into the Great Tribulation as an organization that supposedly represents God—yet it denies Christ. We are moving very close to that today, by the way.

To the church of Laodicea the Lord Jesus Christ gives a word of warning, and He gives a word of wooing. He says in Revelation 3:17, "Because thou sayest, I am rich, and increased with goods, and have need of nothing. . . ." In other words, "You say you're rich—you have many buildings, you have a tremendous program, but thou 'knowest not that thou art wretched, and miserable, and poor, and blind, and naked.'" Did you know that the church in this country—and that includes the Roman Catholic and all the others—as far as the buildings and physical wealth are concerned, is the wealthiest organization in America? The church today, if it would pool all of its assets, could buy Standard Oil Company and the Rockefeller holdings to boot. It is wealthy, but powerless in this hour in which we live.

Back in the early days of the church, the pope was counting his money when one of the real saints of that period walked in on him. When he saw that he had intruded he turned to leave, but the pope said to him: "No longer can the church say, 'Silver and gold have I none.'" And this saint as he was walking out said, "That's true, sir, but no longer can the church say to the impotent man, 'Rise and walk.'"

You and I are in the presence of a mad world, and the church at this hour seems to have no spiritual message for the mad world that we live in. Therefore we find that at the end of the Laodicean period Christ is absolutely outside of the organized church. When He says in Revelation 3:20, "Behold, I stand at the door, and knock," it's an invitation coming from the outside, a personal invitation, the same kind of invitation He gave when He was rejected by His own people as the King. It was right after He pronounced His judgment upon Chorazin and Bethsaida and Capernaum that He said, "Come unto me, all ye that labor and are heavy laden, and I will rest you" (Matthew 11:28). And here in Revelation He gives a personal invitation, "Behold, I stand at the door, and knock; if any man hear my voice, and open the door, I will come in to him, and will sup with him, and he with me." This, my friend, is His response to the total apostasy of the organized church.

Now how did this apostasy come about? What has happened that has brought the organized church into what is not yet a total apostasy, but is moving in that direction fast? Well the Epistle of Jude is the epistle on the apostasy. It has also been called the introduction to Revelation, and it certainly is that.

Beloved, when I gave all diligence to write unto you of the common salvation, it was needful for me to write unto you, and exhort you that ye should earnestly contend for the faith which was once delivered unto the saints. (Jude 3)

There is a tradition that Jude actually started to write on some other great theme. For instance, he might have been planning to write on salvation as Paul did in Romans, or he might have written on the church as the body of Christ as Paul did in Ephesians. Or he might have written on this matter of fellowship, as John did in his first epistle. But whatever the subject was that he intended to write on, the Spirit of God had him push that aside. Knowing that the faith was going to be in jeopardy, He wanted him to write on that theme.

For there are certain men crept in unawares, who were before of old ordained to this condemnation, ungodly men, turning the grace of our God into lasciviousness, and denying the only Lord God, and our Lord Jesus Christ. (Jude 4)

Now I would like to bring to your attention a translation of the Bible that is practically unknown, because it was done by an Englishman who made his own translation. But he has what is probably the best translation of verse 4:

For certain men have wormed their way into the church. Long before this they were designated for judgment, impious creatures they are who twist the grace of God into a justification of blatant immorality and who deny our only Master and Lord Jesus Christ.

According to this verse, the ungodly men who would come into the church would do two things: They would bring about in the church a departure, an apostasy in two directions.

First, there would be blatant immorality, and they would espouse it and support it. They will be licentious, loose, dissolute. And may I say to you that earlier in my life this passage of Scripture seemed so far removed from the church as I knew it that—I'll be very honest with you—what Jude wrote here made no impression on me at all. My response then was: "You mean that people who would come into the church would actually espouse immorality? It can't be! The church stands as a bulwark against that sort of thing."

The second departure of these ungodly men is to deny our only

Master and Lord, Jesus Christ. This denial of Him and the teaching of immorality are the two departures the church will take.

Now not only Jude speaks of this, but Paul wrote to Timothy, "For the time will come when they will not endure sound doctrine; but . . . they shall turn away their ears from the truth, and shall be turned unto fables" (2 Timothy 4:3, 4). And Peter wrote, ". . . Even denying the Lord that bought them, and bring upon themselves swift destruction. And many shall follow their pernicious ways, by reason of whom the way of truth shall be evil spoken of" (2 Peter 2:1, 2).

BLATANT IMMORALITY

Now I'm going to confine myself to a limited number of very specific incidents that illustrate the first of these two departures from the faith. The first example that I want to give is of a church here in Southern California many years ago. I have the bulletin of this church, and the heading of this item is: "Is Your Mind All Made Up?", which we might translate into: "Are You One of These Narrow-minded, Bigoted Fundamentalists?" That's the sense of it, you understand. But you can be sure that the assistant pastor who wrote it is broad-minded!

As I write this article, I'm preparing to leave for a four day national planning conference for homophiles in San Francisco. This will be the second such meeting for this particular group, and the discussion will include such items as *Who Can Represent the Homosexuals in this Country? What Should be the Attitude of Homosexuals Toward Heterosexuals?* and *What Can Be Done to Ease the Persecution of the Homosexual?* I will be attending the conference in my capacity as chairman of the Southern California Council of Religion and the Homophile, which is composed of ministers and homosexuals who meet in order to establish communication between the church and homosexuals. Now I realize that some persons are extremely offended at the thought of ministers even talking to homosexuals, and the purpose of my writing this article is to state that many of the homosexuals I have met are persons with high moral standards. Also, I am quite sure that we have much to learn about homosexuality. We do not have an adequate definition of who the homosexual is, and we certainly have much to learn about why some persons are homosexual. If you have your mind all made up on this subject, relax a little, discuss your position with somebody with a different point of view and maybe you'll change.

Well, before I was saved I discussed things like this quite thoroughly in places where I would not want to go today. And I wonder where some of these pastors have been all their lives. This was in a *church* bulletin! Are you worried about what homosexuals think about heterosexuals? Apparently some people are. Now what kind of communication does this planning conference want to establish with homosexuals? Are they going to give the gospel to them? That's not in the cards at all, I can assure you. Notice that there is no reference to the fact that God condemns homosexuality in no uncertain terms. And as for the statement he makes about some homosexuals having high moral standards, this is the "playboy magazine" approach to morality we are seeing in our day, where sin is being made to appear sophisticated. And boy, are you a square if you can't go along with it! And some preachers feel like they have to go along with it. But I'm not going along with this crowd, I can assure you of that. Oh, my friend, God loves the homosexual as much as He loves anyone else, and He gave His Son to pay the penalty for his sin. Who is going to tell him this good news if the church doesn't tell him?

But who would ever have dreamed that this once-great church would ever get so far away from their original purpose. I never dreamed I would live to see the day.

Now the other example I want to give comes from Portland, Oregon. While I was up there some time ago their newspaper, *The Oregonian*, came out with an article about a woman police captain who worked with runaways. In this interview she said that the greatest opposition she had was coming from the church. The church has established there, as some have here, a place for these young people to meet. This police captain, testifying on proposed amendments to the 11:00 P.M. curfew law for city parks, cited the case of a fifteen-year-old girl from another state who was hidden from the police by church workers. She said this incident was typical and that the police were foiled in their efforts to find the child. According to this police captain, the girl was sequestered by these churchmen, and when

found was high on drugs and had been bused to a center for birth
control pills and then spent the night partly unclothed with four older
males—in a church center! The ministers of this church were called
in by their church federation, and do you want to hear their answer
for all this? It was: "There must have been a breakdown of communication somewhere."

My friend, may I say to you, it is happening exactly as the Bible
says, that men would come in, slip in, worm their way in, ungodly
men who would turn the grace of God into blatant immorality. That
is happening. I never dreamed that I would see in my day the church
combining what years ago was only found in the corner poolroom,
the corner saloon, the gambling den, and the red-light district! They
have it all now under one roof, a hangout for hoodlums. And the
condition of the church in Los Angeles and certain of its centers is
even worse than what I've related to you. In fact, some time ago a
wiseacre here in Los Angeles wrote:

> The Joneses in our town used to lie, cheat, drink, play cards,
> gamble and dance. They had no standing with the better people of
> the community. Then we had visitation evangelism, and they lined
> up the Joneses in the biggest church in town and they joined. (They
> weren't converted, but they joined.) Now the Joneses lie, cheat,
> drink, play cards, gamble and dance, but they're widely respected
> because they are members of the leading church in town.

What an awful picture this is!

Now there are a multitude of instances like this that I could relate,
but these examples are sufficient to show that the apostasy is not new
and is being fulfilled exactly as Jude predicted.

DENIAL OF CHRIST

Now I would like to pass on to the second part of this prophecy,
about those who deny our only Master and Lord Jesus Christ. It is
in this direction of doctrine that there has been the most grievous
departure from the faith. There has been the repudiation of the whole
spectrum of Scripture. And I think that I have the evidence to back
up this statement. This quotation was written at the turn of the
twentieth century:

Towards the end of the last century unconverted and evil men crept in unawares to the professional ministry of the Gospel. They began to criticize instead of expounding the Bible, to deny its blessed truths instead of proclaiming them. Men who were paid to preach the Gospel and, in some cases, had sworn to do so, have been occupied in an ignoble effort to black out its searching light and deny the great fundamentals of Christianity. It is no longer, "thus saith the Lord," but "thus saith the scholars, scientists or critics" who sit in judgment, not only upon the Word of God, but upon God Himself, daring to tell us what is and what is not worthy of God, thus measuring Him by the plummet of their own darkened mind.

As I said, that was written at the turn of the century. And I'd like to begin to bring you down through the years to our day, because actually the liberals recognized what was happening before the fundamentalists woke up to what was happening. I want to give you an excerpt from an editorial that appeared in *The Christian Century* on January 31, 1924.

Two worlds have clashed: the world of tradition and the world of modernism. There is a clash here; it is pronounced and as grim as that between Christianity and Confucianism. Amiable words cannot hide the difference. "Blest Be the Tie That Binds" can be sung in the *Te Deum Sed*, but it cannot bind these two worlds together. The God of the Fundamentalist is one God; the God of the Modernist is another. The Christ of the Fundamentalist is one Christ; the Christ of the Modernist is another. The Bible of the Fundamentalist is one Bible; the Bible of the Modernist is another. The church, the kingdom, the salvation, the consummation of all things—these are one thing to the Fundamentalist and another thing to the Modernist. Which God is the Christian God? Which Christ is the Christian Christ? Which Bible, which church, which kingdom, which salvation, which consummation are Christian? The future alone will tell. But the issue is clear and the inherent incompatibility of these two worlds has passed the state of mutual toleration.

A *liberal* magazine came out with that! And yet when some of us came out of the liberal machine, we were criticized as being fighters and come-outers. May I say to you, the liberals were the first ones to

recognize that we live in two different worlds today, and I'm glad
that they stated the case so clearly.

One of the leading liberals of the past was Dr. Harry Emerson
Fosdick. Some may still remember hearing him speak on the radio.
Dr. Fosdick wrote a book titled *The Peril of Worshiping Jesus,* and in
it he made what was then a startling statement (it is not so startling
today): "The world has tried in two ways to get rid of Jesus, first
by crucifying Him and second, by worshiping Him." Evidently Dr.
Fosdick rejects the clear teaching of Scripture such as Hebrews 1:6
and Revelation 13:8.

And way back in the '30s a survey of Christian ministers revealed
that 48 percent of those in the ministry at that time denied the grand
particulars of the Christian faith.

Then in 1963 *The Christian Century* contained this statement:
"Nothing is so pathetic in modern Protestantism as its confusion over
its own faith." It is interesting to see that they are the ones who said
that time would tell which was the real God. They have been following
the liberal, and now they have to say that Protestantism is pathetic.
And this is one time that I have to agree with *The Christian Century*
thoroughly. These conditions within the church which Jude warned
about have been building for a long time—"ungodly men turning the
grace of our God into lasciviousness, and denying . . . our Lord Jesus
Christ."

APOSTASY—THE WORD OF GOD

If we want to see how far the church has moved away from the
faith, we need to examine how it treats the Word of God. Even the
liberals recognize this—the real test lies in your attitude toward the
Bible and your viewpoint of it.

I understand that many of the pulpits in Germany are inscribed
with this motto: "God's Word Stands Forever." I can't quote the
actual German, but that's the English interpretation. In the back of
my pulpit there is written, "Sir, we would see Jesus," but in Germany
they have, "God's Word Stands Forever." That's a tremendous statement! And it was a German, Emil Brunner, who said this: "The fate
of the Bible is the fate of Christianity."

But another German, Professor Otto Michael of Tübingen, said,

"The Bible remains the theme of preaching for modern theology *but it's no longer the authority for life and thought*. Among the people, generally, its content is rather well-known, *but it is not honored as the divine rule of faith and practice*." That's an important distinction, and it's true in our evangelical circles, as we will see later on. Professor Michael goes on to say, "So, Germany, today, lacks a chart for life. It unites other nations, but cannot supply spiritual direction for itself or for them as long as the Bible is unrecognized as the dress for the body of the Word of God." Although he was speaking in regard to Germany in his day, you could say the same thing about the United States today.

In our last political conventions, did the Republicans mention the Word of God? Did the Democrats mention it? God have mercy on the United States! These Germans have been through a great deal. The Bible provides the direction for Christianity, and the nation of Germany lost its direction when it got away from the Word of God. Maybe that's the reason the United States can't lead in the world today. We have departed entirely from the Word of God, and we are looking to men and their programs to solve the problems. The church stands pitiful in this hour.

The notion that much of the Bible is myth has long been held by some Protestant theologians, but they have talked about it publicly only in the last few decades. I'm of the opinion that in the Presbyterian Church when I was in it there were men all around me who would get up and take an oath that they believed the tenets of the *Westminster Confession of Faith* but didn't believe it at all. Yet they would take this oath!

Awhile back I got an insight into what is happening from what a newspaper reporter wrote, although I doubt if he himself recognized what all it meant. Down in Texas there was a meeting of the American Unitarian Association in the Universalist Church of America. An appointed committee gave their report on the goal of the church: "To cherish and spread the universal truths taught by Jesus and the other teachers of humanity in every age and tradition, and express pathetically, in the Judeo-Christian tradition, as love to God and love to man." Now the delegates of this Unitarian-Universalist convention would not accept this report *because they said it sounded too specifically Christian!* They voted it down. They amended it to read: "To cherish, to spread the universal truths taught by the great prophets and teachers of humanity in every age and tradition immemorially, summarized in their essence as love to God and love to man." So the Austin newspaper came out with the headline, "Jesus Ousted By Churches In Merger." They had put Him out. Note that the first statement read "as taught by Jesus and the other teachers." That was bad enough, but it was too good for that crowd, and they said, "Out Jesus goes. We don't even want it to *sound* Christian."

Is Christ outside the church today? If He's going to give an invitation to many people today, He's going to have to knock on the door from the outside because He has already been put out. That is the picture we have of Christ and the organized church today.

I was raised in the Presbyterian Church, and I owe them a great deal. They educated me: I'm a graduate of a Presbyterian prep school, a Presbyterian college, and a Presbyterian seminary. And there are very few Presbyterian ministers today who have that background, I can assure you.

But I got out. The Presbyterian Church has adopted a new confession of faith that denies the Trinity and the Person of Christ! I don't know how any real believer can live with it. The new confession denies the great basic truths of the Christian faith.

Dr. John Gerstner, a professor at Pittsburgh Theological Seminary, once said, "Possibly the greatest loss for Christianity is in the realm of strict doctrine and consistent discipline. The resultant, 'easy-believe-ism' leads to inert nominalism, which is more of a disaster to true Christianity than communism, Romanism, secularism, and sectarianism combined." The apostasy in our churches is worse than any of these other things that men are attacking today. And I could give you multiplied quotations like these, ad infinitum and ad nauseam.

I would like for you to look with me now into another area in which the church has moved, in which it has no business going. And that is in this area of trying to tell the Pentagon in Washington about how to conduct a war.

Anyway, this letter came to me back in May 1936. That's a long time ago. A great many people think that this business of the church getting involved in war politics is new. But this kind of thing has been going on for many years, as this letter proves. It came from a group called the Emergency Peace Campaign of the National Peace Conference. I'll not list the names connected with it—they are some of the old liberals, who are old men now or dead. This is what they wrote: "If we did not think the religious forces of the world could stop war, create the attitude essential to build peace, we would do something other than ask you to join us in this great mission for peace." Now when World War II came along, none of those men dared stand out when we were at war, they all went undercover. But the minute the war was over, they came out in the same way that after a rain certain creatures come out from under the rocks. They began to spring up everywhere in this country, but they were there all the time and totally disloyal, if you please.

I have a quotation here that identifies ". . . organizations of so-called anti-war congresses, usually including students and well-meaning liberals, the resolutions of which are written by communists. . . ." This is taken out of a conservative journal that doesn't indulge in wildfire at all.

Considering that this was what some were doing as far back as the '30s, it's not surprising that in the late 1960s there were two thousand clerics involved in protest against the Vietnam War. You see, all of this has been moving in one direction, and it led some who were nationally known writers to come out against it very definitely, such as the following:

> Today we wish to submit the companion thought that we find it difficult to understand why clergymen who support such wild talk and wild demands think they are helping their churches or contributing to the cause of religion. Among the elements of religion are order, authority, charity and peace, and we find none of these in campaigns of civil insurrection. Of 444 persons arrested in recent street disturbances here, 61 of the adult males, 26 percent, were clergymen.

This appeared in a national magazine.

That is the condition of the church, my beloved, and back of all of this is the rejection of the Word of God and the great premise of the Word of God. And it has been stated like this:

> Where education assumes that the moral nature of man is capable of improvement, traditional Christianity assumes that the moral

nature of man is corrupt or absolutely bad. Where it is assumed in education that an outside human agent may be instrumental in the moral improvement of man, in traditional Christianity it is assumed that the agent is God, and even so the moral nature of man is not improved but exchanged for a new one.

So you see that there is a direct clash today between the basic premise of the Word of God and the liberal church. How far is their departure from the faith? May I say that it has gone way out!

A fellow minister sees that I receive a little magazine put out by Orthodox Jews, and I've appreciated it very much because I've been interested in the writers' reactions to the issues of Christianity. A while back they met with some liberals who were supposedly representing Christianity, and a Dr. Littel of the Jewish group wrote that "the agony of the breakdown of Jewish-Christian dialogue seven months ago was compounded for some of us by the theological nakedness of leading Protestant churchmen. They had no theological basis to rest upon or historical theology." These Orthodox Jews were appalled that the liberal had no conception at all of God's purposes with the nation Israel, and as a result they accused them of anti-Semitism. And, my friend, that's a new twist—theological liberalism that has boasted of its tolerance is now being accused of being anti-Semitic because they are theologically naked!

Now I want to bring this closer to home, and it will probably hurt. We read in Jude that they deny their Master and our Lord Jesus Christ. It's easy for you and me to point the finger at the liberal and say, "He denies the Lord, but those of us who are evangelicals, we are wonderful. We haven't denied Him." I say that the evangelical has largely denied Him. He is our Master and our Lord. If you want to know what I mean by this, I would like you to consider what another man has written, Dr. A. W. Tozer, a great man who has gone on to be with the Lord. Notice what he said:★

Let me state the cause of my burden. It is this: *Jesus Christ has today almost no authority at all among the groups that call themselves by His Name.* By these I mean not the Roman Catholics nor the

★Taken from "The Waning Authority of Christ in the Churches" in *God Tells the Man Who Cares* by A. W. Tozer. Copyright 1970, 1992 by Christian Publications. Used by permission.

liberals, nor the various quasi-Christian cults. I do mean Protestant churches generally, and I include those that protest the loudest that they are in spiritual descent from our Lord and His apostles, namely the evangelicals.

Now this may hurt, but continue reading:

It is a basic doctrine of the New Testament that after His resurrection the Man Jesus was declared by God to be both Lord and Christ, and that He was invested by the Father with absolute Lordship over the church which is His Body. All authority is His in heaven and in earth. In His own proper time He will exert it to the full, but during this period in history He allows this authority to be challenged or ignored. And just now it is being challenged by the world and ignored by the church.

The present position of Christ in the gospel churches may be likened to that of a king in a limited, constitutional monarchy. The king (sometimes depersonalized by the term "the Crown") is in such a country no more than a traditional rallying point, a pleasant symbol of unity and loyalty much like a flag or a national anthem. He is lauded, feted and supported, but his real authority is small. Nominally he is head over all, but in every crisis someone else makes the decisions. On formal occasions he appears in his royal attire to deliver the tame, colorless speech put into his mouth by the real rulers of the country. The whole thing may be no more than a good-natured make-believe, but it is rooted in antiquity, it is a lot of fun, and no one wants to give it up.

Among the gospel churches Christ is now in fact little more than a beloved symbol. "All Hail the Power of Jesus' Name" is the church's national anthem and the cross is her official flag, but in the week-by-week services of the church and the day-by-day conduct of her members someone else, not Christ, makes the decisions. Under proper circumstances Christ is allowed to say, "Come to me, all you who are weary and burdened," or "Do not let your hearts be troubled," but when the speech is finished someone else takes over. Those in actual authority decide the moral standards of the church, as well as all objectives. . . .

Not only does Christ have little or no authority; His influence also is becoming less and less. I would not say that He has none, only that it is small and diminishing. A fair parallel would be the influence of Abraham Lincoln over the American people. Honest Abe is still the idol of the country. The likeness of his kind, rugged face, so homely that it is beautiful, appears everywhere. It is easy to grow misty-eyed over him. Children are brought up on stories of his love, his honesty and his humility.

But after we have gotten control over our tender emotions, what have we left? No more than a good example which, as it recedes into the past, becomes more and more unreal and exercises less and less real influence. Every scoundrel is ready to wrap Lincoln's long black coat around him. In the cold light of political facts in the United States, the constant appeal to Lincoln by the politicians is a cynical joke.

The Lordship of Jesus is not quite forgotten among Christians, but it has been mostly relegated to the hymnal where all responsibility toward it may be comfortably discharged in a glow of pleasant religious emotion. Or if it is taught as a theory in the classroom it is rarely applied to practical living. The idea that the Man Christ Jesus has absolute and final authority over the whole church and over all its members in every detail of their lives is simply not now accepted as true by the rank and file of evangelical Christians.

Does that hurt? May I say to you, that's the picture today of the church.

Now let's get right down to the nitty-gritty: How does all this work in life? A great many people today, members of the church, say, "Oh, I love Jesus! I dedicated my life to Him." But where are these people on Sunday evenings? Where will they be on the night that their church holds a Bible study? Where will they be when there's something that *can* be done for Christ today? Where are they? Well, they are willing to sing the songs but not much else.

Let me illustrate this with a poem that came out during World War II. At that time there had been absenteeism in the plants that supply the needed material to these fellows at Bataan. Some of us remember—we would like to forget it, of course.

One day at dusk during the tragic, bloody battle at Bataan, a 19-year-old lad from Indiana scribbled in poetic form the burden of his heart. Early the following morning he was killed. The burial detail found his poem:

> And if our lines should sag and break
> Because of things you failed to make,
> That extra tank, that ship, that plane
> For which we waited all in vain.
> Will you then come to take the blame?
> For we, not you, must pay the cost,
> Of battles you, not we, have lost.

With this thought in mind, let's make application to absenteeism in our own church.

Here is another piece that hurts—not a poem exactly—it's called "The Empty Pew."

> I am an empty pew.
> I vote for the world as against God.
> I deny the Bible.
> I mock at the preached Word of God.
> I rail at Christian fellowship.
> I laugh at prayer.
> I break the Fourth Commandment;
> I am a witness to solemn vows broken.
> I advise men to eat, drink and be merry, for
> tomorrow we die.
> I join my voice with every atheist and rebel
> against human and divine law.
> I am an empty pew.
> I am a grave in the midst of the congregation.
> Read my epitaph and be wise.

We say we love the Lord, that He is our Master, the Captain of our salvation. But you let a captain in the army call the roll at five in the morning, and the soldiers are all present. There is not a one of those fellows who found it easy to get up to be ready for inspection at five in the morning. Don't tell me today that we evangelicals are not denying Him as our Master and our Lord. We are!

We are living in days of apostasy, and we measure ourselves by those around us. We look at Mr. Jones and Mrs. Smith, and we say, "Boy, I'm better than they are!" Maybe you are, but you can't really call Christ your Captain or your Lord. Do you remember He said that there will be those who after death will stand before Christ and say, "Lord, Lord, have we not prophesied in thy name? And in thy name have we cast out demons? And in thy name done many wonderful works?" But He will say, "I never knew you; depart from me, ye that work iniquity."

I think that we have come to a day of apostasy that is frightful, and it's easy to see what's happening around us and to point it out as I have done here. But what about you and me? I am confident that we are moving into the night and that the time is coming—not too far away—when there will have to be a separation made within the church. If the Rapture doesn't make the separation, then you can be sure of one thing, the world outside is going to make you pay a price for being a Christian.

It's interesting what both Peter and Paul have to say about this. In Peter's second letter we read:

> **Wherefore the rather, brethren, give diligence to make your call-ing and election** [more] **sure; for if ye do these things** [mentioned in verses 5-9], **ye shall never fall.** (2 Peter 1:10)

The apostasy is a falling away, and Peter says here that it might be well for you and for me to give diligence to make our calling and election more sure—because you and I could fall.

When I was in seminary, I sat next to a fine-looking, brilliant young man. He would have been the greatest preacher to come out of our class. He is today a rank atheist! Yet he had ten times the ability and talent that any of the rest of us had.

Paul said, "Examine yourselves, whether ye be in the faith; prove your own selves. . . ." Honestly, in this day of apostasy, when the church everywhere has cooled, what kind of life are you living for Christ? I think that all of us should examine ourselves.

> **. . . Know ye not your own selves, how that Jesus Christ is in you, except ye be reprobates?** (2 Corinthians 13:5)

That last phrase could be translated "except you are disqualified or discredited."

This is what Peter and Paul say to us. You may think in this day of apostasy that you can't be carried away. Well, all of us need to make a personal inventory.

Chapter 10

ANTICHRIST, THE MAN OF SIN

Now we beseech you, brethren, by the coming of our Lord Jesus Christ, and by our gathering together unto him, that ye be not soon shaken in mind, or be troubled, neither by spirit, nor by word, nor by letter as from us, as that the day of the Lord is present.

Let no man deceive you by any means; for that day shall not come, except there come the falling away first, and that man of sin be revealed, the son of perdition, who opposeth and exalteth himself above all that is called God, or that is worshiped, so that he, as God, sitteth in the temple of God, showing himself that he is God.

Remember ye not that, when I was yet with you, I told you these things? And now ye know what restraineth that he might be revealed in his time. For the mystery of iniquity doth already work; only he who now hindereth will continue to hinder until he be taken out of the way.

And then shall that wicked one be revealed, whom the Lord shall consume with the spirit of his mouth, and shall destroy with the brightness of his coming, even him whose coming is after the working of Satan with all power and signs and lying wonders, and with all deceivableness of unrighteousness in them that perish, because they received not the love of the truth, that they might be saved.

And for this cause God shall send them strong delusion, that they should believe the lie, that they all might be judged who

believed not the truth, but had pleasure in unrighteousness.
(2 Thessalonians 2:1–12)★

ANTICHRIST, THE MAN OF SIN

Across the pages of Scripture passes a character who is awesome
and appalling. This menacing figure is mysterious; he is hazy and
enigmatic. Sometimes he's a shady character. Again, he is an evil
influence. Then again, he is an angel of light. There is actually no
crystal-clear, cameo-cut presentation of him. He moves on the border-
line of the natural and the supernatural.

Who is this man who is called "that man of sin" in 2 Thessalonians
2:3? Some expositors from the very beginning have seen him as only
an evil influence in the world. We will look at that passage where the
apostle John speaks of him as "that spirit of antichrist." Of course,
this does not preclude him from being a person, which I believe he
is, and I think most accept that today. John does identify him as a
person, and John alone calls him by the name Antichrist. This does
not mean, of course, that only John refers to him; Antichrist has many
names in Scripture. Just as most crooks have aliases, Antichrist has
more aliases than any person I know of. He has thirty names which
are given on the pages of Scripture. Also, many figures of speech are
used in God's Word to speak of him, to set him before us, and they
occur again and again. Also, there are many types of him in Scripture,
and I'll be referring to that later in this message.

Now let's nail down some facts concerning this very elusive character to see if he is a person or an influence, or both. We can begin by
saying that the FBI hasn't been able to get his fingerprints, and they
have gathered no facts concerning him. They do not have a dossier
on him, yet Scripture pinpoints some means of identification as well
as the time he appears. I think that the time he appears is the all-
important question. And this will be the principal subject of this
message.

Let's look at the name Antichrist for just a moment. Notice first
the preposition *anti* that appears before the name of Christ and which

---

★All Scripture quotations from the *New Scofield Reference Bible* unless otherwise noted.

forms his name. *Anti* has two meanings. It can mean "against." It also can mean "instead of." It can be a substitute, and it can be a very good substitute or subterfuge for something. It means "in place of" or "in imitation of."

This, then, raises the question: Is he a false Christ, or is he an enemy of Christ? Where is the emphasis placed?

ENEMY OR IMITATOR?

Let's turn first to the epistles of John and see what John has to say about him. I'm going to consider every reference that he has given concerning him. The first is in 1 John 2:18. He begins by saying, "Little children, it is the last time," yet it has been nineteen hundred years since John wrote that. We've been living in the last days for a long time.

> **Little children, it is the last time; and as ye have heard that antichrist shall come, even now are there many antichrists, by which we know that it is the last time.** (1 John 2:18)

Notice that John not only says there is *going* to be an Antichrist, but already in his day there were many antichrists.

Now what was the thing that identified an antichrist? It was one who denied the deity of Jesus Christ. That is the primary definition of Antichrist, as we are told in the following verse:

> **Who is a liar but he that denieth that Jesus is the Christ? He is antichrist, that denieth the Father and the Son.** (1 John 2:22)

So you see, Antichrist is against Christ, and he denies the deity of Christ. We see now he is an enemy of Christ.

John will continue this in the fourth chapter:

> **Beloved, believe not every spirit, but test the spirits whether they are of God; because many false prophets are gone out into the world. By this know ye the Spirit of God: every spirit that confesseth that Jesus Christ is come in the flesh is of God; and every spirit that confesseth not that Jesus Christ is come in the flesh is not of God; and this is that spirit of antichrist, of which ye have heard that it should come, and even now already is it in the world.** (1 John 4:1-3)

What is the spirit of antichrist? It is that which denies the deity of the Lord Jesus Christ. For example, and I say this dogmatically, the rock opera *Jesus Christ Superstar* is antichrist. It denies the deity of Christ. I don't want to be ugly, but I must add that every liberal preacher who denies the deity of Christ is an antichrist—but not *the* Antichrist. You are antichrist when you deny the deity of Christ. You are an enemy of Jesus Christ. That's very important, I think, to see.

The Lord Jesus Himself, you remember, said that many would come in His name and they would deceive many. They would be pseudo-christs; they would pretend to be Christ. And John says: ". . . And this is that spirit of antichrist, of which ye have heard that it should come, and even now already is it in the world."

John nails it down. That is antichrist.

Now in his second epistle John gives the other side:

For many deceivers are entered into the world, who confess not that Jesus Christ cometh in the flesh. This is a deceiver and an antichrist. (2 John 7)

He is a deceiver. He pretends to be Christ. On one side he is an enemy of Christ. On another side, he is a deceiver.

How can we reconcile these two aspects of the person of Antichrist? How can Antichrist, when he appears be an enemy of Christ, at the same time pretend to be Christ? Well, this has troubled me for a long time, and I have given a lot of thought to it. Probably anybody else would have discovered it in a minute, but it took me a long time to discover it.

Now I want to turn your attention to the thirteenth chapter of the Book of Revelation. And if you will forgive me, I am going to quote my own translation—which I do not recommend, as I call it the McGeeicus Ad Absurdum translation! All I've attempted to do is to lift out of the original Greek the meaning of the words. It is a little different and I hope a little clearer. Here are the first four verses:

And he stood on the sand of the sea; and I saw a [wild] beast coming up out of the sea, having ten horns and seven heads, and on his horns ten diadems, and upon his heads names of blasphemy. And the [wild] beast which I saw was like unto a panther, and his feet were as the feet of a bear; and his mouth

as the mouth of a lion: and the dragon gave him his power; and his throne, and great authority. And one of his heads as though it had been slain unto death; and his stroke of death was healed; and the whole [inhabited] earth wondered after the beast. And they worshiped the dragon [this is Satan worship, by the way], because he gave his authority unto the beast; and they worshiped the beast, saying, who is like unto the beast? And who is able to war with him?

Now I want to drop down to verses 11–14:

And I saw another [wild] beast coming up out of the earth, and he had two horns like a lamb, and he was speaking as a dragon. And he exerciseth all the authority of the first [wild] beast in his presence. And he maketh the earth and the dwellers therein to worship the first [wild] beast, whose wound of death was healed. And he doeth great signs, that he should even make fire to come down out of heaven into the earth in the sight of men. And he deceiveth the dwellers on the earth through the signs which it was given him to do in the presence of the [wild] beast; saying to the dwellers on the earth that they should make an image to the beast who hath the stroke of the sword and lived.

In this passage that I've quoted from Revelation 13, there are two beasts represented. The first beast is Antichrist, the enemy of Christ. The second beast, the false prophet, is like a lamb—but he's not a lamb. He's a wild beast underneath. Now this is the one who pretends to be Christ. And you will recall the Lord Jesus in the Olivet Discourse repeatedly warned about one coming in His name. He said, "Many will come in my name and say, 'I'm Christ.' Don't be deceived by that." Now we today have so lowered our conception of the Person of Christ, that I think we would accept any man who could bring peace to this world. I do not think the world would ask whether he came from heaven or hell, and I don't think they would care. They would take him. They would elect any man who could bring peace to this world today, and that man will be Antichrist. He will be a false Christ who will bring in a period of peace.

Here in Revelation 13 is presented the first aspect of Antichrist. Let me go over this again rather carefully.

1. We are told that "he stood on the sand of the sea." *He* refers back to the dragon in the preceding chapter. There the dragon is identified as Satan. Satan is the one who brings this beast up out of the sea.
2. "The sea" is representative of the Gentile nations. So out of the nations of the world he is coming.
3. The beast rising "out of the sea" pictures the first ruler. He will not be a Jew.
4. The second beast, "and another wild beast" (verse 11), has to be a Jew in order to be accepted by the Jews.

So you see, two men are presented on the pages of Scripture, and both men represent Antichrist. There are many antichrists. These two will head up all that the Word of God has to say concerning the Antichrist who is to come. This again is my own translation:

And he stood on the sand of the sea; and I saw a [wild] beast coming up out of the sea, having ten horns and seven heads, and on his horns ten diadems, and upon his heads names of blasphemy. (Revelation 13:1)

Then in the following verses he goes on to describe him.

Is Antichrist Rome reunited? Some expositors look at this "beast" as the nation of Rome which is to be brought back together. Others regard him as the Antichrist who puts it together. May I say to you that I think it refers to both. You cannot have a king without a kingdom; you cannot have a kingdom without a king. If you don't believe that, ask Constantine II, exiled king of Greece, who escaped to Italy. He is no king—he doesn't have a kingdom. He is out of a job and has had a hard time. A true king must have a kingdom. When you have a kingdom, you have to have a king. This "beast" refers to both the kingdom and the person.

Is he someone from the past? Now verse 3 says something that has disturbed a great many of us—it has disturbed me, I can assure you. Again my literal translation:

And one of his heads as though it had been slain unto death; and his stroke of death was healed; and the whole [inhabited] earth wondered after the beast. (Revelation 13:3)

There is a belief abroad that this will be some man who has lived in the past whom Satan will bring back from the dead. Some believe he will be Nero. The early church believed he would be Nero. Also a great many of the church fathers believed that he would be Judas Iscariot. And right now in prophetic circles in this country a belief is circulating that Antichrist will indeed be Judas Iscariot. Now I dismiss all this speculation absolutely, and I'll tell you why I have to dismiss it. It is because of the fact that the head of the "beast" described here was wounded and he is brought back to life. Can Satan resurrect anyone from the dead? The answer is absolutely he cannot.

I believe this refers to the kingdom of the "beast"; this is the Roman Empire that fell apart and will come back together again. And it's like a resurrection. The "beast" himself will not be raised from the dead. I do think some kind of chicanery will be used concerning him, but I do not think that he will die and be raised from the dead. Satan cannot raise the dead.

Now I want to turn to a passage of Scripture that I feel is very important in this connection. Note now the words of the Lord Jesus. He is giving the reason that He can say, "He that heareth my word, and believeth on him that sent me, hath everlasting life." Why? Actually there are three reasons He can say that, one of which is that He raises the dead, and He is the only one to whom the Father has given that power.

> **For as the Father raiseth up the dead, and giveth them life, even so the Son giveth life to whom he will.** (John 5:21)

Only God can give life. And now the Lord Jesus, who is God, says He gives life also. Now let me drop down in this passage to verse 25:

> **Verily, verily, I say unto you, The hour is coming, and now is, when the dead shall hear the voice of the Son of God; and they that hear shall live.** (John 5:25)

Whose voice? The voice of the Son of God. Only Jesus Christ can raise the dead. Satan cannot do that. Therefore, Antichrist could not be Nero. He could not be Judas Iscariot. He could not be anybody who has already lived. He will have to be some new person that appears on the scene. He goes on to say regarding Christ:

> . . . **All that are in the graves shall hear his voice, and shall come forth: they that have done good, unto the resurrection of life; and they that have done evil, unto the resurrection of damnation.** (John 5:28, 29)

What does He mean by "they that have done good"? They came to Him with the question:

> . . . **What shall we do, that we might work the works of God? Jesus answered, and said unto them, This is the work of God, that ye believe on him whom he hath sent.** (John 6:28, 29)

Today the good work God asks you to do is to believe on Jesus Christ. It is the believer who will hear His voice and be raised. Then later on, as I understand it, the Old Testament saints are to be raised to enter the Kingdom, during the Millennium, at the end of the Great Tribulation. Then at the end of the Millennium, the lost are raised for judgment. Only Jesus Christ can raise the dead.

Have you ever noticed that no so-called faith healer can raise the dead? God gave that sign to the apostles; not only could Simon Peter and Paul and the others heal the sick, they also raised the dead. And when you find one of these "faith healers" abroad today who is raising the dead, let me know. I'll go see him then, but not until then. Power to heal the sick and raise the dead was given to the apostles. It's been given to no one else! Only the Son has power to raise the dead. My, this is a tremendous fact today! Therefore, I don't see how in the world the Antichrist could be Judas or anyone else who has already died.

How can he imitate Christ? Now let's look at this other aspect of Antichrist. He's a false christ, a pseudo-christ. In 2 Thessalonians there are several things I would like to refer to. First of all, will you notice that he's called here the "wicked one." That's another one of his aliases.

> **And then shall that wicked one be revealed, whom the Lord shall consume with the spirit of his mouth, and shall destroy with the brightness of his coming, even him whose coming is after the working of Satan with all power and signs and lying wonders.** (2 Thessalonians 2:8, 9)

So Antichrist will perform miracles. He will be a miracle worker. And do you know that he's the only miracle worker the Scriptures promise for the future, with the exception of the Lord Jesus Christ? He's the only one. For this reason I'm not interested in "miracle workers" today. I am afraid of them.

A family who had belonged to a church I went to pastor in Nashville had gone into spiritualism. The pastor who had retired suggested I go to visit them. I went to see them, and they said, "Why, Dr. McGee, we sat for fifteen years in that Presbyterian church, and we never saw anything happen. We went into spiritualism and, just like that, things began to happen." And I said, "I believe you. But why would anybody with intelligence sit fifteen years with nothing happening? I think I would have moved before then." I feel sorry for people who have been sitting in churches for fifteen years without anything happening. My friend, something ought to happen if you've been sitting in God's house listening to God's Word! The second thing I said to them was: "The terrible truth is that you have come into something that *does* have power, but have you ever questioned the source of that power? John says to try the spirits. See whether they are of God or not. Had it ever occurred to you that this may be Satan?" Oh, they had never thought of that. "Well," I said, "it might be well to try it out. We have no miracle worker today except one that will come finally from Satan." And I said, "We walk today by *faith*." God's people find that so hard, don't we? We want to *see* something. We want to *hear* something. We want to *experience* something. And I believe in all of that, but I think the important thing in this world in which we are living is to be able to walk with God by faith.

Now this one we call Antichrist who is to appear denies the Deity—but he assumes deity.

And I beheld another beast coming up out of the earth; and he had two horns like a lamb, and he spoke like a dragon. And he exerciseth all the power of the first beast before him, and causeth the earth and them who dwell on it to worship the first beast, whose deadly wound was healed. And he doeth great wonders, so that he maketh fire come down from heaven on the earth in the sight of man, and deceiveth them that dwell on the earth by

means of those miracles which he had power to do in the sight of the beast, saying to them that dwell on the earth, that they should make an image to the beast, that had the wound by a sword, and did live. And he hath power to give life unto the image of the beast, that the image of the beast should both speak, and cause that as many as would not worship the image of the beast should be killed. And he causeth all, both small and great, rich and poor, free and enslaved, to receive a mark in their right hand, or in their foreheads, and that no man might buy or sell, except he that had the mark, or the name of the beast, or the number of his name. Here is wisdom. Let him that hath understanding count the number of the beast; for it is the number of a man; and his number is six hundred threescore and six. (Revelation 13:11-18)

He acts like he's a lamb, but he's a wild beast. He's Antichrist. He pretends to be Christ, and he will be the religious ruler of the world. And he will work with Antichrist, the political ruler of the world.

Part of the mystery in trying to identify Antichrist has been the belief that he is one person and that we must have one person to fulfill the demands of Scripture. However, the first "beast" represents the first aspect of Antichrist that denies the deity of Christ and is the enemy of Christ. The second "beast" represents the second aspect of Antichrist. He is a wolf in sheep's clothing in that he imitates Christ. And both together are *the* Antichrist. Both are against the living and true Christ. And that's the reason the Lord Jesus Himself said twice in the Olivet Discourse, "Many will come in my name. They will deceive many." And that is the tragic thing.

TWO DEPARTURES?

I want you to notice in 2 Thessalonians 2:3 something very, very important. "Let no man deceive you by any means; for that day shall not come, except. . . ." Notice the reference to "that day." What day is that? It is the Day of the Lord; it is the day that the apostles asked Jesus about. You remember that they came to the Lord Jesus when He went to the top of the Mount of Olives and asked Him first, "When shall these things be?" (Matthew 24:3). When will there not be left here one stone upon another? (See verse 2.) He told them that when they would see Jerusalem compassed with armies they would know the time had come. That happened in A.D. 70. I'm of the opinion that several of the apostles were there. Perhaps they climbed up on the battlements of the walls of Jerusalem and looked over. When they saw the standard, the eagles of the Roman government of Titus there, I think one apostle nudged the other and said, "This is what He was talking about. This is it! It has come to pass." Titus destroyed Jerusalem just as the Lord Jesus said, and not one stone was left upon another. Let me repeat what I said in another message—it bears repeating. If you doubt that one stone was not left upon another, look at the wailing wall in Jerusalem today. The thing that amazes me about the western wall is the kinds of stones that are in it. There are stones from Solomon's temple, from the temple days of Ezra and Haggai and from every other period. One stone was not left upon another when Titus took Jerusalem. And that prophecy was fulfilled.

They had another question: What is the sign of the end of the age? Now that is what Paul is talking about in 2 Thessalonians 2:3. The Lord Jesus labeled the end of the age as the Great Tribulation period. I didn't label it. No evangelical labeled it. The Lord Jesus is the One who labeled it the Great Tribulation period (Matthew 24:21). He said there would be nothing like it in the history of the world.

Now let's look at this again:

Let no man deceive you by any means; for that day shall not come, except there come the falling away first, and that man of sin be revealed, the son of perdition. (2 Thessalonians 2:3)

The word I'm interested in here is "the *falling away* first." And when I made a study of this word, I just had to stand up in my study and say, "Hallelujah!" What a wonderful revelation it was to see the root meaning of the word. Now the word in Greek is *apostasia* and it comes from *apostasis*. The root word means "departure" or "removal from." And the verb means "to remove, to depart, to leave." It comes from two words: *histemi*, meaning "to stand," and *apo*, meaning "away from." From this we get our word *apostasy*. Apostates, we understand today, are men who held the truth at one time. They've stood for the truth of Scripture and now they *apohistemi*, they stand away from it.

That's one meaning of the word. But that's not all the meaning of this word. The primary meaning is "a departure." Paul says that day shall not come until the "falling away" or "departure." What departure is he talking about? Well, the same departure he talked about in his first epistle to the Thessalonians. That's the Rapture of the church. The church is going to depart from this earth. The Rapture is the removal of the church, the departure of the church from the earth. Paul dwelt on that in his first epistle when he was answering their question about their loved ones:

> **For the Lord himself shall descend from heaven with a shout, with the voice of the archangel, and with the trump of God; and the dead in Christ shall rise first; then we who are alive and remain shall be caught up. . . .** (1 Thessalonians 4:16, 17)

This is an *apohistemi*, that's a departure. And to me the word that Paul uses is marvelous because it speaks of two things. It speaks of two departures, because the whole church is to apostatize:

1. The true church is to leave the earth;
2. The professing church will just move away from the truth.

The Lord Jesus said, "When the Son of man cometh, shall he find [the] faith on the earth?" (Luke 18:8). That is, will He find that the body of truth, the apostles' doctrine, is still held? In the original Greek the question is phrased in such a way that it demands a negative answer. The professing church will have departed so far from the faith that in the seventeenth chapter of Revelation it is called the harlot. The true church, called the Bride of Christ, has been caught up to meet Him. That departure must come first. As we saw in 2 Thessalonians 2:3, ". . . that day shall not come, except there come the falling away first, and that man of sin be revealed, the son of perdition." In other words, the Antichrist cannot appear until the true church departs from this earth. Now we have this twofold meaning. Some shall depart from the faith, and some shall depart from the earth. The departure of the true church from the earth brings in total apostasy; so that what the Lord Jesus said about not finding faith on the earth when He comes will be fulfilled.

Now from the viewpoint of the earth, it will be a departure. From the viewpoint of heaven, it will be a rapture; they will be caught up—*apostasia*. That will be the leaving, the departure, of the true church. I think that the world is going to say at that time, "They're gone. They've departed. They've left us." And if they are ever to say, "Hallelujah," that's when they'll say it. The world will rejoice at first. Antichrist will make them believe that they're entering the Millennium when actually they will be entering the Tribulation. That, I think, is the big lie. The world will think they're bringing in the Millennium. And, my friend, haven't you voted already for many candidates who promised to bring peace to this world? Didn't Woodrow Wilson promise it as far back as 1917? And hasn't peace been the platform of many men since then? Don't misunderstand—these men are sincere. They're not antichrists. But they tried to bring peace to the earth. You and I both know that when the man appears on the scene who tells this war-weary world, "We're going to have peace, and I'm going to bring it," they will say, "Bring him on. We turn it all over to him." And the world would take him today in five minutes if he appeared. Only God is holding him back. God is not going to let him appear until He calls out His church, and He alone knows when that time will be fulfilled.

The world will be rejoicing as the Antichrist begins his rule. But it's going to be the saddest day this earth has ever seen, because it means the departure of the church and the entrance of the world into an awful period identified by Christ as the Great Tribulation.

I saw this illustrated some time ago. We were out at the airport getting ready to take a plane to go back East. We had quite a bit of time to spend because we always get there early. So I spent some time walking around. There was a plane getting ready to leave for the Hawaiian Islands, and I am always interested in going to the Hawaiian Islands, so I just looked at the folk who were going. Most of them were going out for a holiday. But I saw a couple sitting there, a soldier boy in uniform, a fine looking young fellow, and beside him the prettiest little wife you've ever seen, holding a fine looking baby. And they were both sad. Everybody else going to the Hawaiian Islands was anticipating the fun they were going to have, but he was on his way to Hawaii to join his outfit going to Vietnam. There sat that fellow and there sat the girl. They weren't saying anything. They were just staring out into space. The little boy didn't know what it was all about, so he was having a big time. When the call came to board the plane, they stood up. I saw him put those great big arms around both of them, his wife and that little boy. And he kissed both of them. Tears were coming down his cheeks and tears were coming down her cheeks. The little boy, he was still having a big time. And then the fellow picked up his little old bag he had there, started out to the plane, and disappeared. The girl stood there, then she went over to the window and waited till the plane pulled out to get on the runway. I watched her as she went away carrying that baby and carrying that bag you women have to carry when you've got a baby. She was weighted down. I never felt as sorry for anyone as I did for that girl. I wondered what the future held. Was there a father or a mother she would go to, or would she have to live alone and take care of that baby by herself? I don't know, but it was sad to see.

I thought, *That's the way it's going to be on this earth someday when the departure, the Rapture, takes place.* The earth will rejoice for awhile, but then a great company of people are going to begin to wake up. They will find they've been deceived. The man who promised peace is Antichrist, not Christ at all. He has taken them in; he has absolutely deceived them.

JUST LIKE AHITHOPHEL

There are many types of the Antichrist in history and on the pages of Scripture. I think Judas is probably the most accurate type. But for another illustration I would like you to look at one that may have escaped your notice. He is Ahithophel. Maybe you haven't even heard of Ahithophel. You can read his story in 2 Samuel 15–17. Ahithophel was one of the counselors in the inner circle that counseled David. David looked to him as he looked to no other man for advice. Then word came to David that Absalom, his favored son, was stirring up a rebellion. It broke David's heart that his own son was leading a rebellion against him. David was warned by those who loved him that the thing was underhanded, that those whom he thought were true to him were not true to him. They had deceived him. So David left the city of Jerusalem and went up the ascent of Mount Olivet. Then word came to him that Ahithophel had gone over to Absalom.

This was a low blow to David. It was bad enough to have his own son rebel against him, but now Ahithophel, his chief counselor, the man whom he knew and trusted, had betrayed him. Weeping and with his head covered, David went out over the Mount of Olives, back down into the wilderness again. David had been deceived. Ahithophel, I think, is a picture of Antichrist who will deceive this world someday.

Now I want to turn to Psalm 55, a psalm that David wrote with this rebellion as the background. There's a storm brewing:

I would hasten my escape from the windy storm and tempest.

There was an undercurrent, and David now is getting away from it.

Destroy, O Lord, and confuse their tongues [the tongues of these who were plotting the death of David]; **for I have seen violence and strife in the city.**

We think today that violence and strife in the city are something new. David saw it in Jerusalem. Perhaps there were those carrying placards conducting little protest meetings in front of the palace saying, "Down with David. Up with Absalom." And David says, "There's strife and violence in the city."

Day and night they go about it upon the walls; mischief also and sorrow are in the midst of it. Wickedness is in the midst thereof; deceit and guile depart not from her streets.

David said, "When I walk down the street, Mr. So-and-so speaks to me, and I'm not sure whether he's my friend or not now. I've heard he's been plotting against me." David says, "I'm getting out of Jerusalem." Now listen to him:

For it was not an enemy that reproached me; then I could have borne it. Neither was it he that hated me that did magnify himself against me; then I would have hidden myself from him.

He's talking about Ahithophel.

But it was thou, a man mine equal, my guide, and my familiar friend.

"Why, Ahithophel—he's my friend, and now he has betrayed me." He's a Judas Iscariot.

We took sweet counsel together, and walked unto the house of God in company.

David just bursts out with this cry of judgment:

Let death seize upon them, and let them go down alive into sheol; for wickedness is in their dwellings, and among them.

Now, David, what are you going to do in a time like this? Listen to David.

As for me, I will call upon God, and the LORD shall save me.

David, what are you going to do when all of the foundations are going out from under you? He says, "I'm going to trust the Lord. I'm going to rest in Him." Friend, we're living in dangerous days. Whom do you trust today—really? Whom do you rest upon? Now listen to David—he's not through.

The words of his mouth were smoother than butter, but war was in his heart; his words were softer than oil, yet were they drawn swords.

He says, "Old Ahithophel, that sly, slippery snake that he was, just wriggled his way right into the palace; he put his arm around me and said, 'You know, David, I love you. I'm going to serve you.'" And David says his words were like melted butter, smooth as oil, but in his heart was war. What will you do, David?

Cast thy burden upon the LORD, and he shall sustain thee; he shall never suffer the righteous to be moved. (verses 8–16, 21, 22)

David says, "The thing I'm going to do is trust in God. I can't even trust Ahithophel. I can't trust in men, but I can trust God."

As we move into the end times we're seeing the thing that Paul said would take place during the last days of the church. Men would be traitors and high-minded, and you would not be able to trust them. These are days when God's people need to trust the Lord as they've never trusted Him before.

TO KNOW HIM!

Now I want to make a practical application. Very frankly this character, the Antichrist, who passes across the pages of Scripture, I see as two persons: one against Christ; another attempting to be Christ. But both of them are awful deceivers and terrible enemies of Christ. I don't ever expect to see either one of them. I don't want to know them. But I want to say this to you: I want to know the Lord Jesus Christ a little better. Even Paul, when he got to the end of his life, said:

That I may know him, and the power of his resurrection, and the fellowship of his sufferings. . . . (Philippians 3:10)

I want to know Christ, not Antichrist. I want to know not just about Him, I want to know *Him*. I want the Holy Spirit to take the things of Christ and make them real to me. This is the Book where He does it, the Word of God. That's the reason I'm interested in getting His Word out, because through this Book you're going to know Him.

Let me conclude with an illustration that comes from my Southland before the Civil War.

There were many boats in those days that plied up and down the Mississippi River. It was a great artery of commerce. Also many passenger boats went up and down the river. When two boats met it was the custom for everyone to run on deck and wave at the folk on the other boat. Now that may not seem very exciting to you, but for them it relieved the monotony of the trip. On one occasion when two boats were passing, a black fireman came up on board. He stood at the rail next to a very elegantly dressed gentleman. When the approaching boat came abreast of them, he nudged this elderly gentleman with his elbow and said excitedly, "Look, look, yonder's the captain! See the captain! Do you see the captain?" His insistence was a little irritating to this gentleman. He drew himself up to his full height and said, "Of course I see the captain. Every boat has a captain. There is nothing unusual about a captain." The man looked at him almost in disgust, and he said, "You see that captain over there? He's different. I used to work on his boat and I fell overboard one day. I can't swim. That captain saw that I was going down. He took off his coat, he took off his cap, and he jumped into the river.

When I was going down for the third time he rescued me. That captain saved my life. And ever since then I just love to point him out!"

Well, friend, the Lord Jesus Christ is the One who has saved us from sin, and He is the One we love to point out. Actually, the important question to be able to answer is not "Who is Antichrist?" The vital question for you and me to answer is the Lord Jesus Christ's question: "Who do men say that I, the Son of man, am?" (Matthew 16:13). Can we say that He is the Son of God, God manifest in the flesh, the One who has saved our souls from sin? When we can say that, we have answered the most important question of life.

Chapter 11

WHEN RUSSIA COMES DOWN AGAINST ISRAEL

Why would Russia, as we see it today, have any interest in invading Israel?

I think you'll find satisfying answers to that question in the classic passage of Ezekiel's tremendous prophecy, chapters 38 and 39. It is without doubt one of the great prophecies of Scripture, as you will see. To get in the atmosphere of this, let's begin with the first eight verses of Ezekiel 38:

> And the word of the LORD came unto me, saying, Son of man, set thy face against Gog, the land of Magog, the chief prince of Meshech and Tubal, and prophesy against him, and say, Thus saith the Lord GOD: Behold, I am against thee, O Gog, the chief prince of Meshech and Tubal: and I will turn thee back, and put hooks into thy jaws, and I will bring thee forth, and all thine army, horses and horsemen, all of them clothed with all sorts of armor, even a great company with bucklers and shields, all of them handling swords: Persia, Ethiopia, and Libya with them. . . .

Here we have mentioned the nations which will be allied with Russia in the last days. Persia, of course, would be Iran today. Ethiopia and Libya are in Africa.

> . . . all of them with shield and helmet: Gomer, and all his bands [Germany]; the house of Togarmah [Turkey] of the north quarters, and all his bands: and many people with thee. Be thou prepared, and prepare for thyself, thou, and all thy company that are assembled unto thee, and be thou a guard unto them. After

many days thou shalt be visited: in the latter years thou shalt come into the land that is brought back from the sword, and is gathered out of many people, against the mountains of Israel, which have been always waste: but it is brought forth out of the nations, and they shall dwell safely all of them.

Now if Russia should come down against Israel tomorrow, it would not be a fulfillment of this prophecy. Because God makes it very clear that when the nations listed here come down in fulfillment of this prophecy, it will be when the nation Israel is dwelling in safety. And at the time of this writing they are anything but safe in the little land of Israel.

Now may I say first of all that when I entered the ministry, even when I began work on my doctoral degree, I did not at all accept the fact that Russia was the nation referred to in Ezekiel 38 and 39. I had attended my denominational seminary which taught amillennialism and did not believe that Russia was being referred to in this portion of Scripture. But since it was the view of many Bible expositors whom I respected, I began to make a study of this passage on my own and attempt to arrive at a decision whether or not this could possibly be Russia.

Well, I would like to present three points of proof, three lines of identification that convinced me. One line of proof would be enough, but there are three here that convinced me beyond a shadow of a doubt that Russia is the enemy referred to in chapters 38 and 39.

LANGUAGE

The first proof that I would like to mention is the linguistic phenomenon—that is, the language that is used. Some of the words are quite remarkable—you'll find them nowhere else in the Scriptures. I turn first to Ezekiel 38:2 and note the word "*chief*, prince of Meshech."

And the word of the LORD came unto me, saying, Son of man, set thy face against Gog, the land of Magog, the *chief* prince of Meshech and Tubal, and prophesy against him, and say, Thus saith the Lord GOD; Behold, I am against thee, O Gog, the chief prince of Meshech and Tubal. (Ezekiel 38:1-3; emphasis mine)

If you compare an *American Standard Version,* the *New King James* and some other newer versions of the Bible, you will notice that there is a change in translation. The word "chief" has been changed to the Hebrew word *rosh,* and it literally means "head," or "beginning." *Rosh* is a proper name, however.

It was the learned Dean Stanley's exhaustive history of the Eastern church (not only exhaust*ive* but exhaust*ing*) published a century ago, that contains a note on the Hebrew scholar Gesenius that the Hebrew "rosh" is mistranslated "chief" in the English version, that it should be "russ" or "Russia." And Stanley added this comment: "It is the only name of a modern nation found in the Old Testament" ("modern nation" in the sense of coming into existence during the past few centuries). That's quite remarkable, coming from the source that it does.

Another historian wrote, "Rosh, taken as a proper name in Ezekiel, signifies the inhabitants of Scythia from whom the modern Russians derive their name." In 1533, Ivan IV, known as Ivan the Terrible, came to power. (I understand that his portrait still hangs in the museum in Russia today.) He was the first to assume the title of czar of Russia, taking, if you please, the name of the people who had migrated from the area around the Caspian and Black Seas and probably earlier had come up through the Tigris-Euphrates Valley. For those who believe that the United States is in prophecy, I'd like to take note of that. Two of the greatest scholars I suppose that we've ever had have made the statement that Russia is the only modern nation that is ever mentioned in the Word of God. My friend, the United States is never mentioned in the Word of God.

"Son of man, set thy face against Gog." And the word "Gog" here is not so much the name but the title of the ruler. And "gog" is a tartaric word that means "roof", it means the person who is at the top, on the roof. And I can't think of a better name for the dictator than to call him the boy on top, he's the one on the roof. This certainly would be the picture of a dictator.

"Set thy face against Gog, the land of Magog, the prince of Rosh [Russ or Russia], Meshech, and Tubal, and prophesy against him." Now Josephus has said that Magog founded those who from him were named Megagites, but who by the Greeks were called Scythians. And

Russia was first called Muscovy, which was derived from Meshech, until about 1533.

So that what we have here is a linguistic phenomenon—a name of a modern nation. And added to that are these two words, *Meshech* and *Tubal*. In Hebrew they are lots closer to *Moscow* and *Tobolsk,* the Russian side and the Siberian side, both that are mentioned here. And I say to you that this is indeed a remarkable thing.

GEOGRAPHY

Then there is the geographical phenomenon. Another way that this nation is identified is that it is located in the north. And you will find that identification in Ezekiel 38:6, 15: "the north quarters," and, "Thou shalt come from thy place out of the north parts." Again you will find it in Ezekiel 39:2, "And I will turn thee back, and leave but the sixth part of thee, and will cause thee to come from the north parts, and will bring thee upon the mountains of Israel."

And we also need to understand that directions in Scripture always relate to this nation Israel. When God says it's in the north, He does not mean north of California, or north of where you live. He means north of the land of Israel. When God says south, He means south of Israel. And when God speaks of it being west, He means it's west of Israel. And when He speaks of coming from the east, He's speaking of east of the land of Israel. It has no reference to the United States or to any other part of the globe. And I don't care whether you point north, northwest or northeast, you are pointing to the Russian republics. It is the kingdom that is definitely in the north. And the very interesting thing is that it would be difficult to find another kingdom in the north that would meet the requirements of Scripture. The geographical phenomenon is the second reason (and we believe it is a valid reason) for believing that Magog is Russia.

BASIC PHILOSOPHY

Now the third, and to me the most convincing one of all, is the philosophical (or ideological) reason. It is that there has come into existence a nation whose basic philosophy fits that described in Ezekiel's prophecy.

World War I brought circumstances into a position for the first time in the history of the world where a nation whose basic philosophy, whose whole political economy, was based on atheism. This was something that the world had never seen before, that had never existed in the past.

Somebody says, "But what about the great nations of antiquity such as Egypt and Babylon and Syria, also Persia and the Median Empire? Not one of them was an atheistic empire. All of them were polytheistic—that is, they worshiped many gods. The reason mankind was not atheistic in ancient times was that they were too close to the time when God had created human life, and it would be very difficult for them to deny His existence. After all, Noah had children who knew a man who knew a man who knew Adam. And when you are that close to Adam, and Adam tells you about coming from the hand of God, it is mighty hard for anybody to become an atheist.

Back in the time of Moses God gave no commandments about atheism. His first two commandments were about polytheism: "thou shalt have no other gods before me" and "thou shalt not make unto thee any graven image." It was a warning against polytheism, not atheism. As man began to get away from God and move away from His revelation, atheism came in. But even as far along as the time of David, we find written in Psalm 14, "The *fool* hath said in his heart, There is no God"—today he is a college professor! How far we have strayed through the centuries! In our day it is considered blasé and sophisticated to deny the existence of God. In David's day you would have been a fool, and in Moses' day you wouldn't have even been in existence. You might have worshiped the sun, moon and stars, but you would not have been godless.

Joseph Stalin said, "We have deposed the czars of earth. We shall now dethrone the Lord of heaven." And that has been the whole thesis and philosophy of the Russian way of thinking since the revolution.

It was when their rocket went by the moon, you will recall, that they made this statement which was aired on the Moscow radio back in December 1960:

> Our rocket has bypassed the moon. It is nearing the sun. We have not discovered God. We have turned lights out in heaven that no man will be able to put on again. We are breaking the yoke of the

gospel, the opium of the masses. Let us go forth, and Christ shall be relegated to mythology.

Did they think that God was hiding out there somewhere behind the moon or some other planet? How utterly ridiculous and preposterous! But their statement is a revelation of their hatred and bitterness against God.

And they were shocked to hear our USA astronauts read the first chapter of Genesis from the moon, and they asked on radio, "Was it really a joke?"

May I say that I could give you quotations galore showing that the communistic system and the nation of Russia even today are absolutely atheistic, as far as the rulers and those who are in power are concerned. For the first time in the history of the world a nation has emerged with this atheistic philosophy.

GOD'S STRANGE WORK

Now the very interesting thing is that God says in Ezekiel 38 and 39, "I'm against you." Notice how strong the statement is. "Thus saith the Lord GOD; Behold, I am against thee." Now I want to say to you, that this troubled me at first. When I began to study this, I wondered what right has even God to condemn the nation before it even appears in history? That's not like Him. In the Old Testament you'll find that God always was gracious. God was always slow to anger. God always wanted to save. And even Isaiah says that judgment is His strange work. He is in the saving business, that's the whole thought of both the Old and the New Testaments.

You will recall when the people of Israel came into the Promised Land, that they conquered it in battle. Some of the so-called higher critics say, "Wasn't it terrible that they went in there and destroyed Jericho and so many of those people!" Have you ever read what the harlot Rahab said to Israel's spies? She said, "We have heard how the LORD dried up the water of the Red Sea for you, when ye came out of Egypt. . ." (Joshua 2:10). When did that happen? Forty years before that. My friend, may I remind you that God granted Jericho forty years more. He kept His people out in order to give the people of Jericho and all Canaan an opportunity to make up their mind whether they would accept Him or not. Isn't forty years long enough? I believe if there had been any hope of their turning to God that He would have given them even more time. God is "slow to anger and of great mercy."

Abraham thought God was rather severe in His judgment of Sodom and Gomorrah. And God told him that if he could find someone down there who was righteous, He would save him. Abraham had to give up. He couldn't find anyone down there. He was afraid even Lot wouldn't make it. My friend, God is gracious.

God sent that message out—even to the brutal nation of Assyria. God sent His prophet Jonah to Nineveh. Jonah couldn't understand why God would send him up there—that's the reason he didn't want to go. He said, "I don't understand this. What is Your concern for Nineveh and these brutal Assyrians?" God said,

And should not I spare Nineveh, that great city, wherein are more than sixscore thousand persons that cannot discern between their right hand and their left hand; and also much cattle? (Jonah 4:11)

And God saved the entire city!

God's wonderful mercy makes His judgment of Russia more remarkable. But God says here, "I'm against you." And they haven't even come into existence. Why is God against them? Because they came into existence as militant atheists. Although they had the Word of God, they set themselves against Him and destroyed every evidence in their manifestos. Centuries before communism declared itself against God, He beat them to the draw and said, "I'm against you." And this is the only nation, up to the present hour, that could possibly fulfill this particular statement that God has made here.

Men in high places, ever since World War II, have felt that Russia would not move in any direction but toward the South, and that in preparation they have been stirring up the Arabs. Another report is that the Arab block intends to invade Israel as soon as it is ready again. Only the date is uncertain. Both Russia and Germany wish Israel to be exterminated, and they have both encouraged the Arabs. That is one of the things which has made this area the most sensitive spot on the earth.

Now we are told in the Word of God that Russia is going to come down out of the north parts, and they're going to come down into the land of Israel. That is the direction God says they are going to move. He says it again and again,

> **And after many days thou shalt be visited: in the latter years thou shalt come into the land that is brought back from the sword, and is gathered out of many people, against the mountains of Israel, which have been always waste: but it is brought forth out of the nations, and they shall dwell safely all of them.** (Ezekiel 38:8)

Now I want you to notice *why* they are coming down. God gives a very good reason. And I think that we can see that today.

> **And I will turn thee back, and put hooks into thy jaws, and I will bring thee forth, and all thine army, horses and horsemen, all of them clothed with all sorts of armour, even a great company with bucklers and shields, all of them handling swords.** (Ezekiel 38:4)

God said that Russia is to move southward. The little nation of Israel knows that her neighbors are living for the day when they can push her into the sea.

Notice again the remarkable language of Ezekiel 38:4: "I will turn thee back, and put hooks into thy jaws, and I will bring thee forth." There have been those who have interpreted this to mean that God is going to put hooks in the jaws of Russia and bring them up out of the land of Palestine. The very interesting thing is when you read this chapter and the next, you find that Russia is not ever going to *come out* of the land. God says of that invading army that comes against Israel:

> **And it shall come to pass in that day, that I will give unto Gog a place there of graves in Israel, the valley of the passengers on the east of the sea: and it shall stop the noses of the passengers: and there shall they bury Gog and all his multitude: and they shall call it The valley of Hamon-gog. And seven months shall the house of Israel be burying of them, that they may cleanse the land.** (Ezekiel 39:11, 12)

God intends to bury them right there in that land. In fact, God says that it will take seven months just to bury the bodies.

Since the invading armies will not be coming up out of that land at all, what does God mean by "I will put *hooks* into thy jaws, and I will bring thee forth"? That is the remarkable thing God says concerning a powerful war-machine nation that has totally rejected Him! In effect, God says, "I'm baiting a hook for you, and you're going to take it, and you are going to come down into the land of Israel."

Now I do not know all the bait that God has for that hook, but I do know that He has on it some very interesting bait.

WARM WATER PORT

First of all, may I say to you that Russia must have a warm-water port. And they have made several efforts to get one. The coast of Palestine along the eastern shore of the Mediterranean Sea is the proper place for the Russians to get a warm-water port that will be available to them. They are looking in that direction. After all, why should they want to move north and get another frozen port? They have enough of those right now. But if they could move into the Mediterranean they would have a warm-water port the year around. God says, "I'll put hooks in their jaws, I'll bring them down into that land."

OIL

There is another hook that obviously is in their jaws, the one with which we are most familiar, and that is oil. The largest oil reserves in the world are not in Texas. I made that statement in Houston, Texas, and I almost had to leave town! But the largest oil reserves are today in the Middle East, and Russia has been after that oil. Any modern nation with a war machine and with modern gadgets must have oil.

It was back in 1955 that an article appeared here in a Los Angeles paper captioned: "Russia Hungers for Arabian Oil." They must have the oil that comes out of that area.

God for millions of years has been storing barrels of oil in the

Middle East. He said, "I'll put hooks in their jaws and bring them down into this land."

THE DEAD SEA

There's a third hook and this is the one He's really loaded. I do not mean to be irreverent, but had you met the Lord ten billion years ago over in that land, and you had said to Him, "I don't understand something that You are doing here. You are running water down there in the Dead Sea and just letting it evaporate. And that's the only place You do it like that. Why in the world are You doing it?" I think the Lord would have said, "Well, I have something in mind. I'm baiting a hook. Because a few billion years from today I'm going to have a nation come down to get the chemicals that I'm storing up here. And it will have to have them." Chemicals are something else that a modern nation has to have. And God has been storing them up down through the millions, and I think billions of years. Don't be afraid of that—God is the God of eternity. He has had plenty of time. He's in no hurry. He's been pouring the chemicals into the Dead Sea, and only basic salts are being taken out of there—magnesium salt, sodium salts—by the simple process of evaporation. But they haven't even touched most of it today. It's estimated—and I saw these figures several years ago—that the value of the chemicals in the Dead Sea were worth then twenty-seven trillion English pounds. That's a lot of money! That was way back when things were not as expensive as they are today. There is no telling what those chemicals are worth now. They would be priceless to any nation in time of war, and they rest there in the heavy waters of the Dead Sea. "I'm going to put hooks in your jaws," God said, "and I'm going to bring you down into that land."

WHEN WILL IT HAPPEN?

Now when will Russia come down? I'm not giving dates, and I hope you'll understand that. This is a place where very fine men who study prophecy differ. On my desk I have books that give six different interpretations as to time, and they're all written by men for whom I have great respect. But God has identified it far enough that I think you can see certain things. Let me just point to one or two.

We are told in Ezekiel 38:8,

After many days thou shalt be visited: in the latter years thou shalt come into the land. . . .

Then in 38:16,

And thou shalt come up against my people of Israel, as a cloud to cover the land; it shall be in the latter days. . . .

Repeated again and again are the "latter days" or the "latter years" or the "last days" or the "time of the end," as Daniel uses it. These are technical terms that relate to God's purposes with the nation Israel.

Now when you come to the New Testament you will find that "in the last days" is referring to the last days of the church, right before the Lord takes the church out of the world.

But the last days for the nation Israel begin with the "great day of the Lord," which, according to Joel's prophecy, is nigh. It is the Great Tribulation period that is yet in the future. We are told that during that period Russia will come down against Israel. Many of us believe that Russia and her allies will come down in the middle of the seven-year Tribulation period. It would seem, as Daniel divides it and as John in the Revelation divides it, that something *triggers* the Great Tribulation period. In the first half of it, when Antichrist appears, he appears as a prince of peace. I'm confident he presents himself as the Messiah. The nation Israel will receive him as such. But they will find out they have been deceived the minute he runs an idol into the temple. However, at first they apparently will go after him, as will the other nations of the world.

We are told that the entire world is going to worship the Antichrist. Why? Because he's going to bring *peace*. We have spent billions of dollars in our efforts to bring peace to this world. The nations of the world want peace at any price. There are many people who are willing to surrender to anyone in order to have peace, because they feel that nuclear war is something that would be frightful beyond words. And it would be.

Therefore when Antichrist appears (there's a vacuum being created right now for his appearance) and promises peace and *produces* peace, the world will go after him. And if that man appeared today in Western Europe, for that is where he will first appear, they will not ask whether he came from heaven or hell. They won't care where he comes from if he will just bring peace.

So the first half of the Tribulation, a period of three and a half years, I think will be a time of peace, a false peace by the Antichrist. They are going to have a real summit conference in that day. The Antichrist will be there, and whoever is ruling Russia at that time will participate. The first one to break the peace treaty will be Russia because in the middle of the Great Tribulation there begins the war of Armageddon, a campaign of three and a half years. It will be Russia that first comes down against little Israel. *At that time I believe that Russia will catch the world off balance because she has made the world believe that she is interested in peace.* There will be no hope of Israel's survival, but God will intervene with some great convulsion of nature when judgment comes down upon this invading horde.

Now that's the beginning of Armageddon—not the *battle* of Armageddon—you think of a battle being fought in a day or two, maybe a week or two; nowhere in the Bible is it called the battle of Armageddon. It is a campaign. It is the *war* of Armageddon. And it apparently lasts for the final part of the Great Tribulation period. It appears that Russia must go down in defeat in order for Antichrist to become a world ruler. And Antichrist *will* become a world ruler. The thirteenth chapter of Revelation makes it clear that the entire world is to *worship* him and go after him.

Russia, therefore, must go down against Israel. How will they go down? Well, God makes it very clear how He intends to manipulate them. Notice this:

> **And I will turn thee back, and leave but the sixth part of thee, and will cause thee to come up from the north parts, and will bring thee upon the mountains of Israel.** (Ezekiel 39:2)

It is God who will bring them "from the north" and "upon the mountains of Israel."

God says, "I will leave but the sixth part of thee." The literal translation of that would be, "I will sixth thee." Or let me give you what is probably the best translation of all: "I will afflict thee with six plagues."

Now what are these six plagues? God says when Russia comes down, there will be no deliverance for the nation Israel. Don't you know even today if Russia should move against her—unless America or some other nation would intervene—there would be no hope for that little nation? It would be absolutely exterminated. Israel would disappear from off the face of the earth. But God says that cannot happen because He will move in Israel's behalf.

> **And it shall come to pass at the same time when Gog shall come against the land of Israel, saith the Lord GOD, that my fury shall come up in my face. For in my jealousy and in the fire of my wrath have I spoken. Surely in that day there shall be a great shaking in the land of Israel.** (Ezekiel 38:18, 19)

Now listen to this language: "*And I will plead against him . . .*" or "I will enter into judgment against him with six plagues." What are they?

> **. . . With pestilence and with blood; and I will rain upon him, and upon his bands, and upon the many people that are with him, an overflowing rain, and great hailstones, fire, and brimstone.** (Ezekiel 38:22)

Pestilence, blood, overflowing rain, great hailstones, fire and brimstone. These are the six plagues. In effect, God says, "I will deal with this nation personally."

Does this remind you of something else in Scripture? Does this remind you of the record in Genesis 19, of how God intervened and dealt with Sodom and Gomorrah? These two cities of the plain had reached the place where God says that He gave them up. He sent no messenger, no prophet to Sodom and Gomorrah to warn them of impending judgment.

The apostle Paul in the first chapter of Romans says that certain individuals, certain cities, certain nations reach a certain place where God gives them up. He has no word for them at all. You mean the God of mercy? Yes, the God of mercy. You mean the God who is a Savior? Yes. He gives them up as He gave up Sodom and Gomorrah. He had absolutely no message for those cities. God says, "With fire and brimstone I am against thee, O Gog. I'm *against* this godless outfit. I will deal with them personally and will bring down this judgment upon them."

Now the very interesting thing is that although God had no message for the cities of Sodom and Gomorrah, He sent two angels into the doomed city to tell *His* man that he had to get out. God said, "As long as you are in the city, Lot, I cannot destroy it. You'll have to get out of the city." And when Lot left the city, judgment came. May I say to you—and I do not want to press this—but what a picture of a future day! God says that judgment can't come upon this world until He gets His people out. The Great Tribulation cannot come, it *cannot* come, my beloved, until God removes His people. Now I know there are people today who would argue, "But the church is in a state of apostasy, and the church *needs* judgment." I agree to all of that, and I do not know how much trouble the church (meaning the body of genuine believers) will go through before it leaves this earth. I am of the opinion there is suffering ahead for the church, but not the Great Tribulation period. On the other hand, the "make-believers" will have no part in the Rapture but will face the judgment of the Great Tribulation.

Again, will you look at Lot as recorded in Genesis 19. If you ask me, old Lot was as miserable a failure as any man I know of. And if I had only the information given in the Old Testament and you asked me, "Do you think old Lot was saved?" I'd say, "Well, personally, I don't think so. I don't think he made it." Lot was a rascal. He went down there and made his home in the city of Sodom. He invested in it. He lost all of his children—they even *married* Sodomites! You remember that the record says he went around to his sons-in-law and said to them, "Look, get out! God is going to *destroy* this city!" The sons-in-law laughed—they thought he was kidding. They probably said something like this, "You don't mean that. You are not living like a man who believes this city is going to be destroyed. You're living just like it's going to be here forever. Run on. We're not listening to you." Poor old Lot, nobody listened to him. He had no witness at all. He had lost his testimony. But he got out himself. God saved him.

My friend, God is going to take true believers out of this world. I think many of us are going to be ashamed as we stand before Christ at His coming. And I'm not sure that our friends and neighbors get very excited when they hear us say, "We believe the Lord is coming." They are saying, "You sure don't live like it. You're not living today like you believe the Lord is coming." But the Word of God says that *He is* coming. One of these days He will bring judgment upon this earth. Real judgment. Fire, if you please. That's the language of Scripture. God says, "I'll deliver My people," and He has told us that we are to look for Him. We are not looking for judgment, but we are "looking for that blessed hope, and the glorious appearing of the great God and our Saviour Jesus Christ" (Titus 2:13).

I'm not looking for Gog or Magog. I'm not looking for Antichrist to appear. But I am seeing a stage being set for Russia's move against Israel. I do not know how close we are. I see not only one sign but the multiplication of all these signs about us and believe they are setting the stage. It looks as if God is getting ready to move again in the affairs of this earth. Thank God today that He has said,

> . . . **He that heareth my word, and believeth on him that sent me, hath everlasting life, and *shall not come into judgment;* but is passed from death unto life.** (John 5:24; emphasis mine)

In our day there is no protection, no shelter, that can deliver you from the judgment that is coming except the blood of Jesus Christ. He is the only safe place in this world for any person to be.

Now God is slow at moving. Since it took Him millions of years to bait a hook, I don't think He's in any hurry today to move. Actually, I get a little impatient; I wonder why He doesn't move. But He says that He's patient, He is longsuffering, not willing that any should perish, but that all should come to a knowledge of the truth. And the reason He didn't come last night was because there were some people today who were saved. Our Lord wanted them saved. Although I do not know when He will come, I do know this: He is coming some day. And when He does, it will be too late to get out of our present-day "Sodom" for the judgment will be here.

Editor's Note: Dr. McGee preached this sermon on Russia in 1969, many years before the changes that have occurred there since 1990. However, Russia is named in Ezekiel 38 and 39 as the king of the north and will have a significant role in Bible prophecy. Also, the situation in Russia could change just as quickly again. Perhaps God has allowed a little time for the spread of the gospel in this thirsty land.

Chapter 12

ARMAGEDDON

Armageddon has caught the imagination of man. Every great war or threat of war always raises the awesome image of Armageddon. Again and again that word occurs in the literature of the world. After World War I, for instance, a motion picture was made called "The Four Horsemen of the Apocalypse," which depicted World War I as being the final war of mankind. Then, when World War II took place, the world was shocked by the blitz of Britain and then the release of the atomic bomb. Many folk said, "*This* is it—this is Armageddon."

From that day down to the present hour there has been a real uneasiness in the hearts of men about the future. A great number of books have been written by outstanding scholars in this connection. Armageddon is an event that has captured the imagination of every student of Scripture and, of course, a great many sensational things have been said about it.

To bring our subject into focus, let us consider two key passages of Scripture referring to Armageddon:

And the king shall do according to his will; and he shall exalt himself, and magnify himself above every god, and shall speak marvellous things against the God of gods, and shall prosper till the indignation be accomplished: for that that is determined shall be done.

Neither shall he regard the God of his fathers, nor the desire of women, nor regard any god: for he shall magnify himself above all. But in his estate shall he honour the God of forces: and a god whom his fathers knew not shall he honour with gold, and silver, and with precious stones, and pleasant things.

197

> Thus shall he do in the most strong holds with a strange god, whom he shall acknowledge and increase with glory: and he shall cause them to rule over many, and shall divide the land for gain.
>
> And at the time of the end shall the king of the south push at him: and the king of the north shall come against him like a whirlwind, with chariots, and with horsemen, and with many ships; and he shall enter into the countries, and shall overflow and pass over. He shall enter also into the glorious land, and many countries shall be overthrown. . . . (Daniel 11:36–41)

I shall break off the reading at this particular juncture and turn to the Book of Revelation:

> And the sixth angel sounded, and I heard a voice from the four horns of the golden altar which is before God, saying to the sixth angel which had the trumpet, Loose the four angels which are bound in the great river Euphrates. And the four angels were loosed, which were prepared for an hour, and a day, and a month, and a year, for to slay the third part of men.
>
> And the number of the army of the horsemen were two hundred thousand thousand: and I heard the number of them. And thus I saw the horses in the vision, and them that sat on them, having breastplates of fire, and of jacinth, and brimstone: and the heads of the horses were as the heads of lions; and out of their mouths issued fire and smoke and brimstone.
>
> By these three was the third part of men killed, by the fire, and by the smoke, and by the brimstone, which issued out of their mouths. For their power is in their mouth, and in their tails: for their tails were like unto serpents, and had heads, and with them they do hurt.
>
> And the rest of the men which were not killed by these plagues yet repented not of the works of their hands, that they should not worship devils, and idols of gold, and silver, and brass, and stone, and of wood: which neither can see, nor hear, nor walk: neither repented they of their murders, nor of their sorceries, nor of their fornication, nor of their thefts. (Revelation 9:13–21)

These are two rather unusual passages of Scripture dealing with our subject, the time of Armageddon.

The Word of God depicts a war in the dimensions of a real global conflict. Actually, World War I and World War II do not meet those specifications. Though they were the largest wars that have taken place in the world, they should not be called "world wars" because in World War I most of South America and most of the Orient were excluded. In World War II a few more nations were involved, especially in the Orient, but by no stretch of the imagination could it be called a *global* conflict. However, the war that is depicted in the Word of God beggars description as to its vastness, the number of nations that are engaged, the size of the armies that participate, the intensity of the conflict, and the issues that are involved in it.

The general public has a rather hazy conception of Armageddon as it is presented in the Word of God. To begin with, a world war in Europe is not Armageddon because that is not to be the location of it. There is a hazy conception and different interpretations as to the place, the time, the forces involved, and the purpose of it.

PLACE OF ARMAGEDDON

One commentator made this statement: "It is some place of a spiritual nature." Now that, my friend, is not exegesis! It doesn't tell you one thing—"some place of a spiritual nature" is even self-contradictory. The Scripture is much more definite than that.

It seems, however, that all commentators agree that Armageddon is the ultimate and final victory of God over the opposing forces of evil. Or, to put it in good old Americana, it is when our side wins. That is the way a great many folk look at Armageddon.

Now let's see what the Scriptures have to say. You may be shocked, if you don't already know, that Armageddon is mentioned only one time by name. There are many references to it, as we shall see, but the only time it is given a name is in Revelation 16:16: "And he gathered them together into a place called in the Hebrew tongue Armageddon."

Let us go back and begin at verse 12 in this very interesting section:

And the sixth angel poured out his vial upon the great river Euphrates; and the water thereof was dried up, that the way of the kings of the east might be prepared.

> And I saw three unclean spirits like frogs come out of the mouth
> of the dragon, and out of the mouth of the beast, and out of the
> mouth of the false prophet.
>
> For they are the spirits of devils, working miracles, which go
> forth unto the kings of the earth and of the whole world, to gather
> them to the battle of that great day of God Almighty.
>
> Behold, I come as a thief. Blessed is he that watcheth, and
> keepeth his garments, lest he walk naked, and they see his
> shame.
>
> And he gathered them together into a place called in the Hebrew
> tongue Armageddon. (Revelation 16:12-16)

Note the phrase in verse 14: "the battle of that great day of God
Almighty." The word *battle,* according to Dr. M. R. Vincent, an
outstanding Greek scholar, means more than a single battle; it means
war. If you want a more accurate scriptural term, it is the War of
Armageddon. It is a conflict that cannot be put in a single battle
context.

The word *Armageddon* itself means "hill of Megiddo." The Scriptures refer to the *hill* of Megiddo and to the *valley* of Megiddo and to
the *town* of Megiddo. This very famous area is the place where Josiah
was slain, the place where Saul was slain, and the place where Ahaziah
was slain. In the Book of Joshua, Megiddo is listed among the towns
taken by Israel when they came to the Promised Land. Deborah and
Barak fought at Megiddo, and Gideon fought the Midianites in this
particular area.

The Valley of Megiddo is part of the Plain of Esdraelon. The Plain
of Esdraelon is about twenty miles long and fourteen miles wide. I
have pictures that I took of it, and you can easily see across it. Also,
I visited the very interesting ruins of Solomon's stables at Megiddo.
He reconstructed Megiddo as one of his chariot towns, and that is
where he stabled his horses. They were extensive stables!

The geographical location of this area is quite interesting, for out
of Lebanon there extends what is known as the Great Rift, beginning
at the Dog River and then turning south. In that Great Rift is the
Sea of Galilee, the Jordan Valley, the Jordan River, and the Dead Sea.
Then the Rift continues on down through that area and even extends
into Africa. The armies of the great nations of the past have marched

there. At the entrance of the Dog River is what is called "the calling cards of the nations." Carved in a rock cliff are the inscriptions of the great rulers who have marched through there and left a record of their exploits. I spent an entire morning at that remarkable place. Nebuchadnezzar came through there, the Assyrian forces came through there, the armies of Egypt came through there, as did all of the other great nations and great generals. Alexander the Great penetrated the land there, which enabled him to take Asia. Napoleon came through there and declared that great plain to be the finest battlefield in the world. General Allenby came through that valley, and by knowing the topography of the land he was able, without firing a shot, to take Jerusalem from the thousand year rule of the Turks.

The final conflict, however, is not confined or localized to Megiddo or the Plain of Esdraelon. The Word of God has a great deal to say about it.

For I will gather all nations against Jerusalem to battle; and the city shall be taken, and the houses rifled, and the women ravished; and half of the city shall go forth into captivity, and the residue of the people shall not be cut off from the city.

Then shall the LORD go forth, and fight against those nations, as when he fought in the day of battle. (Zechariah 14:2, 3)

It is very important to see that the culmination of the War of Armageddon will be when the Lord Jesus Christ returns to the earth.

And his feet shall stand in that day upon the mount of Olives, which is before Jerusalem on the east, and the mount of Olives shall cleave in the midst thereof toward the east and toward the west, and there shall be a very great valley; and half of the mountain shall remove toward the north, and half of it toward the south. (Zechariah 14:4)

Remember that there is that Great Rift that runs north and south through that whole area. Now God says that when the Lord Jesus comes, the entire topography of the land will change. Instead of the valley running north and south, it will run east and west from the Mediterranean Sea on into the Dead Sea. This will be a tremendous transformation of the topography of that land!

There is more information given in the twelfth chapter of Zechariah, in which Jerusalem is mentioned twelve times and the expression "in that day" is used seven times. Let me remind you that the expression "that day" in the Old Testament is a reference to the Great Tribulation and the Millennium which is to follow it.

> **Behold, I will make Jerusalem a cup of trembling unto all the people round about, when they shall be in the siege both against Judah and against Jerusalem. And in that day will I make Jerusalem a burdensome stone for all people: all that burden themselves with it shall be cut in pieces, though all the people of the earth be gathered together against it.** (Zechariah 12:2, 3)

Now let me call your attention to something that is exceedingly strange. Although the fulfillment of this prophecy will not be until the end times, we have noted something that has been going on for years. Every nation in the history of the world that has attempted to control Jerusalem has been destroyed or has gone into decline. The day that Great Britain took the sphere of influence over the land of Israel and began to control Jerusalem—from that day to this—we have seen the decline of Great Britain from the first-rate nation of the world to the third-rate nation it is today. Personally, I do not think this is an accident. God said through Zechariah that He would "make Jerusalem a burdensome stone for all people," and I think that God wants us to keep our hands off that nation. I hope my nation will do that, by the way. A great many people think we ought to intrude in the affairs of Israel on one side or the other, but Israel is a sensitive spot on this earth as far as God is concerned.

> **In that day, saith the LORD, I will smite every horse with astonishment, and his rider with madness: and I will open mine eyes upon the house of Judah, and will smite every horse of the people with blindness.**
>
> **And the governors of Judah shall say in their heart, The inhabitants of Jerusalem shall be my strength in the LORD of hosts their God.** (Zechariah 12:4, 5)

I'll not be tedious by quoting the rest of that prophecy, but it will pay you to read the entire chapter. Not only is it fascinating, but it is a picture of a great day that is yet to come.

Another prophet, Isaiah, sheds more light on the War of Armageddon by telling us that it will extend down into the land of Edom:

> **Who is this that cometh from Edom, with dyed garments from Bozrah? this that is glorious in his apparel, travelling in the greatness of his strength? I that speak in righteousness, mighty to save.**
>
> **Wherefore art thou red in thine apparel, and thy garments like him that treadeth in the winevat? I have trodden the winepress alone; and of the people there was none with me: for I will tread them in mine anger, and trample them in my fury; and their blood shall be sprinkled upon my garments, and I will stain all my raiment.** (Isaiah 63:1-3)

Bozrah is a city of Edom, and the old interpretation of the "dyed garments" is that it pictured Christ in His crucifixion. However, it has nothing to do with His first coming because it is the blood of His *enemies* that has stained His garments, not His own blood. He is coming from the War of Armageddon, as He is the One who will end it.

In the prophecy of Joel we find that the War of Armageddon will also extend to the Valley of Jehoshaphat which is east of Jerusalem:

> **For, behold, in those days, and in that time, when I shall bring again the captivity of Judah and Jerusalem, I will also gather all nations, and will bring them down into the valley of Jehoshaphat, and will plead with them there for my people and for my heritage Israel, whom they have scattered among the nations, and parted my land.** (Joel 3:1, 2)

This reveals the fact that the War of Armageddon is not confined to one local spot but is spread over the entire Near East. Not only that, but in Ezekiel 38:9 we are told that when Russia comes down they will come down like a cloud to cover the land; so the entire land is involved:

> **Thou shalt ascend and come like a storm, thou shalt be like a cloud to cover the land, thou, and all thy bands, and many people with thee.** (Ezekiel 38:9)

TIME OF ARMAGEDDON

Into what time frame does the War of Armageddon fit? I say this very cautiously because this is a subject about which many Bible expositors disagree. I believe that we have to put the War of Armageddon into the context of the Great Tribulation period. There are fine expositors who say that it takes place *before* the Tribulation; others say it takes place *after* the Tribulation; but I can't see that it could take place any time except *during* the Great Tribulation period, and for me the Book of Revelation makes that very clear:

> **For they are the spirits of devils, working miracles, which go forth unto the kings of the earth and of the whole world, to gather them to the battle of that great day of God Almighty.** (Revelation 16:14)

Now "that great day of God Almighty" begins with the Great Tribulation period. This corresponds with the Hebrew way of reckoning days, by the way. Remember that at the creation of the earth, God marked off the creative days by saying, "The evening and the morning were the first day. . . . The evening and the morning were the second day," etc. While you and I begin a new day when the sun comes up, God begins it when the sun goes down. And the "great day of the Lord" begins in darkness, the darkness of the Great Tribulation. The prophet Joel confirms this by saying that the Day of the Lord is "a day of darkness and of gloominess, a day of clouds and of thick darkness" (Joel 2:2). Several other prophets express that same concept because they consider it rather important.

Many of us believe that in the middle of the Great Tribulation period Russia will come down into the land of Israel, and that triggers the conflict described in Ezekiel 38 and 39.

The Antichrist will come to power on the program of *peace*. Even in our day the world wants peace desperately, and it will accept anyone who would be able to bring global peace—I don't think it would care if the man came from heaven or hell. The United States has spent billions of dollars throughout the nations to try to bring peace in the world. A great many folk hang onto the United Nations with one faint hope that maybe it will bring peace. As I interpret the Scripture, for the first three and one-half years of the Tribulation the Antichrist will succeed in establishing global peace. But out of the north Russia will trigger the War of Armageddon by coming down and invading the land of Israel, according to Ezekiel 38. God will intervene on behalf of His people and will destroy the invaders:

> **And I will plead against him with pestilence and with blood; and I will rain upon him, and upon his bands, and upon the many people that are with him, an overflowing rain, and great hailstones, fire, and brimstone.** (Ezekiel 38:22)

This naturally stirs up a turmoil throughout the world. The peace that Antichrist had settled down on the world was a false peace. In the summary of these prophetic events (see Revelation 6) the rider on the white horse of peace is followed by the rider on the red horse of war.

FORCES INVOLVED IN ARMAGEDDON

A great many forces are involved. All nations are going to march against Jerusalem. Let me quote Revelation 16:14 again:

> **For they are the spirits of demons, working miracles, which go forth unto the kings of the earth and of the whole world, to gather them to the battle of that great day of God Almighty.** (Revelation 16:14)

The armed forces of every nation of the world will march against Jerusalem. There will be no help for the people of Israel in that day. In our day we have seen them look to Russia and get no help there, and they have looked to other nations and have been turned down. May I say to you that in that future day they will look to the north, the east, the south, the west and find no help in any direction. Then they will have to look *up* for the first time.

The thing that makes the War of Armageddon brand new, different from anything yet that has happened on this earth, are the forces that come out of the East. This is *new*. The Orient has not been involved except in World War II, and we did not fight them in the West—we fought them in the Pacific. Japan did not move out of the East into the West at all; she made no motion in that direction.

The thing that makes this extremely interesting is that the Book of Revelation says that this is something that will take place in that day. Notice the ninth chapter of Revelation again:

And the sixth angel sounded, and I heard a voice from the four horns of the golden altar which is before God, saying to the sixth angel which had the trumpet, Loose the four angels which are bound in the great river Euphrates. (Revelation 9:13, 14)

That river has been a *boundary*. In fact, the meaning of the name *Hebrew* is "the man from the other side." Abraham is called a Hebrew in Genesis 14:13, which means he came from the other side of the Euphrates River. That has been the boundary between the East and the West. If Kipling was accurate, "East is East and West is West, and never the twain shall meet," the Euphrates River has been the separating point. Now God says He is going to pull the rug out and is going to let the hosts out of the East march beyond the Euphrates for the first time.

Note Revelation 16:12. "And the sixth angel poured out his vial upon the great river Euphrates; and the water thereof was dried up, that the way of the kings of the east might be prepared." That's the white man's dilemma today, I can assure you, because in that area is the majority of the population of the world. You put India and China together and let them march out there before us, and you will see that the white man is outnumbered. The East has never moved so far into the West. Oh, Genghis Khan came, Solomon came, but they were stopped. Islam attempted to come up into Europe, but Charles Martel stopped it. They also attempted to come through Australia and were stopped there. But the Orient so far has never yet moved. Why? Well, I don't know. Napoleon said that China was a sleeping giant, and God pity the generation that wakes it up. Well, we have waked it up. And out of the Orient will pour these multitudes in this final conflagration. May I say to you, it is breathtaking to comprehend.

Let me turn to the eleventh chapter of the Book of Daniel and lift out three verses here:

And at the time of the end [not the end of the time but the time of the end, meaning the Great Tribulation period] **shall the king of the south push at him: and the king of the north shall come against him like a whirlwind, with chariots, and with horsemen,**

and with many ships; and he shall enter into the countries, and shall overflow and pass over.

He shall enter also into the glorious land [that's Palestine], **and many countries shall be overthrown. . . . But tidings out of the east and out of the north shall trouble him** [that's Antichrist who is troubled by this gigantic movement out of the East]: **therefore he shall go forth with great fury to destroy, and utterly to make away many.** (Daniel 11:40, 41, 44)

We find marching at this time something that actually is tremendous. They're marching from every direction against Jerusalem. I am not at this point going to attempt to fill in details. It's breathtaking to begin with, and you may say this is oversimplification to leave it like this, but I'm going to leave it. I'd rather do that than to do what was done a number of years ago. A man of God, a man whom I respect, an excellent preacher, went out on a limb in prophecy. He identified the king of the south as Great Britain and named Mussolini as Antichrist! That sounds absurd in our day. And that's the danger of trying to nail down specifics, especially in a day when we are not told to try to figure out all the details. Let's keep in mind that the true believer is not looking for the battle or the War of Armageddon or for the time of Armageddon. We are "looking for that blessed hope, and the glorious appearing of the great God and our Saviour Jesus Christ" (Titus 2:13). I'll leave it at that particular juncture.

PURPOSE OF ARMAGEDDON

The War of Armageddon is, first of all, a great rebellion against God. Consider this language:

And they worshipped the dragon [Satan] **which gave power unto the beast** [Antichrist]: **and they worshipped the beast, saying, Who is like unto the beast? who is able to make war with him? And there was given unto him a mouth speaking great things and blasphemies; and power was given unto him to continue forty and two months.** (Revelation 13:4, 5)

Forty-two months is the last half of the Great Tribulation period. During that period Antichrist is a world dictator, and it is the worst period the world has ever seen.

And he opened his mouth in blasphemy against God, to blaspheme his name, and his tabernacle, and them that dwell in heaven.

And it was given unto him to make war with the saints, and to overcome them: and power was given him over all kindreds, and tongues, and nations.

And all that dwell upon the earth shall worship him, whose names are not written in the book of life of the Lamb slain from the foundation of the world.

If any man have an ear, let him hear. (Revelation 13:6–9)

And then he goes on to say:

He that leadeth into captivity shall go into captivity: he that killeth with the sword must be killed with the sword. . . . (Revelation 13:10)

The message to God's people who remain on the earth in that day (God have mercy on them!) is not to resist—this is Satan's day. God is taking His hands off for this brief period of time. This is hell's day on the earth, because God will let Satan have that. It's a rebellion against God. The rebellion of man began as just a little pimple on the surface in the Garden of Eden. Now the sin of man leads to the man of sin and to humanity's great running sore of rebellion against Almighty God.

During that period they are going to try to exterminate every vestige of God on the earth. They are going to drive Him from His universe if they can. Naturally, they are going to come against the city that has represented God down through the ages. And at this particular time there will be 144,000 witnesses from the tribes of Israel. The church (meaning every true believer of the church age) is gone. The church will have been caught up to meet the Lord in the air and will be with Him in heaven during this period. On the earth there will be these witnesses, and their headquarters will be Jerusalem. So, for those men from every quarter who want to get rid of God, the starting place will be Jerusalem, of course, and the target will be those who are witnessing for Him. If they can destroy the witnesses, they will have gotten rid of God on the earth. By the way, that's exactly what multitudes are attempting to do even at this very moment.

Now we may not be able to pinpoint the beginning or the course of Armageddon, but we sure know how it's going to end.

END OF ARMAGEDDON

And I saw heaven opened, and behold a white horse; and he that sat upon him was called Faithful and True, and in righteousness he doth judge and make war.

His eyes were as a flame of fire, and on his head were many crowns; and he had a name written, that no man knew, but he himself.

And he was clothed with a vesture dipped in blood: and his name is called The Word of God. And the armies which were in heaven followed him upon white horses, clothed in fine linen, white and clean.

And out of his mouth goeth a sharp sword, that with it he should smite the nations: and he shall rule them with a rod of iron: and he treadeth the winepress of the fierceness and wrath of Almighty God.

And he hath on his vesture and on his thigh a name written, KING OF KINGS, AND LORD OF LORDS. (Revelation 19:11–16)

This gathers up all the prophecies that tell about all nations being gathered against Jerusalem. Christ is coming to the earth. He is coming to put down the rebellion that is here on this earth. One of the purposes of His coming and one of the reasons that Armageddon must take place is that there is rebellion in the heart of man today. Rebellion is actually being held back a great deal, although it may not seem like it. The Spirit of God is hindering evil, but when He is removed for that brief Great Tribulation period, the rebellion will break out on this earth in a tremendous way.

A former president of the United Nations General Assembly, Dr. Charles Malek, a Christian from Lebanon, made this statement:

> If I were asked to choose between the dialectical materialism of the Soviet and the practiced commercialism of the West, I'm not sure

I would choose the Western brand. . . . We have lost the sense of the eternal battle raging between Christ and the devil.

And Armageddon is the consummation of that rebellion. Christ's return to the earth brings it to a conclusion. We have lost the sense of there being a struggle going on in the world today. However, the pitched battle between light and darkness, between right and wrong, between God and Satan, between that which is good and right and that which is evil and wrong will culminate in this tremendous War of Armageddon.

Christ is going to put down this rebellion that is in the heart of man. It is quite interesting to note the men who have led in rebellion and their final reaction. Let me give you a remarkable quotation from George Bernard Shaw that is rarely used. Near the end of his life he wrote an article entitled "Too True to be Good" which contains this paragraph:

> The science to which I pinned my faith is bankrupt. Its counsels, which should have established the millennium, have led directly to the suicide of Europe. I believed them once. In their name I helped to destroy the faith of millions of worshipers in the temples of a thousand creeds, and now they look at me and witness the great tragedy of an atheist who has lost his faith.

How tremendous!

Oh, my friend, the battle between light and darkness has been and is raging, but it seems that Christians are asleep. There is a war, there is a conflict, and many of us have run for cover. Let me quote from Bertrand Russell who wrote in the *Atlantic Monthly* way back in 1951:

> Before this century ends, unless something unforeseeable occurs, one of three possibilities will have been realized. The end of human life, perhaps of all life on our planet. Second, a reversion to barbarism after a catastrophic demonization of the population of the globe. Third, a unification of the world under a single government.

He called it all unforeseeable, and to him it was, but he sensed what was coming. Scripture teaches that one world government is coming, and it will be as godless as it possibly can be. But Christ is coming to put down rebellion. You see, Armageddon is necessary.

The second reason Christ is coming is to get glory to His name.

He is going to declare to a rebellious and Christ-rejecting world that He is God and that He is holy! And I say reverently that it is about time He is doing it, because the world has about forgotten Him. Often I think of a line from the New York play of many years ago entitled "Green Pastures." The man who portrayed God said something like this, "As I look down at the earth, it looks like my children done forgot all about me." Certainly He is not being given the glory due Him. Rather, He is being blasphemed in every way possible in my own country as well as throughout the world.

Mankind needs to be reminded that God created this earth and made it a wonderful home for human beings. Who would want a home on the moon—or on any other planet out there in space? A fine looking fellow many years ago gave me a deed to a lot on the moon! He really did! Friend, I have that lot up for sale today, and I'll be very happy to make you a good price. In our exploration of space we have not found in this vast universe another place where human beings live. Yet here on this earth they are in rebellion against their Creator! If I were God (forgive me for saying it—I don't mean to be irreverent) I would look over this great universe, populated with created intelligences who praise My name, and when I would see little men down there lifting their midget fists against Me, I'd lean over the battlements of heaven and say, "I'm through with you—pooof!" I'd blow them out of existence!

But, my friend, thank God He is not doing that. He *loves* this little earth. He *loves* the human family. He loves us to the extent that He gave His Son to die for us down here! He is patiently dealing with us, but He must get glory to Himself.

Why does God permit Russia to come down against His people? And why does God destroy the enemy? This is not senseless. Listen to God's reason:

> **And thou shalt come up against my people of Israel, as a cloud to cover the land; it shall be in the latter days, and I will bring thee against my land, that the heathen [the Gentiles] may know me, when I shall be sanctified in thee, O Gog, before their eyes.**
> (Ezekiel 38:16)

Russia's godless leaders have been blaspheming God for years, and people ask, "How do they get by with it?" I remember as a boy when I swiped my first watermelon. I actually thought that lightning would come out of heaven and strike me dead. But, you know, after you do that about half a dozen times, you come to the conclusion that God is not going to do anything about it. That is the feeling of mankind at the present moment. They think that God is not going to do anything about their rebellion. God's name is being blasphemed, and God is going to get glory to Himself. Listen to Him again:

> **So will I make my holy name known in the midst of my people Israel; and I will not let them pollute my holy name any more: and the heathen shall know that I am the LORD, the Holy One in Israel.** (Ezekiel 39:7)

He hasn't done that yet, but He is going to do it. This world must know that He is *God*, that He is *holy*, but that He is also the *Savior*.

Now, I conclude with this question: How else but by force should God put down mankind's rebellion? If you are one who likes to criticize God for what He does, how do *you* think He ought to do it?

Suppose that Jesus came back to this earth tomorrow, like He came some two thousand years ago, the man of Galilee, the carpenter of Nazareth, the gentle Jesus. Suppose He goes to the Kremlin, knocks at the door and says to the man in charge, "I'm Jesus. I'm here to take over." Do you think they would say, "Wonderful, we've been waiting for You!"? No, more likely they would put Him before a firing squad in the morning. How do you think He could take over Russia today? He would have to break them with a rod of iron, would He not? Suppose He goes to France. Would they turn over the reins of government to Him? Suppose He goes to Rome. Not long ago I went over the Tiber and listened to a man speak. Although I could not understand what he was saying, I was told that he was telling the world how they ought to do it. Suppose Jesus knocks on the door of the Vatican. The man with the long garment would come to the door, and the Lord Jesus would say, "I'm here to take over." What do you think he would say? I think he would say, "Now look, You've come a little too soon. I am doing so well that I don't really need You." Suppose He comes to the United States and stops by the Democratic headquarters or the Republican headquarters and says, "I am here to take over." I am sure they would say, "We have all our candidates for the next presidential campaign; we don't need You." Suppose He comes to the World Council of Churches today and says to Protestant-ism, "I'm here!" Would they receive Him? Perhaps you think they would. Then why don't they receive Him today? My friend, when He comes the second time He will come exactly as He said—"Thou shalt break them with a rod of iron; thou shalt dash them in pieces like a potter's vessel" (Psalm 2:9).

He is a potentate, a despot. When a despot comes to power, he bowls over all opposition. Whether you like it or not, Jesus Christ will be the dictator on this earth someday. But, my friend, when He is, He will be a benevolent, wonderful dictator, and the earth will be a safe and good place to live. That is the plan in the mind of God. He has a glorious purpose for this earth. He is not going to turn it over to Satan with his minions and to evil men. The Lord Jesus is going to take it back to Himself and rule on this earth as King of kings and Lord of lords. He is the Good Shepherd who has given His life for His sheep. The Lord is my Shepherd; His rod and His staff they comfort me. That rod will someday break down all opposi-tion. That is a great comfort to us who are His own.

But if you are not going to yield to Him now, you will in that day when "at the name of Jesus every knee should bow, of things in heaven, and things in earth, and things under the earth; and . . . every tongue should confess that Jesus Christ is Lord, to the glory of God the Father" (Philippians 2:10, 11).

This is a day when God is not moving to put down rebellion. I am very frank to say that He is permitting it to escalate. Do you know why? It is because He is patient, longsuffering, not willing that any should perish, but that all might come to the knowledge of the truth.

Chapter 13

THE MILLENNIUM
According to Isaiah

What is the Millennium?

Where is the Millennium?

When is the Millennium?

Who establishes the Millennium? And why is the Millennium?

Beginning with Isaiah and continuing through the Old Testament, there is a section of Scripture which is called the prophetic portion of the Bible. Although the predictive element bulks large in this section, the prophets were more than foretellers. Actually, God raised up these men in a decadent day when both priest and king had failed.

Isaiah and all the Old Testament prophets were extremely nationalistic. They rebuked sin in high as well as low places. They warned the nation. They pleaded with a proud people to humble themselves and return to God. Fire and tears were mingled in their message, which was not one of doom and gloom alone, for they saw the Day of the Lord and the glory to follow. All of them looked through the darkness to the dawn of a new day. In the night of sin they saw the light of a coming Savior and Sovereign; they saw the Millennial Kingdom coming in all its fullness. We must understand their message before we can correctly interpret the Kingdom in the New Testament. The correct perspective of the Kingdom must be gained through the eyes of the Old Testament prophets.

We shall confine our glimpse into the Millennium through the eyes of Isaiah, although throughout the pages of Scripture and especially in the Prophets, there is further information regarding this great subject.

Millennium. Where do we get the word? What does it mean? It is like several other important words that are essential for our understanding of the Bible but which do not actually appear in it. The word *millennium* does not appear in the Bible but words that mean millennium do appear repeatedly.

The word *millennium* comes from two Latin words: *mille*, meaning "one thousand," and *annus*, meaning "years." A millennium is one thousand years. In the Greek, the word used is *chilia*. You'll hear that term used by some theologians, and they are always coming up with words so that most people don't know what they're talking about! When theologians talk about chiliaism and millennialism, they are talking about the same event. Both words mean a thousand years, and they have to do with the thousand-year reign of Christ here upon this earth which is mentioned in chapter 20 of the Book of Revelation. That chapter is the only place that gives the duration of the Kingdom, and the phrase "thousand years" occurs there six times. However, the theme of the thousand-year Kingdom which is coming on the earth is a great subject of Scripture.

GOD'S MAGNIFICENT PROGRAM

Actually, the Millennium is merely one phase of God's eternal Kingdom; that is, the "theocratic Kingdom," as Dr. George N. H. Peters calls it—and I like that term so much better. Actually, everything that *has* happened in history, that *is* happening in our day, and *will* happen in the future is all part of God's program in setting up His Kingdom here upon this earth.

Now the Millennium, one feature of God's eternal Kingdom, is a special dispensation that is yet future. The Millennial Kingdom will come to an end, and the eternal Kingdom will begin. That is stated clearly in Scripture. Over in 1 Corinthians 15, Paul gives the order of events, beginning with the resurrection of Christ in verse 20, then he says that those who are Christ's will be raised at His coming.

But every man in his own order: Christ the firstfruits; afterward they that are Christ's at His coming. (1 Corinthians 15:23)

After that, "Then cometh the end." The end of what? The world? No. The Bible does not teach the end of the world. This world that we live in will not come to an end but is going into eternity. Yes, it's to be renovated, made *new*, but it is going into eternity.

> **Then cometh the end, when he shall have delivered up the Kingdom to God, even the Father . . .**

There does come a time when this thousand-year reign will be delivered up to God the Father,

> **. . . when he [Christ] shall have put down all rule and all authority and power. For he must reign, till he hath put all enemies under his feet.** (1 Corinthians 15:24, 25)

Christ is coming into this world someday, and He will come in with great judgment. He will set up His thousand-year reign here upon this earth. And during that thousand-year reign, He will accomplish a purpose. Today He is accomplishing His purpose of calling a people out of this world unto Himself. During the millennial reign He's going to bring this earth under His rule. He will rule with a rod of iron. Those who oppose Him will be dashed in pieces like a potter's vessel. That is going to be a time when Christ will rule arbitrarily upon this earth.

Now let me make this very clear. We have not yet seen a real dictator rule. You wait till Christ rules. When He rules on this earth a bird won't even cheep, a rooster won't crow and a man won't open his mouth without His permission. That'll be a time when His will at last will be done on this earth. And, my friend, even the Millennium would be a hell for any man who is in rebellion against God.

The Bible tells us that there will be some in rebellion, that rebellion breaks out during the Millennium. Christ will judge it immediately because He is going to bring this earth back under the rule of God. That is God's purpose for the earth.

> **For he must reign, till he hath put all enemies under his feet. The last enemy that shall be destroyed is death. For he hath put all things under his feet. But when he saith all things are put under him, it is manifest that he is excepted, which did put all things under him. And when all things shall be subdued unto him, then shall the Son also himself be subject unto him that put all things under him, that God may be all in all.** (1 Corinthians 15:25–28)

Now what does that mean? It means simply this: The Lord Jesus will come to this earth, reign one thousand years, and bring this earth back under the rule of God. When this is accomplished, I take it that He will return back to His place in the Godhead. And this earth then will become what God intended it to be throughout the eternal ages of the future. This is the picture that the Scripture presents.

All the way through the Old Testament, and especially in the Prophets, this Kingdom, this thousand-year reign of Christ on the earth, is set before us. In fact, there is more Scripture—this may surprise you—on this subject than on any other subject in the Bible. The prophets had more to say about this coming Kingdom than anything else. It was their theme song. They sound like a stuck record, saying over and over that the King is coming, the Kingdom is coming, and great blessings will be on this earth.

Now, the prophets spoke of it as coming in the future. And from where you and I are today, it is still future. The conditions predicted have never been fulfilled in the past, and they are not being fulfilled yet, as we shall see.

The Kingdom of God will *not* be established by man's efforts, by human ability. The church is not building the Kingdom today, yet it is geared into a program that will see the coming of the Kingdom. It's not our business to build a Kingdom. This is one reason that I am thankful today to be out of the denomination I was raised in. I used to go to meetings in which there were always brethren building the Kingdom—and you ought to have seen the cheap little "chicken-coop" that we built! Yet we were always talking about building the Kingdom. My friend, when God is ready to set up His Kingdom, He won't need help from any church. In fact, He is going to remove His true church out of the world before He establishes His Kingdom here upon the earth. That is His plan, that is His program, if you please.

Now the Kingdom that we are looking at in these few pages will be confined to what Isaiah had to say on this subject. And believe me, he had a great deal to say about it.

THE KINGDOM OF HEAVEN

This Kingdom—and this is important for you to understand—is the same as we find in the New Testament where it is called the Kingdom of Heaven. That was the message John the Baptist began with: "Repent ye: for the kingdom of heaven is at hand" (Matthew 3:2). When the Lord Jesus began His ministry, He said the same thing.

Now neither John nor the Lord Jesus explained what that phrase meant. That seems to indicate to me that the only ones who miss this are theologians and seminary professors today who don't seem to know what's happening in this world. They try to make something very obtuse, something esoteric out of the Kingdom of Heaven. When you ask one of them what the Kingdom of Heaven is, he bats his eyes, and you think he's going off into a trance, and that it is something that only he and his little clique know. May I say to you that the *common* people who heard John the Baptist and the Lord Jesus understood what they were talking about. The Kingdom we are talking about is just what the Old Testament has been talking about: the Millennial Kingdom coming on the earth.

The Kingdom of Heaven is just simply this: the rule of the Heavens over the earth. When Heaven rules over this earth on which we live, we will have the Kingdom of Heaven condition.

Now look, I had to go to seminary to learn that! But that's all it means. And it's a shame to have to spend years in seminary and just make the discovery that the reign of the Heavens over the earth is all the Kingdom of Heaven can *possibly* mean.

The Millennium will be the time when there will be the full manifestation of the glory, the power and the will of God over this earth. And all agree that this is not in evidence today. You'll not have hospitals, you'll not have graveyards, you'll not have the suffering nor broken hearts and lives when Christ is reigning on this earth. And it's an insult to my Lord to say that the Kingdom of Heaven is being built today and is in existence on this earth. When He is reigning you won't have the tragedy that presently exists throughout the world.

Now we, of course, ask these questions. Why must we have tragedies? God has to vindicate Himself. Why is it that the earth is in such a deplorable condition? Why isn't God reigning on this earth now? Isaiah tells us how it all began. This is where *sin* began, and Isaiah deals with this subject.

WHERE SIN BEGAN

In Isaiah 14:12 the prophet tells about the fall of God's highest creature and that this creature led a rebellion against God to set up a kingdom that was opposed to God. Here is the revelation concerning it, and it is startling indeed.

How art thou fallen from heaven, O Lucifer, son of the morning! how art thou cut down to the ground, which didst weaken the nations! (Isaiah 14:12)

The prophecy of Isaiah goes back into the past and then looks on into the future concerning this creature who is yet to be judged and brought down. Who is this creature that rebelled against God? He is the highest creature God ever created, Lucifer. We know him today as Satan and as the Devil. He has many different names. Our Lord even called him a liar and a murderer.

This highest of God's creatures, according to Ezekiel 28, was "full of wisdom and perfect in beauty." And Satan hasn't lost that beauty. If you could see him today, you would not see an ugly, fearsome being. He would be most attractive. He disguises himself as an angel of light, and his ministers as preachers of righteousness, according to 2 Corinthians 11:14, 15. I do not know why those of us who are gospel preachers can't be handsome, tall, robust fellows who speak with basso profundo voices. Most of us are an unattractive lot. But have you ever noticed Satan's preachers? I heard Judge Rutherford when I was a boy. I want to tell you, he was impressive. I've heard many others who are the leaders of cults, and they all look like ministers of righteousness. Satan, if you could see him today, would be the most beautiful creature you have ever seen. God created him that way.

Now what was it he did? This significant passage refers to the beginning of *sin* in the universe:

For thou hast said in thine heart, I will ascend into heaven, I will exalt my throne above the stars of God: I will sit also upon the mount of the congregation, in the sides of the north: I will ascend above the heights of the clouds; I will be like the most High. (Isaiah 14:13, 14)

You see, Satan does not want to be unlike God, he wants to be like God. When Lucifer, son of the morning, said, "I will," sin entered the universe.

Way back in the past, and we're told practically nothing about this in the Bible, something happened to this earth. Apparently, it happened long before man got here. If you are in Southern California, you may have taken a trip over the Ridge Route and have gone down through that area where you see those great big rocks along the side of the highway. I said to a friend of mine who is a geologist, "When do you think that took place?" and he answered, "Oh, two or three million years ago."

And while out in Arizona another friend of mine, again a geologist with Cal Tech, said, "You want to see what's on top of that ridge?" He took his foot and kicked out the topsoil, and you know what was under that, what made the ridge? A petrified log!

I said, "My there must have been a forest here."

"No, there never was a forest here. These floated in here."

"*Floated* here—in this desert?"

"Yes."

"From where?"

"They floated in from California."

"Floated in from California! How long ago was that?"

"About two hundred fifty to three hundred thousand years ago."

All of this took place before man got to this earth. What does that mean? It means that a great catastrophe took place on this earth. When? The view that I favor is that this catastrophe took place between verses 1 and 2 of the Genesis account, and the earth became without form, and void. Also, I think that the catastrophe was connected with the fall of Lucifer, who became Satan, as we know him today. However, God has given us no details in the first chapter of Genesis.

In the third chapter of Genesis God does tell us that Satan had access to this earth and that he approached our first parents with the same temptations that had affected him—the desire to "be as gods, knowing good and evil."

This is the sin of man right now. This is our problem today. In Isaiah 53:6 he says, "All we like sheep have gone astray; we have turned every one to *his own way*"—those are the three words that tell what's wrong with all of us. You and I want our own way. Have you ever noticed how the little baby in the crib gets red in the face and yells and then holds his breath? You think he's going to die! Do you know why he does that? Because he wants *you to pick him up*. He wants *his* way. It's born in us. We have a nature that says, "We want our way." We don't want God's way. Mankind is in rebellion against God.

God says that He is going to establish His Kingdom on this earth. *His* way is going to prevail some day. That is the meaning of the rule of the Heavens over this earth.

Sin entered the universe when Satan rebelled. Then man rebelled against God—and continues to do so.

God's *process* by which the Lord Jesus will come to the throne—that is, the establishing of the Kingdom here upon this earth and the Millennial Kingdom—is part of the great theocratic Kingdom of God.

I want to hit only some high points. You may have noted that the difference today in eschatology—that is, the difference in interpretation of future things—is always centered around the Millennium. This controversy is not actually around the person of Christ, but rather centers around the Millennium. There is postmillennialism which holds that the church or Christian agencies will correct every evil in the world until Christ has a "spiritual reign" for a thousand years. And not until after that would He return in person to reign over the earth. However two world wars, a worldwide depression and then the atomic bomb put the postmillennialists out of business.

A new group has come up known as amillennialists. They were not much in evidence when I started in the ministry, but by the time I got to seminary they were very much in the fore. In fact, in seminary I was taught the amillennial position, which is that there will be no Millennium other than that which is in progress at the present time! It is because I studied the amillennial position in seminary that I am a premillennialist today. Years ago a man came up to Dr. Beaver and declared, "Dr. Beaver, I am not a postmillennialist and I'm not a premillenialist." Dr. Beaver looked at him and said, "That's pre-*post*erous." And to my judgment amillennialism is a preposterous position.

Now, premillennialism holds the position that in the present age, evil will increase and end in judgment at the second coming of Christ to the earth, at which time *He* will set up His Kingdom and reign in righteousness for one thousand years.

These are the three views of eschatology today, and they all center around the Millennium.

The amillenialist makes the charge against those of us who are premillennial that we believe in only a materialistic kingdom with physical blessings in the future. In fact, a professor at Westminster Seminary has said that what we believe in is a *worldly* kingdom. That is actually not true. I want to answer this, confining our answers at this time solely to the Book of Isaiah, and cite some of the spiritual blessings of the Kingdom that are yet to come.

SPIRITUAL BLESSINGS OF THE MILLENNIUM

Peace

This is one of those wonderful passages of Scripture:

And he shall judge among the nations, and shall rebuke many people: and they shall beat their swords into plowshares, and their spears into pruninghooks: nation shall not lift up sword against nation, neither shall they learn war any more. (Isaiah 2:4)

This will not be experienced until the Millennium. Only then will there be world peace. Until then, you'd better keep your powder dry. You'd better not believe that aggressive superpowers will quit filling their arsenals, because they have lied before and are very capable of doing that sort of thing.

But the day is coming when there *will* be peace. That peace will come when the Prince of Peace rules on this earth. In that day you can beat swords into plowshares. Peace is a great spiritual blessing that is yet in the future.

Righteousness

And the work of righteousness shall be peace; and the effect of righteousness quietness and assurance for ever. (Isaiah 32:17)

In Psalm 85 it says, "Righteousness and peace have kissed each other"—they aren't even on speaking terms today! One of the reasons we cannot have peace on this earth is because we do not have righteousness. However, righteousness will characterize the reign of Christ during the Millennium.

Holiness

> **And it shall come to pass, that he that is left in Zion, and he that remaineth in Jerusalem, shall be called holy, even every one that is written among the living in Jerusalem.** (Isaiah 4:3)

Holiness is one of the things that characterizes the Millennium. The word *holiness* literally means separation, a thing set apart. A believer's spiritual birth, his salvation, sets him apart as holy—that is, separated unto God. But our salvation is in three tenses: I have been saved; I am being saved; and I shall be saved.

Our problem comes in the second tense: "I am being saved." We are told, "Work out your own salvation with fear and trembling. For it is God which worketh in you both to will and to do of his good pleasure" (Philippians 2:12, 13). Yet the believer still has that old sinful nature, and the idea that we can get rid of it in this life is a tragic mistake. "If we say that we have no sin, we deceive ourselves, and the truth is not in us" (1 John 1:8).

Not until we go to be with Christ will we experience the final stage of our salvation. ". . . We know that, when he shall appear, we shall be like him; for we shall see him as he is" (1 John 3:2). Now, my friend, let's not beat around the bush about these things. We are not going to see holiness on this earth until Jesus Christ rules. Believe me, it's going to be holy when He is ruling during the Millennium.

Glory

Not only does Isaiah mention peace, righteousness and holiness, but we're also told here that glory is another spiritual blessing during the Millennium.

> **When the Lord shall have washed away the filth of the daughters of Zion, and shall have purged the blood of Jerusalem from the midst thereof by the spirit of judgment, and by the spirit of burning. And the LORD will create upon every dwelling place of mount Zion, and upon her assemblies, a cloud and smoke by**

day, and the shining of a flaming fire by night: for upon all the glory shall be a defence. (Isaiah 4:4, 5)

Glory is another spiritual blessing during the Millennium.

Joy

Therefore with joy shall ye draw water out of the wells of salvation. And in that day shall ye say, Praise the LORD, call upon his name, declare his doings among the people, make mention that his name is exalted. (Isaiah 12:3, 4)

The phrase "in that day" in Isaiah and in all the Prophets is referring to the Kingdom, to the Millennial Kingdom. "And in that day shall ye say, Praise the LORD," and when *you* say "Praise the Lord" in your church in that day, people won't look at you as if something is wrong. You can say, "Praise the LORD, call upon his name, declare his doings among the people, make mention that his name is exalted!"

Sing unto the LORD; for he hath done excellent things: this is known in all the earth. (Isaiah 12:5)

Joy. That's one of the blessings that will characterize the Millennium. Joy does not characterize the world today. Instead there is dissatisfaction, loneliness, sorrow and heartbreak. But just imagine being on this earth when all is joyful, and everyone is filled with joy!

Comfort

There is also comfort in this same chapter, will you notice it:

And in that day thou shalt say, O LORD, I will praise thee: though thou wast angry with me, thine anger is turned away, and thou comfortedst me. Behold, God is my salvation; I will trust, and not be afraid: for the LORD JEHOVAH is my strength and my song; he also is become my salvation. (Isaiah 12:1, 2)

Full Knowledge

Now here is another wonderful feature: there will be *full knowledge* in the Kingdom. Today we "see through a glass darkly; but then face to face: now I know in part, but then shall I know even as also I am known" (1 Corinthians 13:12)—full knowledge.

> And there shall come forth a rod out of the stem of Jesse, and a Branch shall grow out of his roots: and the spirit of the LORD shall rest upon him, the spirit of wisdom and understanding . . . the spirit of knowledge and of the fear of the LORD. (Isaiah 11:1, 2)

There will be knowledge in that day.

Instruction

Also it's going to be a time of instruction, a time when folks are going to go to school. Right now a great many young people are going away to college, going away to school, trying to learn something—and maybe some of them will. But ours is a day when a great many people are interested in knowledge. During the Millennium there will be great knowledge, and there'll be a great deal of instruction. I'm hoping the Lord will let me teach a class down on this earth, probably the kindergarten class, during the Millennium. I enjoy teaching today and I think I'll enjoy it more in that day.

> And it shall come to pass in the last days, that the mountain of the LORD's house shall be established in the top of the mountains, and shall be exalted above the hills; and all nations shall flow unto it. And many people shall go and say, Come ye, and let us go up to the mountain of the LORD, to the house of the God of Jacob; and he will teach us of his ways, and we will walk in his paths: for out of Zion shall go forth the law, and the word of the LORD from Jerusalem. (Isaiah 2:2, 3)

There will be a great hunger and thirst for God, folks wanting to know about God. We are living in a day when men want to know about missiles, about electronics. But in that day there will be a great hunger and thirst after God—people wanting to know *Him*, wanting to know His Word.

I sure am looking forward to that!

Every now and then I see that eagerness to know God's Word. I think my Thursday night Bible study congregation represented a group like that. I also get a glimpse of it in letters I read from our radio listeners. When I was up at a Campus Crusade conference with a bunch of college kids, I never saw kids as alert as those young people were. And then when I was out in Flagstaff with the Indians one summer, those Indian believers—my, how eager they were—they just hung around me. They let me teach for an hour and a half and still wanted to hear more. It's amazing! We see little indications of thirst for God, but just think what it will be during the Millennium. It'll be wonderful!

May I say to you, I think you ought to equip yourself down here for what you are going to do over there. This is really a training place, a staging area, where we get ready to go over on the other side. And one of these days we are going to move over. So it's time to prepare ourselves for that.

I want to mention just three or four passages that have to do especially with the Millennium. This second chapter of Isaiah has these special features. So let me go over this again and call your attention to what I omitted. These are the special features—the person, the character and the physical facts of His Kingdom.

SPECIAL FEATURES

The word that Isaiah the son of Amoz saw concerning Judah and Jerusalem. And it shall come to pass in the last days, that the mountain of the LORD's house shall be established in the top of the mountains, and shall be exalted above the hills; and all nations shall flow into it. (Isaiah 2:1, 2)

Jerusalem will become the capital of this earth in the Kingdom. Just as Babylon is to be the capital of Antichrist during the Tribulation, so Jerusalem will be the capital on the earth for the Lord Jesus Christ as the Messiah.

And many people shall go and say, Come ye, and let us go up to the mountain of the LORD, to the house of the God of Jacob; and he will teach us of his ways, and we will walk in his paths: . . .

You'll have to go there to the university, in order to learn.

. . . for out of Zion shall go forth the law, and the word of the LORD from Jerusalem. (Isaiah 2:3)

Now God names Jerusalem specifically, and this, of course, refers to the Kingdom.

> **And he shall judge among the nations, and shall rebuke many people: . . .**

This is a worldwide kingdom.

> **. . . they shall beat their swords into plowshares, and their spears into pruninghooks: nation shall not lift up sword against nation, neither shall they learn war any more.** (Isaiah 2:4)

This is one of those remarkable passages.

Then there is another remarkable passage in the eleventh chapter, and let me call attention to several things:

Person

> **And there shall come forth a rod out of the stem of Jesse, and a Branch shall grow out of his roots.** (Isaiah 11:1)

The Kingdom is never established by the church, never by an organization, never by a movement. The world will not grow into the Kingdom of Heaven. But the One who will establish the Kingdom is mentioned in this Scripture as the "rod" and the "Branch," the Messiah who is to come.

This is exactly what John the Baptist meant when he said, "The kingdom of heaven is at hand;" literally the Greek is "in your midst." The Kingdom of Heaven is in your midst because the King is here. And you can't have a kingdom without a king, any more than you can have a marriage without a bride and groom. They are essential. If I say that I officiated in a wedding, you know immediately that a bride and groom were there. There couldn't have been a wedding without them. And neither can you have a kingdom without a king. When John said, "The kingdom of heaven is at hand," he meant the King is here. It couldn't be otherwise, could it? The King had come.

Now, they rejected Him. But here the prophet is emphasizing the necessity of this One coming in the line of Jesse.

He is to come out of the stem of Jesse. Why didn't Isaiah mention David? Did Jesus come from the line of King David? Yes, but David's line had returned to peasantry by the time Jesus came. Jesse was a farmer from Bethlehem. The Lord Jesus was a carpenter from Nazareth—that's the way He was identified when He was here. The stem was of Jesse and a Branch would grow out of his roots.

Notice that the Messiah was to have the fullness of the Spirit:

And the spirit of the LORD shall rest upon him, the spirit of wisdom and understanding, the spirit of counsel and might, the spirit of knowledge and of the fear of the LORD. (Isaiah 11:2)

In John 3:34 we are told that God gave to Jesus the Spirit without measure, the fullness of the Holy Spirit.

And shall make him of quick understanding in the fear of the LORD . . . . (Isaiah 11:3)

One thing that will characterize the Kingdom is that the Lord is going to jack up the IQ of all the people. Won't that be wonderful! There will be no neurotics, no mentally retarded, no dull minds. There will be nobody in the class who will have to say, "Teacher, I didn't get that. Would you go over that again?" They will get the point immediately. I wouldn't mind having my IQ stepped up a little, and maybe you wouldn't either.

Character of Reign

Notice this as Isaiah continues:

But with righteousness shall he judge the poor, . . .

The poor have never had a square deal yet, have they? The politicians talk about all of us before election day, and then they forget us the day after election. The Lord Jesus shall judge in righteousness the poor man. Special interests and labor unions are not for the poor anymore. Capitalists have never been for the poor. Let's face it, friend, the poor man just doesn't have a chance in this world. Thank God for a King who is coming to judge in righteousness for the poor! He is the One I want to see rule on this earth. I like His platform.

. . . and reprove with equity for the meek of the earth; . . .

Meek folk. He says in Matthew 5:5 that the meek are going to inherit the earth, and they are certainly not doing it today.

. . . and he shall smite the earth with the rod of his mouth, and with the breath of his lips shall he slay the wicked. (Isaiah 11:4)

You may want to play that down, but the Word of God doesn't play it down. He will "break them with a rod of iron," according to the second Psalm. The Word of God is very specific. He intends to put down the wicked. He will make no treaty with the godless superpowers of this world. He will make no treaty with the combine of gangsters either in our own country or abroad. He intends to put them *down*— with no apology to anybody. He doesn't need their votes. He doesn't need their influence. He doesn't need their help. He intends to slay the wicked. Thank God, my friend, this earth is yet to get a square deal. And it will never get it until Christ comes. That's the reason the Millennium is quite a wonderful prospect for this earth.

And righteousness shall be the girdle of his loins, and faithfulness the girdle of his reins. (Isaiah 11:5)

Righteousness and faithfulness are two additional spiritual blessings, and they are wonderful.

PHYSICAL BLESSINGS

Now let's look at some of the physical blessings of the Kingdom.

The wolf also shall dwell with the lamb, and the leopard shall lie down with the kid; and the calf and the young lion and the fatling together; and a little child shall lead them. (Isaiah 11:6)

Apparently in the Garden of Eden there was no distinction between wild animals and domesticated animals. They were all tame. The animals would just walk right by Adam, and he named them. Then, after the fall, certain animals became wild, no longer friendly to man.

And the cow and the bear shall feed; their young ones shall lie down together: and the lion shall eat straw like the ox. (Isaiah 11:7)

A fellow came up to Dr. George Gill, a Bible teacher who had a very sharp mind, and said to him, "Doctor, that's ridiculous! Everybody knows that a carnivorous lion eats meat, not hay!" In his inimitable way, Dr. Gill said, "I'll tell you what we'll do. You make a lion; I'll make him eat hay."

If God made the lion and says he's going to eat hay, he will eat hay, my friend, and like it. This will be the Millennium.

And the sucking child shall play on the hole of the asp, and the weaned child shall put his hand on the cockatrice's den. (Isaiah 11:8)

Nothing that is poisonous will be on this earth.

They shall not hurt nor destroy in all my holy mountain: for the earth shall be full of the knowledge of the LORD, as the waters cover the sea. And in that day there shall be a root of Jesse, which shall stand for an ensign of the people; to it shall the Gentiles seek: and his rest shall be glorious. (Isaiah 11:9, 10)

Now he's going to talk about returning the Jews to their homeland:

And it shall come to pass in that day, that the Lord shall set his hand again the second time to recover the remnant of his people, which shall be left . . . .

This is the nation Israel. There can be no Millennium until Israel is back in the land. There are so many things out of socket today. The devil is in the wrong place—he goes to and fro in this earth seeking whom he may devour. He has to be in the bottomless pit during the Millennium. He's out of place today. Christ is not in His rightful place for the Millennium. He will be on the throne of David reigning over this earth. The church is out of place today—it's in this world. The church is to be with Christ in the New Jerusalem. And Israel is out of place today, her people scattered throughout the world, and they must be back in their own land. There will be no Millennium until everything gets in its place.

In that day the Lord will recover the remnant of His people, who shall be left,

. . . from Assyria and from Egypt, and from Pathros, and from Cush, and from Elan, and from Shinar, and from Hamath, and from the islands of the sea. (Isaiah 11:11)

This includes America.

> **And he shall set up an ensign for the nations, and shall assemble the outcasts of Israel, and gather together the dispersed of Judah from the four corners of the earth.** (Isaiah 11:12)

Again, this is during the Millennium which is to be established on this earth.

One more reference that has to do with the physical characteristics of the Millennium is that wonderful thirty-fifth chapter of Isaiah. Now will you note this:

> **The wilderness and the solitary place shall be glad for them; and the desert shall rejoice, and blossom as the rose. It shall blossom abundantly, and rejoice even with joy and singing: the glory of Lebanon shall be given unto it, the excellency of Carmel and Sharon, they shall see the glory of the LORD, and the excellency of our God.** (Isaiah 35:1, 2)

The desert will blossom as a rose in the Millennium. The curse that's on this earth today will be removed. I thought of this again out in Arizona as I drove from Flagstaff all the way up to Page at the Glen Canyon Dam. That is a desolate country, friend, for miles and miles. Now I think there is a beauty in the desert. It's a desolate, stark, almost an ugly beauty, yet it is beautiful. But I said to the folk traveling with me, "You know, it would be wonderful to make this trip during the Millennium. Just think—mile upon mile of roses! The desert shall blossom as the rose."

That's not all. He says something else here:

> **Strengthen ye the weak hands, and confirm the feeble knees. Say to them that are of a fearful heart, Be strong, fear not: behold, your God will come with vengeance, even God with a recompense; he will come and save you. Then the eyes of the blind shall be opened, . . .**

There'll be no blind in the Millennium.

> **. . . and the ears of the deaf shall be unstopped.** (Isaiah 35:3–5)

There will be no need for sign language to translate for those who do not hear. There will be no deaf in that day at all.

Then shall the lame man leap as an hart, and the tongue of the dumb sing. . . .

Even I will be able to sing. I want to sing a solo for you then. It may not seem like the Millennium to have to listen, but I do want to sing along with those who haven't been able to speak. "The tongue of the dumb sing."

. . . for in the wilderness shall waters break out, and streams in the desert. (Isaiah 35:6)

Now let me drop down to the final verse of this chapter:

And the ransomed of the LORD shall return, and come to Zion with songs and everlasting joy upon their heads: they shall obtain joy and gladness, and sorrow and sighing shall flee away. (Isaiah 35:10)

That is the Millennium; that is the hope of this earth. However, that is not the hope of the church. The church's hope is that one of these days we are to be caught up to meet the Lord in the air,

For if we believe that Jesus died and rose again, even so them also which sleep in Jesus will God bring with him. For this we say unto you by the word of the Lord, that we which are alive and remain unto the coming of the Lord shall not prevent them which are asleep. For the Lord himself shall descend from heaven with a shout, with the voice of the archangel, and with the trump of God: and the dead in Christ shall rise first: then we which are alive and remain shall be caught up together with them in the clouds, to meet the Lord in the air: and so shall we ever be with the Lord. (1 Thessalonians 4:14–17)

He will take us to a place that, candidly, is going to be even more wonderful than this earth, the New Jerusalem. But I think we will be able to commute back and forth. What glorious things God has planned for our future!

I wonder today if you are on the way to the New Jerusalem. Our Lord Jesus said, "I am the way, the truth, and the life: no man cometh unto the Father, but by me" (John 14:6).

Chapter 14

NEW JERUSALEM, THE ETERNAL HOME OF THE CHURCH

Let not your heart be troubled: ye believe in God, believe also in me. In my Father's house are many mansions: if it were not so, I would have told you. I go to prepare a place for you. And if I go and prepare a place for you, I will come again, and receive you unto myself; that where I am, there ye may be also. (John 14:1-3)

The fourteenth chapter of John was given by our Lord in the Upper Room, and He introduces something that is entirely new. The first part of the chapter was given to a man to cushion the shock of failure that was to come into his life. Also it was to comfort and put down the fears of this little band of apostles across whose pathway the shadow of the Cross had fallen. Sin was knocking at the door in the Upper Room, demanding its pound of flesh. These men were frightened men, and our Lord was speaking to their hearts. He begins by saying,

Let not your heart by troubled: ye believe in God, believe also in me. (John 14:1)

He is putting, as essential, faith in Himself along with faith in God—which, of course, is the thing that makes a Christian today. I was in a hospital visiting a Christian friend, and after I had prayed with him, the man who was in a bed across the room called to me, "Preacher, will you pray for me?" I went over and talked to him and asked,

"Are you a Christian?" "Well, yes, I believe in God." "That does not make you a Christian," I said, "it simply means that you are not an atheist." Then I gave him this verse, "Let not your heart be troubled: ye believe in God, believe *also* in me." Our Lord begins with His men on that plane, and He continues.

In my Father's house are many mansions: if it were not so, I would have told you. I go to prepare a place for you. (John 14:2)

Now the word *mansion* is a very unfortunate translation. It surely gives the wrong impression. I was a Presbyterian preacher for many years, and I lived in a home that the Presbyterian church calls a *manse*, a shortened form of the word *mansion*. I lived in a Presbyterian mansion—in fact, I lived, I suppose, in a half dozen of them. I moved into my first mansion when I was ordained to the ministry in Nashville, Tennessee. It was an antebellum home—that is, it was built before the Civil War. It had fourteen rooms, and they were spacious rooms! I used to say to folk that on a clear day you could see the ceiling in the living room. I was then single, and I moved into the corner of one of the rooms. Years later I drove by it and shuddered when I looked at it. I thought of this verse, "In my Father's house are many mansions," and I said, "Oh my, I don't want one of those up there!" I certainly would not want to go to heaven and find myself assigned to another mansion! And I am thankful that it does not mean that, my friend. Actually, the Greek word is *moni;* it has no reference to a great big home but means "abiding place." "In my Father's house are many abiding places."

What is the Father's house? When you go out tonight, look up into the vaulted sky above you, and you will see the Father's house. That is His house. Our Lord said, "In My Father's house are many *moni,* many abiding places, many places to live." Now I do not know this, but it is my personal opinion that God has a universe filled with created intelligences, and I do not think He has a vacancy sign out anywhere. I think all the abiding places are occupied, for abiding places are living quarters for some sort of intelligences. I do not mean to suggest that His universe is peopled with human beings—this planet has enough! God does not need any more folk like us, nor any that would compare with us. But God has other created intelligences.

In the Book of Revelation John tells us that he could not even number them when he got a look at them. They are in the Father's house.

When the two-hundred-inch mirror for the Palomar Observatory was being ground, the man who had charge of the mechanical part of the grinding was my neighbor and a very fine Christian. He would come down from Palomar every weekend, and when I would see him I would ask, "What do you see?" Every weekend I would head him off with that question, "What do you see?" Finally, one day after my usual question he wondered why I was so interested. So I told him, "You have that big eye poked into the window of my Father's house, and I want to know what you see up there."

In my Father's house are many abiding places.

He enforces this statement with,

If it were not so, I would have told you.

Then He says,

I go to prepare a place for you.

This place is different from any other in His universe—"I go to prepare a *special* place for you." It is a prepared place for prepared people. The One who was the carpenter of Nazareth down here about two thousand years ago is at this moment preparing a place up yonder for those who are His own. Have you ever wondered about that place He is preparing? Do you wonder what it is like? We are going there some day, and we shall live there eternally.

Then He makes the statement,

And if I go and prepare a place for you, I will come again, and receive you unto myself; that where I am, there ye may be also. (John 14:3)

As far as I know, this is the first time in the Word of God where it mentions that He is going to take someone off the earth out into space. You will not find that in the Old Testament at all. God did not promise anyone in the Old Testament that He would take him off this earth to a place called heaven. The hope of the Old Testament saints was that there might be a heaven down here on this earth, and that is what I understand the expression, *the Kingdom of Heaven,* to mean—

the reign of the heavens over the earth, the day when this earth becomes a heaven. That is the hope of the Old Testament.

When God called Abraham, He called him into a *land*. His promise was not that He would take him out into space but that He would give him a land. God marked it out—north, east, south, and west—put boundaries around it and said, "I am giving you this land for a permanent possession." Abraham took God so literally that when his wife Sarah died, he went to the sons of Heth and said, "I want to buy the cave of Machpelah for a burial place." Why did he want a burial place in the Promised Land? Because he expected to be raised someday from the dead there. God promised Abraham, "I will multiply thy seed as the stars of the heaven," but He never said that He would take him out to one of the stars or give him one of the stars. A heaven on earth is the hope of the Old Testament.

You find that Isaac also was buried in that land. Then you find that old Jacob, who died down in the land of Egypt, had commanded his sons, "Bury me with my fathers in the cave of Machpelah." And when he died they carried him, with a long funeral procession following, into the land of Canaan and buried him in the Promised Land. Why all of that? Because he expected to be raised from the dead in that land someday. Now, if he is to be carried away in a rapture out yonder in space, what difference would it make if he was buried in Egypt or the Promised Land, London, or Los Angeles? But it would make a lot of difference if he is to be raised from the dead in that land.

Even Joseph said, "The day will come when you will leave Egypt and return to the Promised Land. I want you to take my bones with you." Joseph died as a national hero, and his people could not have removed him from Egyptian soil. But there came a day when there arose a Pharaoh who knew not Joseph, and then the children of Israel went out; and the night they left Egypt behind them, they had with them the bones of Joseph. They were taken and interred in the Promised Land. Why? The hope is that someday they will be raised from the dead there. Such is the hope of the Old Testament saints.

But when our Lord took into the Upper Room the men whom He had called out of Judaism, He gave them something that was entirely new,

. . . I go to prepare a place for you. And if I go and prepare a place for you, I will come again, and receive you unto myself; that where I am, there ye may be also. (John 14:2, 3)

The hope He is giving believers today is that someday we are to travel out into space to that place He has prepared. It is interesting that man, in all his recorded history, has had his nose to the grindstone and his eyes fixed on the earth. It is only recently that man has turned his face upward and has started looking into space. Today the great aspiration of our generation is to be able to travel in space. Well, that has been the hope of believers for more than nineteen hundred years! The glorious hope of the church is the coming of our Lord Jesus to take us into space to that home He has prepared.

Now, where is that place? What kind of place is it? I turn to the only chapter I know of in the Word of God where there is a description of it, the twenty-first chapter of the Book of Revelation.

As we look at this chapter, I shall not try to make a comprehensive study, but rather I shall make a few suggestions that may intrigue you into probing deeper into this fascinating subject. I believe that if Christians were more interested in the place to which they are going, they would be more concerned about the way in which they are living down here.

If you have read Bunyan's *Pilgrim's Progress,* which is actually the experience of Bunyan himself, you will notice that when he got up out of the Slough of Despond and started out, the hope that he had from the beginning was this: "I am a pilgrim, and I am on the way to the Celestial City." And when he would fall down, he would always get up, brush himself off and say, "I am a pilgrim on the way to the Celestial City." And when he was incarcerated in Doubting Castle, the key that unlocked the doors and set him free was this promise. When he had mountains to climb, when the way was difficult and discouraging and it seemed as though he would not make it, he got his mind and his heart fixed on that Celestial City.

I believe there are many believers today who have lost sight of this city. They have become discouraged along the way. I say to you, friend, that this world is only a camping place for the night. We all are here temporarily—we are merely pilgrims down here on this earth. We are on the way to the Celestial City. We are on the way to the

New Jerusalem. The thing that would encourage the hearts of many today would be to know a little about this place to which we are going.

> **And I saw a new heaven and a new earth: for the first heaven and the first earth were passed away; and there was no more sea.** (Revelation 21:1)

John here tells us that God is going to trade in this old earth and the old heaven on a new model. He is going to get a new earth—not get rid of earth entirely but merely get a new one. He calls attention to only one great change in His new earth: there will be no more sea. That which covers three-fourths of the earth's surface today will be entirely removed. What a tremendous population can then be put on this earth! Someone asked the other day, when I made the suggestion of the population explosion that will probably take place during the Millennium, "Where in the world will they go, when we don't even have room today?" May I say to you that there will be three-fourths more surface on the earth, plus the fact that the curse of sin will be removed from the earth so that it will produce as it never has before. You will be able to find a parking space in that day; there will be plenty of parking spaces! That appeals to me, because we need more parking space in Southern California, and if we could use the Pacific Ocean, we would have the problem solved!

But these are things that concern the earth, and we are not an earthly people. We are to leave this earth. The thing that interests us is what John sees in the next verse:

> **And I John saw the holy city, new Jerusalem, coming down from God out of heaven, prepared as a bride adorned for her husband.** (Revelation 21:2)

Now, this is the first time the New Jerusalem comes into view. The question is asked, "Is it in existence before this?" I do not know, but I rather think that at the Rapture the church will be brought to this place. I believe this city is to be our permanent home. I think that during the Millennium it will be a matter of commuting back and forth from the earth to the New Jerusalem. Yet the New Jerusalem does not come into view until this point because now eternity opens up and reveals the eternal home of the church.

Notice that the city is a *holy* city. The inhabitants have been made holy in Christ and in no other way. *He* is there. That makes it a holy city.

The *new* Jerusalem is in contrast to the *old* Jerusalem down here on the earth, and it is coming down from God out of heaven.

Now there are men today—better men than I—who believe that the New Jerusalem comes to the earth. I never have been able to see that, I cannot move it that far. I think it comes out into space, and it comes, apparently, within sight of the earth.

The loveliest thing that God could say about it is that it is prepared as a bride adorned for her husband. As a preacher I have had the privilege of seeing over two hundred couples stand before me to be married. This has been one of the delights of my ministry. And I can truthfully say that I never yet have seen an ugly bride. It always is a thrill to me to stand and look down the aisle and watch her come in. I never have seen a bride who was not pretty. I believe that if any girl has a right to be pretty it is on her wedding day. Now don't think that I am being a sentimental old preacher, because I am not. I have seen them before they were married and, frankly, have looked them over and wondered how in the world they would meet the standard. But always on the wedding day they were beautiful. Then I have seen them afterward, and I do not think *beautiful* is the word that should be used in their connection at all. Yet when each one came down the aisle, adorned as a bride for her husband, she was beautiful. Thus God uses the figure of a bride to characterize this city. It is a thing of exquisite beauty.

And I heard a great voice out of heaven saying, Behold, the tabernacle of God is with men, and he will dwell with them, and they shall be his people, and God himself shall be with them, and be their God. (Revelation 21:3)

The New Jerusalem is the temple for the universe of God. This will be the place, apparently, where Israel and the gentile nations of the earth will come to worship. They will come to worship and then return to their homes on the earth.

Now I want you to notice several things that are said concerning this city. Though they are negative, they are very important.

And God shall wipe away all tears from their eyes; and there shall be no more death, neither sorrow, nor crying, neither shall there be any more pain: for the former things are passed away. (Revelation 21:4)

Would you like to move to a city where no one sheds a tear, a city where you would never know disappointment and you would never have occasion to weep? All of us who do counseling have discovered that under the veneer of prosperity and pleasure there are tears.

It is uprooted humanity here in Southern California. Very few have been born and reared here; they have come from some other place. As a result many get into sin, awful sin. At home in their normal environment they might have weathered the storm, but they break their home ties and are carried away. Some have been regular church-goers at home and have given an appearance of being Christian, but they came out to California and the first Sunday they went to Disney-land, the next Sunday they went to the mountains, the third Sunday to the desert, the fourth Sunday to the beach, and by then they had met a couple down the street who drank cocktails. Now they are drinking cocktails with the couple down the street. The next thing you know they are having marital trouble. They go to a marriage counselor or to a psychiatrist, then in desperation they call and want to talk to a pastor. When they come in, we see the tears.

A member of my staff, who has been with us only a couple of years, came to my study the other day and said, "I am tired of seeing tears." I said, "Buck up, old boy, we are going to a city where there will be no tears." He said, "Yes, but I am tired of it here; I see so much." I understood how he felt, because I have been here for forty years, and I am tired of seeing tears also. It will be wonderful to go to that city where there will be no more tears, no more broken hearts.

A columnist in New York made the statement years ago, "For every light that burns on Broadway there is a broken heart." That probably is true. When flying over Los Angeles at night, I hear many exclaim about the beautiful carpet of lights beneath us, and it is a thrill to see; but for every one of those lights there is a broken heart also. Oh, the broken hearts and lives and homes! Can you imagine what it will be like to live in a city where there are no tears?

The second thing that makes the New Jerusalem a wonderful city is "there shall be no more death." No death. That makes it different from any city I have heard of down here. There will be no cemeteries, there will be no undertakers. They all will be out of business in the New Jerusalem. I mentioned this some time ago, and after the service a man came up to me and said, "My little boy was sitting beside me this morning and when you said the mortuaries and cemeteries would be out of business, he looked up at me and said, 'Dad, *you* will be out of business too.'" He was an insurance man. The little fellow was right. I had not thought of that, but the insurance man will be out of business also in the New Jerusalem. No more death. Would you like to go to a place like that? Never again would you have to follow a hearse to a cemetery; never again would you see a loved one encased in a casket and buried. No more death. What a wonderful place this will be!

And then it says, "neither sorrow, nor crying, neither shall there be any more pain." All the hospitals will be closed, doctors and nurses will be out of a job, "for the former things are passed away."

Then we come to something that is quite wonderful:

And he that sat upon the throne said, Behold, I make all things new. . . . (Revelation 21:5)

I love that. Would you like to start all over again? I want to make a confession. I never have been the preacher that I have wanted to be. I never have preached the sermon that I longed to preach. I honestly never have been the man that I have wanted to be. I have not attained, really, my ambition. I have not reached my goal in life. I never have been the husband that I have wanted to be, and I never have been the father that I have wanted to be. As I come to this place in life and look back, I have regrets. I would like to go back and do things differently. And God is going to let me! He says to my heart, "In that city, McGee, I make all things new." We are going to start over, and there will be nothing to hinder us. The sin and weights that beset us and hold us back are going to be removed. I don't know about you, but I want to go to that place where I can *be* and *do* the thing that I have wanted to be and do. When I finish this life, I shall look back and thank God for a Savior who has forgiven me for my sins, but I wish I could live my life over again. "Behold, I make all things new." I would like to move up to that city tonight. Wouldn't you?

Now I want to make a suggestion concerning the shape of this city.

And the city lieth foursquare, and the length is as large as the breadth: and he measured the city with the reed, twelve thousand furlongs. The length and the breadth and the height of it are equal. (Revelation 21:16)

Twelve thousand furlongs is 1,378.97 miles—roughly fifteen hundred miles. It is fifteen hundred miles long, fifteen hundred miles wide, and fifteen hundred miles high. Some men have concluded that it will be a cube; others see it as a pyramid. It is difficult to conceive of either a cube or pyramid projected out in space. Cubes and pyramids are appropriate for earth's buildings but are impractical for space, as spheres are impractical for earthly buildings. I cannot believe that, since God has made everything in space globe-shaped, He would make this square. I do not say this in a dogmatic fashion, for there are many fine Bible students who disagree with me, but I believe that the New Jerusalem is a sphere and these measurements that Scripture gives are the dimensions on the inside of the sphere, a cube within a crystal-clear sphere. I took this problem in solid geometry to a man in the field of theoretical engineering. He worked it out for me and came up with a sphere that is slightly larger than our moon. The diameter of the moon is about 2,160 miles, and that of the New Jerusalem sphere is about 2,600 miles. We live on the *outside* of the planet called earth, but if my theory is correct, our eternal home will be *within* the planet called the New Jerusalem.

Having the glory of God: and her light was like unto a stone most precious, even like a jasper stone, clear as crystal. (Revelation 21:11)

The jasper stone is evidently similar to our diamond. The city from the outside looks like a diamond. I like to think of its being the wedding ring of the church. It will be like a diamond flashing out through God's vast universe. I believe it will be the most beautiful thing that you have ever seen because the twelve foundations, which would be the outer surface, are all precious stones through which the light passes. Varied hues and tints form a galaxy of rainbow colors:

- *Jasper*—perhaps the blue diamond
- *Sapphire*—opaque with a greenish or yellowish color
- *Chalcedony*—perhaps green
- *Emerald*—green
- *Sardonyx*—white and yellow
- *Sardius*—red
- *Chrysolite*—golden lustre
- *Beryl*—sea green, aqua
- *Topaz*—greenish yellow
- *Chrysoprasus*—golden green
- *Jacinth*—violet
- *Amethyst*—purple or rose red

The presence of the primary colors suggests that every shade and tint is reflected from this city. A rainbow that appears after a summer shower gives only a faint hint of the breathtaking beauty of the city of light. I believe it will be the most thrilling sight in the world to see this city. Nothing in all God's universe will compare to it.

The One who is the source of light and life dwells within the city. The New Jerusalem is a light giver. It does not reflect light as the moon, nor does it generate light by physical combustion like the sun. Rather, it originates light and is the source of light, for the glory of God will lighten it.

> **And the city had no need of the sun, neither of the moon, to shine in it: for the glory of God did lighten it, and the Lamb is the light thereof.** (Revelation 21:23)

The New Jerusalem will be independent of the sun and moon for light and life. What a contrast to the earth which is utterly dependent upon the sun and the moon. The sun and moon may even be dependent upon the Celestial City for power to transmit light, since the One who is the source of light and life will dwell within the city. Neither will light be furnished by the New Jerusalem Light and Power Company. The One who is light will be there, and the effulgence of His glory will be manifested in the New Jerusalem unhindered.

> **And the nations of them which are saved shall walk in the light of it: and the kings of the earth do bring their glory and honour into it.** (Revelation 21:24)

The New Jerusalem will be the center of the universe. All activity and glory revolve about this city. The nation Israel and the gentile nations of the earth will walk in the light of it and bring to it their glory and honor. They will not live in the city but will come, as the priests of old came to the holy place in the tabernacle and temple, for the purpose of worship. There will be no need to bring a blood sacrifice, for the Lamb is there in person.

And I saw no temple therein: for the Lord God Almighty and the Lamb are the temple of it. (Revelation 21:22)

This city has no temple because it *is* a temple—God is there and Christ is there. It is the holy place, if you please, because Christ is present. That is the thing that makes it such a wonderful place. The Lord Jesus said,

. . . I go to prepare a place for you. And if I go and prepare a place for you, I will come again, and receive you unto myself; that where I am, there ye may be also. (John 14:2, 3)

We are to be with Him throughout eternity. That, after all, will make it heaven—Christ will be there.

Many folk ask, "Will I know my loved ones in heaven?" We shall certainly know our loved ones in heaven. As Dr. G. Campbell Morgan said years ago when someone asked that question of him, "I do not expect to be a bigger fool there than I am here, and I know them here." Yes, we shall know our loved ones in heaven.

But the wonder of it is that we shall know the Lord Jesus. We say today that we know Him. Actually, we know Him as Savior, but we do not yet *know* Him. I think the thing many of us will want to do is to spend eternity just being with Him and coming to know Him. And if you think you will know Him in an evening's conversation, you are wrong. Did you ever stop to think of all the books that have been written on any one of the sciences such as geology or chemistry? They are the record of man's probing into His work. He did it all. And today He is the One who is holding it together.

I was talking to a man who is working in the field of theoretical science. He pointed out, "The center of the building block of the universe, the nucleus of the atom, has in it protons. Each proton has a positive charge. Like charges repel, unlike charges attract. Here in the center of the building block of the entire universe you have a force that is trying to blow itself apart! What is holding it together? Science does not know. The Bible tells us that by Him, by the Lord Jesus Christ, all things consist or are held together. He is the holding force of the entire universe."

For by him were all things created, that are in heaven, and that are in earth, visible and invisible, whether they be thrones or dominions, or principalities, or powers: all things were created by him, and for him: And he is before all things, and by him all things consist. (Colossians 1:16)

The reason the universe is not flying to pieces at this moment is that *He* is holding it together! It will be wonderful for Him to tell us in that day about this vast universe which He has made. That is something that will engage the brain power of all His redeemed creatures.

I hope you will want to go to this city. Someone may ask, "Well, how do you get there?" That brings us back to where we started.

When our Lord was talking to His men in the Upper Room, He said, "And whither I go ye know, and the way ye know" (John 14:4). Sitting there was one of His disciples, a man who had a question mark for a brain, Thomas. This man had doubts. He raised questions about everything and he always saw the dark side of things. He really was not a very pleasant fellow to have around, and I do not know why our Lord called him. In fact, I have never figured out why He called any of them—who would want Simon Peter, Thomas, Andrew, James, or John? All of them were problem children, every one of them. But I am glad He called them because if He will use them there is still hope for me and there is hope for you. This man Thomas is a doubter. He says, "Wait a minute, Lord. You say that we know where You are going and we know the way. We don't!"

Thomas saith unto him, Lord, we know not whither thou goest; and how can we know the way? (John 14:5)

I am glad he was there. He raised my question—he saved me from having to ask it.

Jesus saith unto him, I am the way, the truth, and the life: no man cometh unto the Father, but by me. (John 14:6)

My friend, Jesus is the way to the Celestial City. He has gone before us, and He is preparing an eternal home for all of us who have become children of God through faith in His name.